# Personology

## Method and Content
## in Personality Assessment
## and Psychobiography

Irving E. Alexander

Duke University Press
Durham and London
1990

Portions of chapter 1 were originally printed as
"Personality, Psychological Assessment, and
Psychobiography" in a special issue of the *Journal
of Personality*, Vol. 56, No. 1 (1988), edited by
Dan P. McAdams and Richard L. Ochberg, and
again in *Psychobiography and Life Narratives*,
McAdams and Ochberg editors, copyright © 1988
Duke University Press. Chapter 3 was originally
published in the *American Psychologist*, vol. 37
(1982), 1009–18.

To my wife and children,
their children, those here
and those yet to come.

# CONTENTS

# PREFACE

Over the course of forty years of professional life my thoughts have been organized around a limited set of questions, although it took me many, many years to become clearly aware of what they were. The first has to do with how one could know what another human being is like in some meaningful, dynamic sense. By this I am stating a curiosity about what constitutes the important signaturelike features of an individual's personality without deriving it from membership in a class or comparison with others. A discussion of that question is contained in the opening essay outlining methodological issues in the study of individuals. One possible direction for solution is explored.

A second question, stemming from the first, deals with the relationship between the extracted picture of the personality and the lived experience that preceded it. Stated in another way: What's she/he like and what in the past could contribute to that outcome? Although I can point to an early fascination with theories of personality (especially those of Freud, Jung, and Sullivan) which likely sparked an interest in the relationship of the then to the now, the answers various theories provided never entirely satisfied me. My chief misgiving was that they were not sufficiently personological. A general outline for personality development was postulated in each theory, and the understanding of the individual derived from a reconciliation of the individual's experience with the features of the general model. Although I was aware of the necessity for ultimately establishing the general framework from which any particular example or instance could be understood, my concern was for the understanding of the particular. Weak, general theories about the development of human personality might serve as the background or context against which the story might be better appreciated or compared with others, but it seemed to me that the individual narrative and its telling was in itself the most compelling unit to be decoded or understood. It was not until I began to speculate on the relationship of each man's life to the theory he produced that the historical personological aspects became so apparent. What were recognized by the psychological world as extremely important intellectual contributions, adding immeasurably to our knowledge about human psychological functioning, were clearly filtered products of the lived experience of each of these men. The essays on Freud, Jung, and Sullivan attempt to make clear some aspects of the relationship between the life and the work utilizing the methodological stance outlined earlier.

On a more practical level I can identify still another question which has had a guiding influence on my thinking and thus on the material I am presenting here. I am by choice, inclination, self-description, and practice, first and foremost a teacher concerned with the question of how to communicate my thoughts to students as well as those with whom I share a psychotherapeutic relationship. It is to this end that I offer the essay on the teaching of these personological concepts.

From what has already been said I hope that I have conveyed the idea that I did not sit down one day with the intention of writing a book. The work grew out of what seemed like unconnected activities over many years. Thoughts on the Freud-Moses relationship began some thirty years ago and culminated in a lecture given in my personality course at Princeton. It was not until the recent past that I went further with those early ideas and finished the essay "If Freud Were Moses."

"The Freud-Jung Relationship" was written in 1977 for a psychiatry Grand Rounds presentation at Duke. Several years later, after positive feedback from students and colleagues here and abroad, it was submitted for publication in the *American Psychologist*. The reflection on Jung's life and work was similarly written in response to an invitation to appear on a special program at the American Psychological Association meeting in Toronto in 1985. The program was devoted to an evaluation of the work of important figures in the history of psychology.

The work on Sullivan was stimulated by a reading of Helen Swick

Perry's biography when it first appeared. I had been lecturing for years on Sullivan's theory and how his life influenced his work. The mysteries of that life as presented by Perry led me immediately to recall various places in Sullivan's writings that had a bearing on these issues. Thus a frantic summer's research and a consequent summer's writing resulted in the essay presented here.

The methodological paper was produced after constant prompting by interested colleagues and students who were involved with me in my yearly graduate seminar on personality assessment. Having thought about these issues for many years and shared my thoughts with decades of students, I felt as though the ideas were generally well known and contained nothing new. When I finally undertook the challenge to commit them to writing, I was pleasantly surprised by their positive impact on colleagues who shared my interest in personology and in psychobiography. The first presentation of this work was at the annual meeting of the Society for Personology, in Chicago, June 1986. It later appeared, in an abbreviated version, in the March 1988 special issue of the *Journal of Personality*. Encouraged by the interest in this group of personologists in the problems of teaching the study of the individual, I ventured to describe the format and the rationale involved in the seminar I had developed over the years.

One additional issue, alluded to and briefly explored in the methodological paper, has occupied my thoughts. It concerns the relationship of this set of ideas, this way of thinking, to the problems of self-understanding and change. The general outlines of my position are clear to me and involve the extraction by therapist and patient, conjointly, of the major messages, scripts, and themas that constitute the drama of that individual life. As for the explication of how the work is done in the therapeutic setting and how the material is utilized in the process of change or revision, these thoughts are still incubating and await a future time to be told.

My intellectual debts have accumulated in the development of the ideas I am presenting and I hope that I have done justice in the narrative to the people whose work has influenced me. Without question the single most important influence on my thinking is Silvan Tomkins. In what is now more than forty years of close personal and professional association, we have shared through our deep friendship much of what we think and feel about humans and their paths through life—ourselves and others. It has been a highly privileged experience for which I will be eternally grateful.

In another vein, I owe much to the many, many students, under-graduate, graduate, and postdoctoral, who have stimulated me over the years by their questions and comments about the material I presented. Among those who helped make mine an especially exciting intellectual journey are Ken Shapiro, Pam Slater, Amy Demorest, and David Lisak.

For more than twenty-five years I have had the companionship of a group of able colleagues, members of a conjoint effort to introduce graduate students to the mysteries of human personality in its various manifestations. Their friendship, support, scholarly achievements, and willingness to exchange ideas have had a positive impact on my working life. Robert Carson, Martin Lakin, and Lloyd Borstelmann were here when I arrived at Duke. Michael and Lise Wallach came at the same time as I did. Harold Schiffman and Irwin Kremen followed close on my heels. In the ensuing years Philip Costanzo, John Coie, and later Susan Roth enriched our ranks. It is really no longer possible to extract their individual contributions to the positive side of my academic career or to the development of this work, but each had a part to play.

On the more practical side, there are people who were of great help in bringing this work to conclusion. At the time I was searching the Sullivan literature, Mark Stein, who had assisted me in my assessment seminar, was extremely helpful. He chased down many leads that grew out of vague traces of my memory. We had intended to collaborate on the Sullivan essay, but he went on to a new post which interrupted our joint effort. The seminar assistant of another year, Amy Demorest, generously gave of her time and expertise in a critical reading of Chapters 1 and 2.

To highlight the contribution of Marge Williams, the administrative coordinator of the Duke program in clinical psychology and hand-holder extraordinaire of generations of graduate students, I must begin by disclosing that I am a person who still composes his work in longhand, largely on the back of discarded notices. When you add to that a rather distinct variation in the legibility of my handwriting depending on unknown circumstances, you may be at the threshold of understanding the magnitude of her secretarial task. Through it all, the writing and the revisions, she maintained a warm, supportive attitude, somehow always finding a way to get my work done despite her considerable departmental responsibilities. It was service beyond the call of duty, for which I am truly appreciative.

Not many people in this mobile world have had the good fortune to have experienced a continuous lifelong friendship that dates back to childhood. Even fewer have enjoyed the benefits derived from the fact that the friend is also a professional colleague. Harold Basowitz has held that place in my life. He is a person with whom I share the ongoing joys and burdens of the world of work and beyond. He has always represented for me a kind of anchoring point, the voice of reason, the soul of dependability, and trust. He has been valuable to me in the development of these ideas through his wise counsel and unswerving support.

Most difficult of all is to find the words to portray the multitude of ways that my wife, Pearl, has contributed to my work and to my existence. From sounding board for germinating thoughts to editorial consultant on grammatical form and clarity of prose, she has offered me much. Beyond that she remains a constant source of encouragement, a limitless source of positive affect of all kinds—a true collaborator.

A final debt of gratitude must be acknowledged to those people who have shared intimate portions of their lives with me. Among them are students, friends, those who have come to me for psychotherapeutic counsel, and those to whom I have gone for similar purposes.

I. E. A.

# CHAPTER 1

# A Personological Approach
# to Personality Assessment
# and Psychobiography

## The Task and Its Background

In this essay I would like to reflect on issues which have engaged me for most of my professional life. How do we know with any degree of certainty anything about the personality of a human being, either the self or another, living or dead? Or, stated in another way, how can we as personologists know or understand the uniqueness of a single personality in much the same way that we can recognize the particularity of a human face? Although I am certain that if I looked at a face I could judge whether there are unusual features that would easily identify it, based on normative factors, there is a unity about a face which makes it that person's own, that person's uniqueness. In fact, we are so clearly aware of this expectation of singularity that we are markedly concerned with look-alikes, twins and others, and rather strongly affected by the possibility of seeing oneself in a stranger, the fascination of the doppelgänger. In a similar vein, we may include the idea that although all faces have essentially the same constitutive elements which are geared to performing the same functions in humans, they are all quite different and each face is identifiable in its own right.

To prepare the path for what is to come, let us now put the face back in its usual context as only one part of the total corporeal entity which defines a human being and return to the problem of identifying particularity. Despite the importance and possible value of the various bodily parts as identifiers, the chief instrument of particularity is ordinarily the face. This is what we associate as being one of two essential elements in recognizing a person: a face coupled with a name. In the realm of personality, let us employ a similar body/face metaphor. For the body we can substitute the variety of descriptors of personality studied in the normative sense—traits, styles, types, motives, ideologies, attitudes, affective dispositions, and psychopathological categories. For the face, I would suggest the more dynamic, sequential, units of personality characterized historically by Murray's (1938) "themas," and Tomkins's (1979) "scripts"—what I shall call the signature elements of personality identification. The search for the signature, at some level of reflection, will likely center on methodological concerns.

In adopting a personalistic stance, I immediately become aware of the fact that, as background, I am assuming some implicit knowledge about commonalities assigned in the Sullivanian sense of "being much more human than otherwise." We feel, we think, we desire, we strive, we fear, we suffer, we enjoy, we compete, we master, the list may seem endless; however, what I wish to center on is how these aspects of human experience are uniquely organized in any one person. Can I ever know this with any reasonable degree of certainty? There are of course those who would argue in the negative that complexity in humans is so great that the task of understanding any single human is really an impossible one and not amenable to the scientific enterprise. I do not resonate to a view in which complexity acts as the major deterrent. I rather see the task as similar to that faced by humans in trying to understand their physical surroundings, a matter to which they were forced to attend. If complexity was the chief criterion influencing the decision of whether or not to proceed, we might still be in the dark ages with regard to our knowledge about the universe. Movement was heavily influenced by an interplay of factors: the framing of specific questions so that the available observations could be scrutinized or ordered in particular ways to provide possible responses, and the framing of rules of logic or order to allow one to extract from the observations that which constituted its particular meaning or essence. We shall follow a similar path in trying to unravel the mysteries of the individual. While I have indicated, in a general sense, the direction this path will take, perhaps it is necessary at this point to present a definitional framework for what I wish to explore in the study of personality. To this end I will borrow generously from Allport's personalistic definition but with significant departures. He defined personality as "the dynamic organization within the individual of those psychophysical systems that determine his unique adjustments to his environment" (1937, p. 48). I have modified the statement to characterize personality as the dynamic organization of human attributes which characterize an individual and his or her approach to the world. Attribute is of course a very general term and covers such things as attitudes, aptitudes, skills, affective dispositions, motives, ideologies, and more centrally, for our purposes, scripts. By this latter term I intend, following Tomkins (1979, 1984), a consistent set of sequential directive clauses which are derivable from imagery and reflect a consistent manner of dealing with emotionally powerful and problematic aspects of lived experience (scenes). In its simplest form, a script may be seen as a stable if-then relationship which may also include indications of any or all of the other above-mentioned attributes. An example might be, "If authority threatens, I will fight back," (an overcoming script). What leads to authority's becoming threatening may identify the relevant "scenes."

### What to Study about an Individual: Data Sources and the Nomothetic-Idiographic Controversy

To study any aspect of human functioning, one must decide what constitutes the essential data. In some realms this is a simple, straightforward problem which can be largely resolved, as in the case of visual acuity, by the data resulting from the monocular reading of a Snellen chart at a distance of twenty feet. For the realm of personality, the issue of what to study and how to study it is variously and incompletely answered. Consider the different ways in which psychologists have gone about this task. They have examined symptoms, dreams, fantasies, spontaneous cognitive and perceptual responses, expressive movement, body language, interpersonal styles, coping styles, and others far too numerous to mention. The methods employed for eliciting data have ranged from face-to-face interviews to personal questionnaires, preference inventories, story telling, object identification, figure drawing, and countless more. Some techniques are designed to get at rather specific aspects of functioning, for example, the Rosenzweig Picture Frustration Study as an indicator of "punitive style" (1945). Others, especially exemplified by the more "projective" instruments like Rorschach's Ink Blot Test (Beck, 1944), and epitomized by Morgan and Murray's Thematic Apperception Test (1935), provide more elaborate pools of data from which inferences about personality functioning may be drawn.

Although the list of human products studied and the multitude of instruments devised to study them is awesome, there is an underlying simplicity about the logic employed in our path to knowing about another. In its most exercised form, it is fundamentally normative and thereby comparative. Individuality is derived from the specific configuration of deviance, in the statistical sense, that one person demonstrates when compared with a "sample" of others on factors assumed to be important in the makeup of the personality. An illustrative example might be provided by the Minnesota Multiphasic Personality Inventory, certainly one of the most heavily used tools for personality assessment in the modern era (Hathaway and McKinley, 1943). Interpretation of the test results is a function primarily of elevation of individual scale scores applied in various combinatorial relationships. Inferences flow from analysis of performance on single scales, or two or three peak scale configurations. The flatter the MMPI profile and the closer to the mean scale score level of fifty, the less informative is the resultant personality picture, as though people with such MMPI profiles do not have distinguishable personalities or else the test is not designed to tell us about such people. To some extent even the interpretation of the more projective devices are also clearly influenced by normative logic. Certainly the analysis of a scored, summarized Rorschach record, no matter what formal scoring technique is utilized, would reflect this fact. Even TAT analysis, where no formal norms exist, is not totally independent of the characteristic stories elicited by any particular card. One would no doubt assign different weights to the role of various needs expressed by the subject as a function of the frequency with which that need is expressed by all subjects in responding to the demand characteristics of any card. Perhaps the only verbal techniques relatively free of normative information are Kelly's Role Construct Repertory test (1955) and Stephenson's item Q-sort (1953). However, even in these instances the derived data are left largely to the ingenuity of the examiner to extract a dynamic picture of a functioning personality.

In reflecting on the variety of techniques available to study personality, I am reasonably convinced that there is important information to be gathered from those which have stood the test of time and remain part of the clinician's armamentarium. No better testament need be gathered than the multiplicity of validity studies that exist in the literature for each test or measurement device. Yet when it comes to the issue of the core identifying aspects of the personality of any particular human being, we tend to run into more difficulty. If we want to make inferences about how he/she handles various aspects of the everyday world, what affects him/her, what interests him/her, how he/she feels about what, what distresses him/her, we must make second- or third-order inferences, usually from group normative data.

There are, of course, people who have clearly recognized these issues and have attempted to gather data from sources that are much more personalistic. Outstanding examples may be found in the various long-term studies carried out in the Harvard Psychological Clinic by Henry Murray (1938, 1955), Robert White (1938, 1975), and their co-workers. Additionally, Gordon Allport in his emphasis on and demonstration of the importance of the study of personal documents charted a path (1942). For Murray's group, the interview was an important source of personalistic data; for both Murray and Allport autobiographical material served this same purpose. Allport (1965) also used personal correspondence as a data source for personality investigation. While these various personalistic sources were by no means novel to the psychological community, they tended to be overlooked, disregarded, or minimized because there were no reliably established methodologies for reducing the massive data sets to more manageable properties. Furthermore, the value of such data remained continually suspect because validity concomitants were difficult to establish.

Perhaps even more cogent reasons exist to help explain why these very person-centered methods remain on the periphery of psychological investigation. We live in a culture which is heavily functionally and technologically oriented, where time and unit cost are primary considerations. Why should anyone study the psychological organization of another human being? If it is to diagnose difficulties in order to prescribe or initiate remedies, the emphasis is placed on the development of brief, rapid techniques which will allow immediate classification and initiation of treatment which moves ever increasingly toward the impersonal. The same is true for all sorts of selection procedures both vocational and educational.

Long-term dynamic therapies of which psychoanalysis was a prime example were clearly outside the model just presented. They dealt with the life of an individual as seen through the imagery of that person. Thus, the interview format and the examination of life history data were clearly the preferred methods of data gathering. However, despite the fact that the investigator or therapist was centrally involved in understanding the person with whom he/she worked, the process of understanding was an emergent, not amenable to systematic examination of the data, nor open to the social check, nor entirely uninfluenced by the participation of the therapist in the process. It also suffered possible confounding by attempting to understand another while at the same time trying to help the other toward changing those aspects of lived existence that were sources of growth arrest. What therapist has not had the experience of reading extensive case history presentations and finding his/her own interpretation of the data was considerably different from the presenter? In fact, it is more likely than not to be the case that the important aspects of the data will not be sufficiently highlighted nor inferential steps clearly enough stated to allow the reader to follow the path of the teller.

Considering all of these admonitions, it is difficult to understand why these sources of data, the life story, the real and fantasized experiences of the individual as revealed through interview, and examination of personal documents remain of interest to psychologists. One approach to an answer may lie in the fact that it is not uncommon among humankind to be fascinated by individual stories of lives lived. Perhaps it is in some ways a substitute for the wish and fear to know one's own story while that story is still unfolding. The differences among stories and the uniqueness of each, despite the similarities in structure shared by all lives, provide hope and sow seeds of wisdom through this shared experience. Certainly an interest in the story of the other must reflect the continuous interest in the dynamic properties of psychological life. What is that person like, how did he/she get to be that way, and how will she/he evolve over time? Its relationship to the continuous saga of the self is apparent.

### The Development of a Personalistic Stance

In my own work, I have followed two related yet different paths in my quest for "knowing" in the personological sense. One direction evolved from my work as a clinical psychologist and graduate teacher where I was constantly reminded that personality assessment was clearly related to problems of personality theory, psychodiagnosis, and psychotherapy. Fortunately, my early training in assessment under Silvan Tomkins at Princeton was not confounded with training in psychopathology. It followed a paradigm established in the thirties at the Harvard Psychological Clinic headed by Henry A. Murray. The major emphasis was on how the data reliably revealed the prominent features of an operative, functioning, intact, individual personality. The data were read, combed, confronted, analyzed with the intent of understanding as much as one could about the way in which another human being experienced the world. This search is vastly different from one in which the outcome is directed toward establishing a person's membership in a set of classes indicative of psychopathology or descriptive of gross aspects of personality functioning. A major difference between the two approaches is that the results of the former can easily be directed toward answering the questions intended by the latter. The reverse is, unfortunately, a low probability event in anything other than a global sense. To designate someone as an obsessive, or hysteric, or depressive, or schizophrenic will place the focus on particular salient aspects of functioning but say little about the dynamics in that individual leading to that particular form of functioning. More destructively, it is likely to lead to inferences made about an individual by virtue of assigned membership to a class rather than leading to a search within the individual's own material to tell what he or she is like. What is illustrated here once more are fundamental differences between nomothetic and idiographic approaches to knowledge about the mysteries of personality. The former focuses on prediction as the critical goal, the latter on understanding, even when prediction is also clearly desirable.

As my work evolved, it was directed toward a limited set of aims, either resolving particular issues of clinical decision making or teaching graduate students about the intricacies of personality assessment. In either case, the work was likely to be carried out with a live subject at some particular point in the journey through his or her life span. In my clinical work, it could have been a person of any age and in varying states of psychological distress, from moderate to intense. In my graduate teaching the subjects studied were almost exclusively reasonably well-functioning students by all obvious criteria, with no psychiatric history, and usually in the senior year of college. Subjects were usually studied for extended periods of time, one to two semesters, using a variety of methods and data sources, including personal documents (autobiography), extended interviews, objective and projective tests (see chapter 2). Subjects originating in the clinical situation were studied much more briefly, usually with a limited time for interviews and a selected battery of tests.

A second avenue of interest for me in personological study was stimulated by the appearance in the mid-fifties of Ernest Jones's three-volume biographical study of Sigmund Freud, the life and the work (1953, 1955, 1957). In my study of personality theory with Tomkins, both as his student and colleague at Princeton, we had often discussed the possibility of describing personality by the limited number of "guiding messages" or "scripts" which were central to an individual. We were both fascinated by the obvious similarities and differences in the lives of personality theorists and how this might be reflected in the products of the work itself. Jung had stimulated my interest in this line of investigation as well in accounting for differences in Freudian and Adlerian psychology in his *Two Essays on Analytical Psychology* (1916/1966). It is there that he points to the correspondence between Freud's objective and Adler's subjective psychology as reflective of differences of temperament between the two men (pp. 42–43), a prelude to his introduction of psychological types.

My first efforts to pursue this interest in the relationship of the life to the theory were reflected in a series of lectures to undergraduate and graduate students in the mid-fifties in a course entitled "Theories of Personality." In reading Jones I had become intrigued with the evolution of Freud's relationship to male authority figures throughout the course of his life. In these lectures I traced what was salient in the relationship of Freud to his father, the failure of the father to live up to the hero image, the continued search for the father-hero substitute through Brücke, Breuer, Charcot, and even Fliess. The live search which, no matter its initial promise, ended in disappointment, was abandoned to return to an earlier, regressive solution in fantasy. The progression was from Hannibal and Alexander the Great, his childhood heroes, to Moses, who became a prominent figure in his adult life. This led to my surmise that what he wrote about Moses in 1901,

1914, and in the last decade of his life during the 1930s, was powerfully suggestive of unconscious conflicts that he suffered at those times (see chapters 3 and 4, this volume). It was an exciting venture into the realm of psychobiography which whetted my appetite to continue along the personological path.

Slowly, through the pursuit of what seemed to be two disparate endeavors, I began to realize that the ideas Tomkins and I had so fervently discussed as colleagues in the 1950s, and since, concerning the consistency, lawfulness, understanding of, and (under specific circumstances) even predictability of the individual's responses in the world, were more satisfactorily explored by studying the products of that individual within the framework of that person's life rather than in comparison with the products of others or as derivations from nomothetic postulates.

### Personality Assessment and Psychobiography as Personological Tasks

The study of lives in progress, more generally represented by personality assessment, and the study of lives already lived, psychobiography, do present a variety of differences in approach and interest. The former, almost by definition, suggests an exposition of what that person is like in present time and an analysis of the forces that helped to shape or mold that product. One might also be concerned about the continuities and discontinuities over time in that progression and perhaps what the future might hold for such a person in a variety of different contexts.

The study of a life already lived is more likely to call attention to the explanation of those aspects of the life history which do not seem to flow easily from either common sense derivations or simple psychological principles. Perhaps this makes more understandable our fascination with those of unusual stature or accomplishment or notoriety. The steps between who they were and how they got that way may not be apparent to the untutored eye.

The problems of personality assessment and psychobiography only partially overlap but in a very important way. They are alike in that they both demand an inclusive description of personality at some point or points in time and a set of connectors which relate the person to the influences which led to that particular configuration. They differ in that in a life already lived one entirely eliminates the problem of prediction and is directly led to the importance of the problem of understanding.

### The Critical Descriptive Unit to Study

Despite the fact that the study of personality has been concerned with a host of important and largely unresolved issues such as the impact of early experience on personality development, stability and change in personality over time, and the centrality of disposition as opposed to situation in predicting behavioral outcomes, the most fundamental questions that are asked relate to those we have already introduced. The first involves a description of what the individual is like at some referential point in time (e.g., now, as a child, in old age), and the consistencies over the life span. The second involves the link between outcome and the factors that were influential in producing it. On first blush the descriptive question seems relatively straightforward. We are all accustomed in our everyday lives to dealing with this question endlessly. When asked about another person with whom we are familiar, we are very likely to respond with large caricature-like brush strokes indicating in an informative way the identifying characteristics of that individual: how he/she looks, what his/her function is in the world, what are his/her obvious traits of character, the dominant aspects of his/her behavior, what he/she values, what he/she enjoys, what distresses him/her. This kind of information, although substantial and perhaps important in deciding such issues as whether one is interesting, attractive, likable, safe—issues which are central to whether a relationship is pursued or not—deals mainly with what Jung termed the persona aspects of personality, or one's face to the world: how one wishes to present oneself to others. The methods of data treatment which I am about to describe can be used to deal with these questions. However, beyond this level of functioning there lies another level, less accessible to conscious presentation but no less important in determining how an individual lives and experiences in the world. It consists of relatively fixed if-then sequences, scenes, and scripts, which run themselves off when triggered by appropriate stimuli, largely independent of conscious control. Their origins may be multiple. Frequently they follow the pattern indicated by Tomkins in his discussion of nuclear scripts, namely that such a script is likely formed under circumstances in which a positive-affect state of more than moderate frequency, intensity, and duration is replaced by a negative-affect state with similar qualities (1984). The ensuing script emanating in response to such a "scene" may then deal with the anticipation of repetition of such changes, strategies for return to the former desired state, strategies to avoid the feared expected negative state, or any or all of the above. But not all scripts are nuclear scripts. Any set of consistent if-then or means-end relationships which are largely unavailable to an untutored consciousness but clearly revealed in the imagery of the individual whether in dreams, fantasies, or more usually studied written and oral productions may be considered under this rubric. It is to the extraction of these sequences that we shall turn our major attention.

Now one might ask of what value it is to have identified such units of human experience. In essence, these largely consistent but hidden sequences may be the critical elements leading to the understanding of an individual in terms of what she/he thinks and feels, as well as to the ultimate predictions of his/her responses to the exigencies of the surrounding world. The contention expressed here is that identifying the major scripts of an individual through the study of his/her own unique experience as expressed in imagery will be of greater value in understanding his/her path in the world, helping her/him to deal with unmanageable internal and external forces and/or predicting her/his responses under known or controlled circumstances, than personality designations produced through normative comparisons, such as traits, typological designations, and psychopathological categories.

### Preferred Data and Suggested Treatment: Two Approaches

Let us now turn to the considerations of how these important units of personality structure may be extracted from imagery produced by the experiencing individual. The most satisfying data sources are those which deal with the spontaneous recollection from memory of various aspects of life already experienced, as in a freely produced autobiographical essay or directed interviews about particular aspects of lived experience. The critical distinction that is being made here is between the data of memory and how it emerges as opposed to the data of present conscious reflection as in opinions, preferences, professed values and the like. The former contain the promise of less contamination as data sources and may in fact be the basic underpinning for predictions about the latter. To extract scripts from living subjects it is preferable to work from data in which the individual is describing people, places, and incidents that seem to be the significant memory remnants of lived existence. Alternate data sources could be different forms of personal documents, diaries, letters, recorded dreams, and if none of these are available, imaginative responses to standard stimulus configurations such as those provided by the TAT. Of course, in psychobiographical work adequate samples of the written or recorded oral productions of the subject constitute a major vein of source material.

Once gathered, a central problem is how to treat the data so that it will lay bare its order and thereby reveal the basic messages it contains. These are ordinarily embedded in the complexity of functions served by written and verbal communication. In an oversimplified but fundamental sense, one might conceive of this process as the investigation of a dynamic system which operates from a limited set of organizational principles which are holographically manifested in widely differing contexts. The different contextual frameworks frequently obscure the constancy of the underlying principles. The parallel to decoding the flow of a psychotherapeutic hour to the ear of a dynamically oriented therapist is clearly brought to mind.

In principle two major avenues of approach to the data have occupied my thoughts over the years. One is more directly related to the image offered by the therapeutic hour. It involves letting the data reveal cogent properties by sifting the material through a network of rules designed to call attention to importance. The sifting has a twofold purpose: to reduce the data to manageable proportions and to break the conscious communicational intent of the content. The former needs no extended explanation at the moment. It will be treated at length in what follows. The latter may not be quite so obvious. Most interpersonal communications have a purpose which involves the relationship or intended relationship between the teller and the hearer or reader. Do you agree, like, understand, sympathize, feel pained, etc.

with my effort? These are typical outcome expectations of interpersonal communications and demand of the recipient some response. This is the usual mode of social communicative interaction to which we have become accustomed and which we must discard in treating the data. The set must be directed away from the understanding or judgment of content to the awareness of what is important to the individual and the underlying elements of process that make for that importance. Personality assessment and psychobiographical study are all too often geared toward judgment outcomes, reflected by the use of psychopathological descriptors to provide the basis for understanding rather than the search for the dynamic directives which make the understanding of that person's experience possible.

The second avenue of approach to the data involves asking the data a question, the answer to which the investigator feels is relevant to unravel the intricacies of the subject's personal view of the world, e.g., what are his attitudes toward women? Or the question could be directed toward how some aspect of personality functioning operates in this person. For example, the data might reveal a subject for whom fear is clearly the most frequent negative affect expressed in imagery. The ensuing questions might involve minimally a search for who or what triggers fear in this person and how fear is relieved. In this instance we would again be reducing the data by attending to only certain aspects of it at any one time and clearly breaking the set of content by isolating the relevant data from its total context.

Having expressed the two general directions of search, let us now take each in turn to explicate them more fully.

### Letting the Data Speak

The first of the methods intends a sorting of the raw data using a set of rules designed to identify what in the material demands further scrutiny because of its importance. The identifiers which have been extracted over years of working with this sort of material are to be found in the psychological literature of learning and perception as well as in the literature of personality and psychotherapy especially as it derives from Freud and classical psychoanalysis. These "principal identifiers of salience" as they shall be called are by no means exhaustive nor necessarily nonoverlapping. At present they number nine. We shall list them and discuss each one separately in turn.

1. Primacy
2. Frequency
3. Uniqueness
4. Negation
5. Emphasis
6. Omission
7. Error
8. Isolation
9. Incompletion

### 1. Primacy

The association of "first" with importance has a long-standing history in folklore and in human customs and mores. Certainly in psychology the idea is upheld in the importance assigned to early experience in the development of personality. The first as the "foundation stone" upon which structures are built is also a common metaphor in language. The first as "the key" to the unfolding of meaning is also a prevalent idea in our culture. We can see its expression in the teaching of theme or story writing in which paragraphs are initiated with a topic sentence whose meaning is then elaborated in the ensuing sentences.

The fundamental importance of primacy was adopted as a critical one in psychoanalytic thinking about personality and psychotherapy and is wonderfully illustrated in the opening paragraphs of Ernest Jones's autobiography. After two complex sentences locating his date and place of birth, the geography of the surround, and the relationship of his father to the area, he goes on in a second paragraph to comment:

> It is the common experience of psychoanalysts that a patient intimates in the first hour of the treatment, and often in the very first sentence, the most important secrets of his life, although this is done in such a veiled way that it may take months or years of arduous work before it is possible to read the inner meaning of them. Were I in the position of such a patient, the opening sentences of this book could be put to a similar use. I know that the essential story of my life lies hidden in those sentences, though

they need a minute examination to decipher it or even discern its elements. (Jones, 1959)

Anyone familiar with Jones's life story will immediately see major aspects of that story reflected in the two seemingly innocuous sentences giving simple background information: the importance of being first and a leader, and its variant, being the bypassed center between two powerful forces.

The fundamental idea of the importance of primacy can be carried beyond that expressed by Jones in his example and has undoubtedly been done by therapists who will treat the opening communication in any hour as a salient bit of information which may either be the foundation stone for or the key to what ensues. It is a small step to extend this line of thinking to any sort of material spontaneously produced by a person whether it be in personal documents or in a face-to-face interview format.

### 2. Frequency

Of all the indicators of importance, frequency of appearance probably needs the least justification, although there are complications involved if one assumes a direct relationship or straight-line function between frequency and recognition of importance. There is something paradoxical about experience in this regard in that beyond a certain point as frequency increases, awareness of importance seems to decrease. We are more likely to become accustomed to what is involved and salience declines only to be reintroduced experientially by the contrast of absence. Freud was clearly aware of this relationship when he turned toward the study of the ever present (but overlooked) as a source of critical knowledge about personality. Dreams would certainly fall into this category, since dreaming is an act which by its omnipresence tends to be devalued in importance. For the most part, though, we are tuned to frequency or repetition as increasing signs of certainty and thus by implication of importance. When someone tells us the same message about himself repeatedly but short of monotony we are likely to assign importance to that message. However, the kind of importance a frequent message has may be complex in terms of its value for the discovery of scripts. In many instances frequency may be an expression of powerful conscious value schemas. When frequency is coupled with other salience indicators it may reveal less conscious sequential consistencies. In listening or reading through material, if one isolates sequential "units" of material or information, and follows them in terms of means-end structures, frequent or repetitive sequences will stand out in bold relief. If when mother is mentioned in a recalled incident and the outcome is clearly positive, it does not take many repetitions of this sequence, despite contextual variation, before the obvious associational relationship will be posited as existent and important.

### 3. Uniqueness

As an indicator of salience, uniqueness can be employed in a variety of ways. It may actually be pointed out by the subject as a frame for the unit of communication. An example might be one in which an experience is prefaced or followed by the statement, "Nothing like this ever happened to me before or since," or "It was the most unusual thing that I ever went through." More subtle however are the signs of uniqueness that arise from either departures of expression from those commonly held in the general language, or more importantly, clear departures from the usual language expressed by the subject. The sudden appearance of street parlance in an otherwise formal presentation might be such a sign.

Uniqueness refers not only to verbal expression but also to the content of what is being expressed. Were one to examine a sequence in which a certain outcome would be clearly expected and find instead a different and unexpected outcome without explanation, it should be taken as a sign of salience, that which needs to be examined further. A powerful example from the autobiographical sketch of a paid student volunteer in a graduate personality assessment course concerned an incident which he recalled from his first year in elementary school. At the end of the school day he returned home to find his mother hanging from a rope in her bedroom, a description which he followed only with the statement that he was sent off to a private school shortly afterward. Uniqueness in this instance is signaled not only by the event itself but the response elicited in the report by the subject.

Uniqueness as a salience indicator is clearly related to assumptions of probability theory. It is the defeat of the null hypothesis at a high level of examiner confidence. What must inevitably be kept in mind in invoking this criterion of importance are the various baselines with which the selected material is being compared. There are the nomothetic ones that emanate from general cultural expectations, e.g., loss of an intimate leads to negative affect. There are also those which are personalistic and emanate from the norms established by the investigated subject, e.g., the unmistakable expression of affect in an otherwise highly controlled subject. The issue of the individual baseline is clearly treated in the work of Lamiell (1981).

### 4. Negation

While sometimes coupled with either frequency or uniqueness, negation deserves an independent discussion as a mark of salience. Freud (1959), in a small paper originally published in 1925, called attention to the importance of negation statements by patients in the analytic hour as indicators of hitherto repressed, unconscious material making its way to the surface thinly disguised by the cover of unlikelihood or impossibility. Imagine, for example, a therapeutic interview in which a dream about the father is mentioned, followed by the statement, "Let's move on to something else. *It's not* that I think talking about father would drive me crazy, it usually leads to a feeling of helplessness." Freud's assumption about negation, namely that one can entertain the likelihood of the statement by eliminating its negative component, is but one of the possibilities available. We shall, at the moment, only point to imagery framed negatively as being tagged for further study without assuming the exact nature of its importance, or how directly it might reveal a significant dynamic sequence.

### 5. Emphasis

Since all salience indicators are in some fashion forms of emphasis, we shall restrict our explication to rather specific instances of its appearance. In general, we are aware of emphasis when it is called to our attention deliberately by the teller, e.g., "I want you to know that . . . ," or "A critical event in my life was . . . ," or other obvious forms of accent or underlining in oral or written communication. Whether such units necessarily contain important material remains open to question. In some instances the material may be so identified by the teller without revealing properties of importance. It truly says only "pay attention." The possible reasons for accenting attention may be myriad but not necessarily indicative of underlying means-end regularities. For example, one could emphasize an experience one had in the service of establishing a bond with an attractive, new acquaintance. In such an instance the communication, "*I will always* remember *the great* warmth I felt from the first moment I set foot in your country. The atmosphere just felt *absolutely* right to me," may be filled with emphasis indicators without leading to the uncovering of an important means-end sequence. If we try to extract such from the communication, it would look like: your country = warmth, or in translation, you and your country are synonymous and thus "from the beginning you have stimulated positive affect in me." The sequence emphasized could be treated as an important communication which can be decoded but not necessarily as a script. Other instances of emphasis may reflect clear, commonly held, human expectations which are not at all hidden from the subject's awareness, e.g., an incident which in its abstract form could be characterized by the sequence—hard work + perseverence leads to success and accompanying positive affect.

More subtle forms of emphasis and perhaps more suitable for our purposes are those that are not obviously intended by the teller but yet signal in some clear and unmistakable way. We may categorize them under the headings over, under, and misplaced emphasis. Overemphasis can usually be detected when the hearer or reader begins to wonder why so much attention is focused on something considered to be commonplace. "I just could not get over the fact that this person, a native of the country, from whom I as a tourist had inquired about directions, took such pains to make sure I understood how to find my way. From that moment on I adored my visit to ———," would be an example of a passage chosen by the criterion of overemphasis for retention in the reduced data pool. Its ultimate transformation might be: unexpected attention (kindness) when in distress → euphoria. This may be a negative analogue of the expectation that when one is in trouble no help is expected.

Underemphasis would be inferred when the question is raised as to why so little attention is paid to something which seems important. To describe a high school career in several pages and embed a single sentence to the effect that, "In my senior year I was elected president of the student body" would illustrate this point. A previous incident used to illustrate uniqueness, the discovery of mother's suicide, would also qualify as an example of underemphasis. Misplaced emphasis is indicated when means-end sequences seem to stretch credulity limits in that appropriate means are present or implied but not attached to the announced outcome. Consider the following example in which the subject says, "Although I studied music in conservatories and with renowned teachers for twenty years, I have always felt that my success as a concert pianist was due to my father's strong confidence in me." Other forms of this phenomenon abound as in dwelling on the humorous in an essentially tragic unfolding or stressing its opposite, the danger in an essentially benign sequence.

### 6. Omission

To know when something is missing one must begin from the baseline of what exists when completion is reached. The standards of comparison may be given or implied by the subject or may be invoked by using either cultural or logical criteria. An example of a given or implied standard can be gleaned from an autobiographical essay in which the subject identifies all family members, then goes on to describe events that include interactions with all but one. The use of a cultural norm might be exemplified by the description of high school years without mentioning significant friends or social interactions. The use of logical criteria usually follows a sense of unease when a story or sequence of events is being related and steps critical to the smoothness of flow are missing. An illustrative example might be one in which the subject describes a memory involving a punitive action toward him by the mother after she had accused him of hostile behavior to a sibling. The retelling goes on to include the subject's feelings as a result of the mother's actions but speaks not at all to the issue of whether he had in fact treated the other child in the manner suggested. What is omitted is attention to or consideration of the subject's role in a sequence with a negative outcome which must then be investigated for its repetitive properties.

Perhaps the most prominent form of omission encountered in this kind of material is not connected with cognition but rather with affect. Frequently written and even oral narratives get reduced to action sequences with affect removed and thus are of limited value in understanding consistent means-end patterns, especially the role of affect in their evolution. One could see the confusion that might arise from a set of salient bits of data extracted from a subject in which the expression of disapproval on the part of an intimate authority figure sometimes leads to escape, sometimes to inactivity, sometimes to confrontation, and sometimes to contrition. In order to sort the data further in the search for order, one could focus on the authority variable and differentiate that more specifically. Are the responses more consistent as a function of the sex of the authority, age of the authority, and so on. Or one could look at degree of culpability expressed by the subject and consequent outcome. Each of these possibilities might reveal consistencies. A more fruitful source of potential clarity may lie in the examination of the affect likely produced but not reported by the negative message received and the relationship between affect and outcome. Does shame or fear or anger in this subject lead to a consistent outcome and do these outcomes differ? The omission in imagery of affect in general, or specific affects, would lead to a search for the particular circumstances which govern relevant affective experiences and their consequences.

### 7. Error or Distortion

A large part of Freud's discussion of the parapraxes in *Psychopathology of Everyday Life* (1938) deals with the role of error in its variety of forms including slips and distortions as indicators of important, hidden motives. In his treatment he gives countless examples of its manifestation in both oral and written productions. In many instances the appearance of error is recognized by the subject and as such called to the attention of the observer. This is especially true with slips. Factual error, such as time, place, or person distortions, and misquotations are easily recognizable if the data in question are also part of the observer's store of knowledge. However, when one is relating personal experience, all sorts of errors may go undetected in that criterion templates are not available for comparison. Not infrequently the subject may muse over the causes of past error which may suffice to alert the observer. Such an instance might be given in the communication, "I always had difficulty as a child in pronouncing my sister's name even though it seems quite simple in retrospect." While the association of an ever present attribute or representation of sister with difficulty is clearly present and not consciously understood, the association serves as a marker for further investigation of that relationship and those belonging to the general tags to which sister belongs, e.g., sibling, female, for consistent sequential imagery.

Despite the fact that the observer has no absolute check against the recalled experience of the other, credibility serves at least as a partial criterion. In written exposition this is sometimes indicated by obvious undetected error by the subject in an otherwise error-free or minimally error-prone sample. An example might be in the statement, "I came from a family of tall people; my father is 6–5, my brother is 6–4, my mother is 9–5, and I am the runt at 5–8." This not only calls attention to the possible importance of the size dimensions in the life of the subject but highlights (error signaled by lack of credibility) the over-valuing of mother on whatever dimension the size variable symbolizes, and by contrast the undervaluing of the writer who is described uniquely as a runt. Underlying these pointers there most likely exists a dynamic set of conditional sequences constituting the subject's view of the family drama.

### 8. Isolation

As a mark of salience, isolation[1] is best recognized by the criterion of "fit." If in reading or listening, one finds oneself asking the question, "Where did that come from?" or "That doesn't seem to follow," it is highly likely that important personal material is contained in the communication. While this seems like a perfectly straightforward statement, one that should easily translate into action by the observer, it may at first contain hidden difficulties. Unless the example is clear and stark, we may find ourselves having to overcome a fair amount of what we have learned to do in successful social communication.

I shall try to expand by illustration what is intended in these condensed statements. To follow a person through an orderly description of an experience which is punctuated by a seemingly irrelevant association or aside ordinarily alerts us to something being amiss. It is usually an indication of something of importance in the mind of the subject, covered over by consciousness which is either stimulated by associative connection to the material being expressed, or of such momentary power that it must make its appearance in consciousness despite the usual rules of order involved in communication. An instance of the former would be: "I remember how we saved a touchdown by our opponents in a high school football game by something we learned from observing their game films.—Oh! Did I remember to bank the fire in the fireplace before I left the house to come here? The films showed that the quarterback. . . ." The associative link might be in the value of preparation in any human endeavor and might lead to the means-end sequences (a) preparation leads to avoidance of negative outcome, (b) failure to prepare leads to anxiety about the possibility of negative outcome.

An instance of the latter, a compulsive rather than associated link, would have likely had a more intrusive or nonsequiturial aspect as in "My job has always been a source of great gratification to me. You know, I feel strangely enough as though someone is listening in on this discussion, but to get back to my job, I started. . . ."

In both examples the likelihood that the communication would be recognized as containing indications of salience is high. Where we are likely to run into difficulty is in more subtle expressions of such phenomena which go unrecognized because the observer as a matter of course supplied the missing connections which would make continuous sense out of discontinuous communicational sequences. This is done all the time in social communication and in fact finds its ultimate expression in long-time intimates who claim that they need not communicate verbally because they know what the other is thinking. While this may in part be true, we should be aware of its opposite as represented by Carson McCullers (1940) in *The Heart Is a Lonely Hunter*, a story which begins with two deaf mutes and proceeds with a variety of other relationships in which congruence in communication is extant only in the mind of each beholder. The following example is offered to further illustrate the point in question. In an autobiographical statement, the subject reports, "As a young child my parents were never terribly happy about my eating habits. By the time I was ten I was sent off to a private school where I did well in my studies. Now as an adult I eat everything." This sequence may elude many readers as being an instance of isolation and possibly containing script-like aspects because causal attributions may automatically be made between the clauses so that the sequence is interpreted as one in which the subject was sent to private school to remedy his poor eating habits and the program was successful. On closer examination one may notice the logical gaps between the sentences which calls attention to the salience of the sequence, from which may be extracted through contiguity the possible means-end expectations that not pleasing authority → separation → independent success → adoption of parental norms. The phenomenon of "reading in" is well known to any teacher who has ever had to grade a long set of essay exams. Key words in an answer constitute an important part of rapid search. The extent to which the reader supplies the connectors may not always become obvious until a more careful rereading is demanded.

### 9. Incompletion

An obvious form of incompletion occurs when an expository sequence begins, follows a course, but ends before closure is reached. Sometimes the subject may be aware of what is occurring and in verbal discourse simply stop abruptly, indicating that to continue would be too painful. In such an instance, outcome may be known. Other examples may include more subtle changes, where distraction serves to interrupt the narrative flow and there is no return to the original story line. Whether avoidance of outcome or its implications contributes to incompletion under these circumstances is much more difficult to determine.

Still another form of expression of incompletion may be recognized even when story line closure is reached. A case in point might be one in which in describing an event a clear step-by-step sequence is elaborated which leads to a problem or crisis. This is followed by an outcome which lacks an explanatory means-end relationship. In an autobiographical essay, a subject writes, "All through college I dated John. It started as a casual friendship but within a short period of time we found that we enjoyed the same interests and people. By the time we reached senior year we were making plans for a future together. Marriage, while not an immediate prospect, was our ultimate goal. Three years later I married Fred Perkins, whom I had recently met, and moved to Pittsburgh where we have lived ever since." This illustrates an incompleted fragment or portion of a descriptive segment about courtship and marriage which in itself has an aura of completion. Perhaps another aspect of incompletion as a salience pointer is revealed by discontinuities in the narrative even when closure is reached. Discontinuity, however, will not be treated as a separate importance marker since it is likely to be identified through several already mentioned identifiers such as isolation, distortion, omission, or uniqueness as well as incompletion.

The nine identifiers of salience which have been elaborated are clearly not exhaustive but in my own work they have grown to be the ones most relied upon. What must be emphasized is that this set of pointers does not cover all possibilities. Others which immediately come to mind are recency, conflict, inconsistency, and incongruity, which may or may not be clearly covered in the existing set. The investigator in extracting salience should always be prepared to elaborate the principle upon which it is based.

### Transforming the Salient Extractions

I have now introduced a set of markers with which the initial data can be sorted and consequently reduced. What should fall out from invoking such a procedure is a finite number of salient units. A unit may be defined as a number of consecutive sentences which form an entity through shared content. They are, in their completed form, microscopic stories with an introduction, an action, and an outcome. In other instances, they are fragments whose story line is somehow disturbed. A simple example of the former might be illustrated from material gleaned from an assessment interview. The subject in the beginning of the session is responding to a greeting offered by the interviewer. He says, "You know something happened to me today that really upset me and brought to mind the memory of a time when as a child I didn't speak to my father for close to two weeks. My boss called me in to discuss a report which I had just finished after a week of productive and satisfying effort. He chose to dwell on a minor point which he thought might contain an error. This made me very angry and I sat there dumbfounded." The unit has multiple marks of salience: primacy, uniqueness (didn't speak to the father for two weeks), frequency (two of a kind), emphasis (really upset, very angry), and omission (lack of description of the incident leading to anger toward the father). An example of a fragment is contained in a description by a subject of his family members. After simple identifying statements about mother and father he says, "My brother has to be, without doubt, the dumbest guy in the world but beside that he's okay." Salience indicators abound, overemphasis or distortion (without doubt the dumbest in the world), incompletion (lack of relationship between clauses), but no meaningful story is told.

I shall put aside for the moment what might be the next steps in dealing with fragments. I have already indicated that they provide the empirical material from which questions can be put to the original data. Further explication of the procedure will be taken up in our discussion of this general method. Instead I shall turn to the story-line units which have been extracted from the original data sample after filtering by use of salience indicators.

The major task that emerges is how to transform these units into a form that will increase the likelihood of detection of means-end commonality by inspection. The way to do this is by rewriting the means-end sequences in their most obvious general or abstract form. Let us return to the example used earlier to illustrate a salient means-end unit and apply the procedure suggested. The incident involving the boss's response to a submitted report may be roughly diagrammed in the following manner: Independent effort → (leads to) productivity and satisfaction [positive (+) affect] // (which is interrupted by) unwarranted criticism by authority ($\delta$) → anger and inactivity [negative (−) affect]. To diagram all of the salient means-end units in this manner provides a fundamental data source from which a variety of hypotheses about the subject may be derived and also explored. Suppose, for illustrative purposes, that the following additional units had also emerged from the data of the same subject in a single life history interview. The subject says, "Without doubt the happiest days of my childhood were spent in the fields surrounding our house where I gathered material for my butterfly and rock collections which gave me great pleasure. I can recall with some annoyance my mother's exasperated voice finally reaching me and summoning me to a meal. Somehow or other I could never work up much of an appetite." The likelihood of recognizing the stark similarity between the sequential patterns, the means-end relationships and outcomes between the two seemingly disparate descriptions of experience is considerably reduced if the transformation is not made to the abstract or general case. In the transformation process the embedding and all too frequently misleading aspects of particular elements of content drop out with the clear understanding that they can return whenever further inquiry makes it necessary. For example, in the two salient incidents we are discussing, some of what they both share is the means-end sequences that positive affect states are interrupted by authority and that this interruption leads to negative affect outcomes. Although the general pattern is clear, further differentiations then become possible. Does the gender of the authority make a difference in outcome? From these data one could postulate that the sequence is not dependent on the gender of the authority, although gender could have something to do with the intensity of the outcome or the expectation of how much affective change is likely to occur as a result of the interruption. Numerous other questions are immediately suggested by the data, the answers to which may then become the object of search in this or other samples from the same subject. Again, from our examples we notice that although in both instances we have contiguous independent clauses, independent effort → (+) affect, and interruption by authority → (−) affect, one cannot be sure whether these can stand alone or are always expected to be contiguous. One is not sure of whether any appearance of authority would be considered an interruption or whether differentiations can be made about the impact of authority activity when the subject is alone and experiencing positive affect. The fixity or flexibility of these patterns may then become the legitimate focus of inquiry. It would not be difficult to picture that if two people in the world were to exhibit similar sequences that for each there could be different limiting properties. Again, if we could return to the example we have been examining, for one person interruption by authority might lead to a negative affect outcome independent of his affect prior to interruption. For another without the prior positive affect state, interruption by authority could lead to interest or engagement or indifference and thus the conjoining of the two clauses in the sequence is essential to outcome.

There is, then, the possibility of uncovering what are important aspects of the subject's experience, as well as the manner in which those aspects influence experience, their limits, and their affective and cognitive consequences. In addition, if our data sample is large enough and representative enough of the functioning of the subject, we may also be led to hypotheses concerning the range, magnitude, and frequency of the affects in the experiential life of our subject as well as the cognitive motivational referents to which they are ordinarily attached. To explicate this point further, I shall once more return to the two incidents offered by our imaginary subject. Were I to add an unspecified number of data pieces that emerged from my application of the rules of salience to the original data pool, and if I found that no matter the nature of the means-end sequences, the only positive affect to emerge was enjoyment and the only negative one was anger, and these appeared under a variety of conditions and with reasonable frequency, I would be in possession of critical information about the personality of my subject. The same sort of reasoning can be applied to the discovery of any aspect of an individual's psychological functioning. My assumption is simply that what is expressed in imagery and the way that it is expressed is indicative of the repertoire of that subject.

To treat the data in the manner suggested is likely to reveal some number of sequences with repetitive properties. Comparison of the transformed bits selected by salience criteria will serve to provide the basis for judgments about power in the sense of fixity and generality of these identified units. In the case of power, the chief indicator tends to be frequency. To find repeated fixed instances of a sequential pattern, despite changes of context, characters, and time, alerts the observer to the power, in the sense of importance, of that sequence in the experience of the subject. Generality refers more to the issue of pervasiveness, how much play or attention does this sequence get in the overall psychological economy of the subject. For example, the connection between independence and pleasure may be pervasive but modifiable by all sorts of conditional circumstances as differentiators. An illustration might be given by our imaginary subject: "I remember a teacher in high school who had a strong influence on me. We shared a table in the library one time while I was working on a project of mine. At one point we happened to look at one another. He smiled and asked me what seemed to absorb me so intently. Although I was deep in what I was doing, I stopped briefly to explain. We became friends after that, sharing many common interests." Here the situation is again one of independent effort and positive affect being interrupted by an authority figure. However, in this instance the behavior of the authority around the interruption is different from our earlier examples and outcome is changed. What is learned from this is the pervasiveness of the concern with interruption of pleasurable solitary activity in that it becomes a part of the description even when outcome differs. It also provides a differentiator to the sequential pattern in that it is not authority alone that is critical but rather an interaction between the act of interruption and the behavioral context surrounding the interrupter (we happened to look at one another, he smiled, he inquired about my activity). Of course, to increase the certainty of importance of authority in this sequence we would have to search for instances of interruption by peers and younger children and analyze the means-end relationships therein.

To uncover the fruits of such an investigation is not a be-all or end-all in itself. In the best instance it can reveal important aspects of the subject's experience which would otherwise be much more difficult to detect. The observer then is in a much better position to begin to respond with increased assurance to one of the two fundamental questions that beset the investigator of personality, namely, "What's he like?" and "How did he get to be that way?" Consistent means-end patterns are fundamental pieces of descriptive information in dealing with the first of these questions.

In some ways the factoring process which I have been elaborating is no different in limitations than is formal factor analysis. What is extracted is clearly a function of the composition of the original data. If the initial data are sparse or unrepresentative of the subject, one must treat what is extracted with extreme caution and be certain to subject whatever hypotheses that are derived to adequate validation.

What emerges from this sort of examination of the data may be characterized in a variety of ways. In some instances the filtered data may look like single, disparate pieces of a large mosaic whose ultimate form cannot yet be detected. Yet on closer examination certain relationships may begin to take form. To illustrate this point, I shall consider three salient sequences taken from a personal history interview. In their abstract form they were recorded in the following manner:

(1) fear of failure → inactivity; encouragement by nurturant au-

thority → despair and escape → ridicule by peer → anger → renewed activity

(2) rejection by peer → self-examination → self-discovery → excitement → renewed search for intimacy

(3) instruction by authority → mastery → independent attempt → impasse; encouragement by peer → continued effort → solution

While no two sequences are alike in the same sense that was apparent in our earlier examples rewritten in abstract form, we may make certain inferences from the data which then can be followed up or tested. If I look solely at outcomes, I find that no matter what circumstances preceded, the subject winds up either finding a solution to his quest or he remains actively engaged in that process. If I ask what kinds of things can distress this subject, I may postulate that they involve concerns about independent competence and peer relationships. If I ask further about conditions surrounding peer relationships, I find them to be varied but perhaps tending toward the negative side. The consequences of negative action on the part of a peer leads to some internal state which ultimately results in continued search or remedial action. In the situation of positive response from a peer, no intervening state occurs and action leading to positive outcome results. The difference between the two conditions is clear and important. If things go wrong in a peer relationship, the subject feels and reflects and then tries to find a solution. However, solution is not what is indicated by the imagery but rather a continuing active attempt. When, however, a peer is supportive, this leads to activity, the usual outcome of peer interaction, but followed by success.

I shall now contrast this with what we can glean from examination of the self-authority relationships. There are two sequences that are informative in this regard. One is that encouragement by a nurturant authority leads to despair and escape, while the other points to mastery as a result of instruction by authority. I shall set aside for the moment the context (i.e., failure) in which the encouragement by an authority was offered, as at this point I do not know whether the context is critical to the subject's response or not. This would be a question to ask this or other samples of data. However, I do notice that encouragement by a peer was also embedded in a context of failure, yet the outcome of this act was considerably different from that following similar behavior by an authority figure.

What I have attempted to illustrate from a limited data set, three bits of salient means-end sequences, will likely take on added richness, complexity, and question-answering properties when the data sample is enlarged. With additional bits we might have been treated to further insight on the response to expressions of positive affect by authority figures, or whether the positive impact of authority is confined to their instructional role.

Sometimes what may emerge from a salience search seems to have more unitary form, but the scope of the unit, in the example of the mosaic, seems to be focused on one part of the whole. This experience is certainly known to psychotherapists in initial interviews where patients' presentation of problems appears to cover all of their existing imagery, as though they are nothing more than their problems, although many other external signs point out that this cannot be the case. I can imagine, for example, the data emerging either from interview or autobiography about present life circumstances in which the subject says, "Life in general is okay. I really don't have too much to kick about but I sure wish I could find someone that I could feel good about marrying." There follows the recitation of a set of experiences with several marital candidates over a period of some years. When the sequences are reduced and diagrammed, they reveal a basic commonality which puts into stark relief a script with which the subject struggles, one which is perhaps vaguely or only partially available to awareness. The sequential pattern that is revealed is that, desire for intimacy → attempts to establish intimacy → success → fear of being controlled and infantilized → withdrawal, disillusionment, reduction of need → renewed emphasis on other sources of gratification (work). A variant of this pattern is also revealed when attempts to establish intimacy are not initially successful, which takes the following form: desire for intimacy → attempts to establish intimacy → failure → derogation of other and fantasy about more desirable partner → renewed search. In this example I have learned a fair amount about how an important but as yet unresolved aspect of life is experienced. I am, however, not privy to the structure and form of those experiences which are embodied in the opening sentence in which existence is described as generally positive. Again, in such an instance I might have to go back to the original data to ask questions pertaining to what in this subject's experience leads to positive outcome or positive affect.

There are, of course, times when enough salient data emerge to be suggestive of the general features of the mosaic, where with a modicum of speculative glue one can form a somewhat more comprehensive, dynamic view of a functioning organism. If the personality is constricted, the task is somewhat simplified. The richer, more flexible, and more complex the personality, the more the task is complicated by nuance. In such people sequential patterns are much more apt to be influenced by conditional forces, as though finer causal relationships can be discriminated. As an illustration, one might conceive of a number of means-end sequences which fall out concerning male-female interactions from which no simple general conclusions may be drawn but which present a fair number of specific possibilities. The interactional sequence may sometimes be difficult, sometimes harmonious. The actions of the partner may vary from the positive to the negative side and outcomes may not at all be consistent. Yet on closer inspection one may discern particular combinatorial consistencies. Disparaging partners may be responded to differently as a function of what constituted the source or cause for the disparagement, or the combination may be even more complex and depend on not only the provoking stimulus but also characterological attributions assigned to the partner. From these data it might not be possible to respond to a question about the subject's general expectations about members of the opposite sex other than that they are varied. However, one might be led toward very specific hypotheses given specified antecedent conditions.

It was indicated earlier that two general methods were employed in working with the data. The first, letting the data reveal their features frequently leaves one without enough pieces of information to complete a mosaic, or raises provocative questions which cannot be answered from the data extracted by this method. The second approach, loosely characterized as "asking the data a question," can be used either as an independent or complementary source of revealing critical information about the personality.

### Asking the Data a Question

Every student of personality assessment has in some way become familiar with this manner of analyzing data, especially when dealing with the responses generated to stimuli in which ambiguity is an important factor, as in the Thematic Apperception Test and in the Rorschach Ink Blot Test. One need only read Bellak's (1975) brief review of TAT analysis or recall various approaches to Rorschach content or sequence analysis to bring the procedure to mind. For example, one could ask questions for which the tests are not specifically designed and specify the kinds of material which would have to be examined and the criteria to be invoked in order to derive an answer to whatever question is posed. On TAT one might consider vocabulary level, clarity of thought, and logicality of means-end sequences as some of the variables important in making a descriptive statement about the subject's level of intellectual functioning. On the Rorschach, one might extract every percept that deals with a single human or human figures and by assessment of the nature of the interactions be led to important features of interpersonal relating in that subject. A major assumption involved in work with fantasy is, of course, that we are being treated to the repertoire contained in the personality of the subject projected out onto safer, less threatening sources than would occur in an analysis of self.

Although I had been in touch with this method for many years in work with projective materials, its more general possibilities dawned on me somewhat more slowly. Some years ago I was asked to review a then current novel whose subject matter was of some interest to the group. It was a long tome and in considering the degree of knowledge and concern the group members had with the topic, I wondered what I could present them with that might be novel, interesting, and informative. After much thought I took as my task the discovery of what the author's imagery revealed about issues with which the book obviously dealt but which the author did not set himself consciously to resolve or even to make central. Furthermore, they were issues which, if the author were queried, might have resulted in an "I don't know" response or "I have no clear simple response to that question." Think for a moment of asking about Galsworthy's representation of foreigners or working people, or royalty, or children, or males in *The Forsyth Saga*. Are there sequential patterns or consistencies, or scripts, or trait characteristics, or value preferences, or ideological stances represented in the author's imagery which are masked by the persuasive, attention-demanding power of content? My effort on this occasion was quite revelatory. I was able to point to data which placed in bold relief the repertoire of the author with respect to different issues from which a wide variety of inferences or hypotheses could be generated with varying degrees of supportive security.

In referring to novels or projective tests, I have unintentionally discussed this methodological approach as it relates to fantasy material which is at least one step removed from the concrete, memory-based experience of the relater. The possible value of fantasy analysis is related to the assumption that you are tapping both the actual and the potential background source for human endeavor whether ideational, affective, or behavioral (verbal or more grossly motoric). However, in order to make some determination of what value the imagery assigned to another in a fantasy production has to the storyteller, one must make judgments about the degree of identification the teller has with the character described, and this in many instances turns out to be a difficult task. Should similarity be treated as a sign of identification (e.g., sex and age of teller and subject)? Is similarity more consistently indicative of the more apparent aspects of the teller? Should dissimilarity be treated as a sign of lack of identification and thus indicative of the less apparent or hidden aspects of the teller? These are weighty problems which have never been entirely resolved among those dealing with fantasy material. Yet, the richness and order that emerged from my initial use of the method with data from a novel led me to ponder the possibility of its increased value if restricted to the products of personal memory, the recall of incidents from lived experience. In such data, the issue of the relationship of story to teller is much more readily resolved.

The working details of the method involve steps not unlike those already elaborated, in that the basic pool of data must be sorted. This time, however, the criteria for selection are derived directly from the question posed. If one were concerned with assessing the factors leading to success as an outcome in the imagery of the subject, one would extract every sequence or incident appearing in the data in which success was the outcome or a goal in the descriptive unit whether or not achieved. Consequent data manipulations would involve, as in our first method, the reduction of these sequences to their most general or abstract form. The steps that follow reduce the data further by coding and counting conditional or sequential similarities. As an illustrative exercise, we might think of ten units that emerged from an original data pool when the success question was examined. After completing the suggested operations, the results are represented as follows:

| Frequency | Sequence | Outcome | Affect |
|---|---|---|---|
| 4 | isolation + persistence | → success | (+) |
| 2 | competition + peer support | → success | (+) |
| 1 | conjoint effort + instruction | → success | (+) |
| 1 | competition + instruction | → lack of success | (−) |
| 1 | competition + persistence | → lack of success | (−) |
| 1 | competition | → fantasy about success | (o) |

To examine such a summary of the data immediately puts one in touch with or begins to locate the subject's relationship to the issue of success in his or her existence. What becomes apparent is that success can be expected under a broad range of conditions, whether alone, in cooperation with another or others, or in competition with another or others. It also points to the possibility that the usual means leading to success are not as effective when applied in a situation in which competition is involved. Furthermore, it may be noted that although competition may as frequently lead to success or not, only a single additional condition, peer support, appears to be associated with the positive outcome.

Data summarized and displayed in this form can be used to support existent hypotheses about the subject. They are also rich in possibilities for hypothesis formulation. One might begin to speculate about the importance of competition in the life of the subject. One might also be concerned about further understanding the realm of peer relationships in the life of the subject since they appear so critical under conditions of competition. Are they easily achieved by the subject? Some doubt may be cast on that possibility by the fact that solitary activity is so frequent a concomitant of positive outcome. Yet on balance the imagery of the subject reflects a considerably higher incidence of goal achievement (7 to 2), under a variety of conditions, which would lead away from a conjecture about a person in great distress. Of course, as one begins to speculate about more general states of the subject from data as limited as those presented, new questions are raised which can then be put to the data in a similar manner. I might, in pursuing the distress question, extend my analysis to any indications in the data of affective or behavioral consequences of success or lack of success. I have used the term "lack of success" rather deliberately in this example in order to try to minimize complexity and to introduce an important consideration in transposing the original data to the reduced form. The central issue is that one cannot assume that "lack of success" and failure are interchangeable terms unless so indicated by the imagery in the original data. To say "I didn't win first place" or "He broke the tape a fraction of a second before me," or "I almost caught him at the end but we just ran out of distance," is qualitatively different from "My performance in the race resulted in a resounding defeat—my preparation went entirely for naught," or "It made no difference that the outcome was close, I failed to win the gold medal." In the summarized data presented earlier, it may be assumed that two sequence outcomes emanated from statements in which lack of success, not failure, was reflected in the verbal imagery. In this instance it would be most instructive to pose the failure question to the data to uncover what relationship it has, if any, to the imagery attached to lack of success. If it turned out to be an exact duplicate, one could then be more secure in the belief that in this subject anything other than success is interiorized as failure.

Reviewing the summarized data, it should become apparent that frequency is being recorded as a possible indicator of power or importance. This was deliberately done to make a point at its most uncomplicated level. Yet, earlier on, in the explication of our first method we used all salience indicators, including frequency, as power or importance markers. Since in this instance not all of the sequences also meet salience criteria, would there be any gain in conjoining frequency and salience in assigning power? This is of course a question that could and should be answered empirically, not only in its gross sense but also in the finer sense of (if conjoint) whether the function is additive or multiplicative and in what proportions for each variable.

In providing an introductory example for the method of "asking the data a question," I have stayed at a rather specific level of questioning and attempted to provide the kind of material that has the possibility of being considered quantitatively. The method, however, is not restricted to any particular kind of question or any specific consequent mode of analysis. One could, in fact, ask much more global questions relating to the person's sanity or form of psychopathology or trait configuration or personal style characteristics or defenses. In each instance, it becomes incumbent on the investigator to provide the steps of reasoning which led to the formulation of the question posed. For example, in assessing introversion, one might extract all instances in which the subject describes (a) an interaction with another or other persons, or (b) any situation in which decision about choice of activity involves solitary or conjoint participation. Rules could then be specified by which introversive tendencies could be assessed (see Shapiro and Alexander, 1975).

Questions related to present functioning are more likely to be the focus of personality assessment studies. The more global questions are likely to be raised in psychobiographical study where some salience indicators are likely to point out known but unexplained aspects of a life already lived. Recent psychobiographical studies in this vein by psychologists are Runyan's (1981) review of the various explanations of why Van Gogh cut off his ear, Anderson's (1981) analysis of a period of severe despair in the life of William James, and my own effort (chapter 6) to understand Sullivan's two missing years.

In these studies the investigators are dealing with actual events in the life of the subject whose explanation might provide greater insight into personality structure or make mystery-shrouded life events more coherent. There are, however, instances in which the critical data are indirect, but logical assumptive steps are provided to link the disguised material to the experience of the subject. Certainly, in recent years, many investigators dealing with the intricate relationship between Freud's life and his work have pointed to the possibility that many illustrative items in his writings attributed to patients were really his own. Yet another indirect example from Freud's life is contained in the figure of Moses, whom Freud wrote about in one fashion or another at various times during the last four decades of his life. If one follows Jones's (1957) suggestion that Moses served Freud as a strong identification figure, and adds that it was a figure upon whom his unconscious conflicts could be projected and played out, an analysis of Freud's writings on Moses turns out to be quite revealing. In each case—at the turn of the century after a visit to Rome in part to view Michelangelo's Moses, in 1914 in the anonymous (but later claimed) paper on the Moses of Michelangelo (1959), and in his final completed book, *Moses and Monotheism* (1938/1964)—one can draw parallels between the conjectured life of Moses and Freud's own life at that time. Thus to ask the broad question of the meaning of Moses in the life of Freud, and to resort to that which Freud wrote about Moses to answer the question, is as revelatory in its way as the more direct sources of personal experience, his personal documents (see chapter 4).

### Further Issues Stemming from the Methods

Thus far I have presented a position defending the importance of the personological approach to the understanding of human functioning. What has given me pause, over time, as I attempted to grapple with what a person was like or how a person got to be that way, was how did I know what I thought I knew, and with what degree of certainty could I hold my belief. These same issues remained no matter the data source (personal documents, interviews, standardized tests), or the conditions under which the data were gathered (therapeutic hour or assessment laboratory). In attempting to deal with these issues initially, I was most taken with the possibilities open to fantasy analysis, especially as represented by TAT protocols. One does not need to stretch the imagination too far to recognize that what I have presented as methodological approaches, ways of thinking about data, grew partially out of work with this test, especially as it was represented by Tomkins (1947) and the use of Mill's canons of logic.

One of my first attempts to deal with the problem of certainty with inferences drawn from responses to TAT cards was to introduce the idea of an inquiry or limits testing, a la Rorschach, when the TAT as designed was already completed. The reasoning, as I now reconstruct it, was similar to that offered in the methods I have briefly described. I was trying to locate, from the specific story description, which aspects were critical in the repertoire of the teller to the particular development portrayed. Examination of other stories in the record was not always helpful in this regard. For example, let us imagine the following sequence extracted from a story[2] given by a female to card 4 which Murray describes as "A woman is clutching the shoulders of a man whose face and body are averted as if he were trying to pull away from her": demand (for intimacy) → rejection (by other) → fear (of loss of other) → compliance → stability (of relationship) + unhappiness. If one were to find in a ten-card set of stories a repetition of this entire sequence or parts of the pattern, e.g., rejection → fear (of loss) → compliance → unhappiness (especially if the stimulus card was less conducive to themes of rejection and unhappiness), there would be increased security in the inference that the sequence is meaningful and important in the life of the subject. The issue that was raised, however, was that if frequency did not appear in the data, especially if the mass of data was limited, were there other ways to assess its value? The inquiry was conceived of as a mini-experiment, a way of varying the variables and assessing their impact on criterion measures. In the sequence outlined, a variety of steps could be taken. The subject reviews the story with the examiner and is then asked to conjecture responses to "what if." One could examine whether demand itself is a necessary precursor of rejection or whether the particular demand for intimacy was critical to what ensued. To investigate this possibility, the inquiry could proceed with "what if he had reneged on some of the household responsibilities and she had demanded that he carry them out?" Or to investigate further the fixity or flexibility of expectations in male-female relations, one could change the subject's initial communication from demand to request or plea and examine outcome. Further, one could ask whether there were other things the heroine could have done and what outcome they might have produced. When a sequence is an habitual one for the subject, e.g., rejection → fear → compliance → unhappiness, it is striking how few alternatives can be imagined or how stable outcome remains no matter the variations in antecedent conditions. Inquiry, although cumbersome, highly dependent on cooperative subjects, and more amenable to leisurely, extended laboratory- or teaching-based investigations, did yield important leads toward the style of working that eventually emerged. For one, it led to the idea of asking the data a question, especially one that is suggested by the data, in that an inference can be clearly made but its limits or power are not yet known. With a large enough data base, personal documents, creative productions, life history interviews, psychotherapeutic sessions, one has the possibility of making limits and power assessments of any sequential pattern uncovered by salience indicators.

What I have attended to thus far is how to extract from an individual's verbal productions, particularly those relating to personal experience or creative narrative, material central to the description and understanding of his or her individual personality. The usual question that I have been asked when describing my approach to data has been, "Okay, so you can find these things that go together, their relative degree of invariance, the conditions that modify them, perhaps even the connections to their historical antecedents; now how do you put them all together? Don't you need a theory?" My response to this query has changed from time to time, as though it is still evolving, and I am not sure how it will eventually conclude. Over the years I have been taken with the theoretical stances of a number of extremely creative thinkers, most notably Freud, Jung, Lewin, and Tomkins. Despite my admiration for the genius of the first two and the influence their work has had on the background of my thinking, I have always come away dissatisfied when I took the data in which I placed some confidence after applying my way of working and tried to fit it into a Freudian or Jungian mold. My imagery concerning this task reverts to shoe fitting when accurate size and width indicators are not available. Any experienced salesman can make a reasonable enough estimate so that you are very likely to be able to insert your foot. The degree of comfort you will experience may be problematic, especially if he has a limited stock or your contours do not fit in with the general style in which his shoes are made. Even if the shoes are able to be worn despite their discomfort, there is no clear indication of what ultimately may result as a function of the grossness of fit, no matter how elegant the design, quality of the leather, or expense of making the final product. If your foot has to be shoehorned in, or the leather stretched, or the product purchased because it was all that was available, I am not sure it is the best shoe for you. Theories that are written to apply to mankind as a species and then used largely to deal with individual people give me pause. The understanding of the individual case depends on whether the observer has the flexibility to deal with "error variance" by using theory as a springboard rather than as a restrictive binder. Lewin's emphasis on the lawfulness of the individual case (1935) and Tomkins's basic position taken in script theory (1984) are much more in line with my own sense of direction. I see such work as structural, providing a framework within which the individual dynamics may be described. Each person is a story, a theory, described in a major way by the prominent scenes and scripts of that person's life.

The methods of approaching data that I have outlined, or the manner of putting things together, do not presuppose a particular stance on the psychological nature of human beings. Data that emerge from the approaches suggested may be put together conceptually with any kind of theory attractive to the investigator. It remains incumbent, however, on the investigator to make clear the connections.

Cogent examples, particularly instructive for our purposes, are provided in two recent papers by Carlson (1981, 1986), who offers an analysis of a single salient memory of a subject, and later her dreams before and after psychotherapy using the major ideas found in Tomkins's (1979, 1984, 1987) script theory. Carlson's work is especially valuable, not only as an attempt to demonstrate the explanatory power of Tomkins's ideas, but also as a rich, yet concise, introduction to these important, novel, and provocative views.

In my approach to the treatment of data, several important questions must be considered. One belongs under the general rubric of "reliability," a standard issue in the psychological literature. Reliability as it relates to the data of personal imagery may be considered in many forms. There is the question of typicality or performance stability. In the usual test instrument, designed to measure some stable entity, it is assumed that the questions asked will draw consistent responses from subjects in order to have the possibility of assessing the test's value. Personal documents, autobiographical memories, and life history interviews seem on a logical, common sense level to fulfill the consistency criterion. People talking about their own lives have a story to tell. Although often complex and convoluted, focused on different times and experiences, the major happenings and their construals are likely to reflect a high degree of reliability. When we leave the within-subject consistency question and move to the reliability question as it pertains to any manipulation or transformation of the original data, we are in more troubled waters. In the methods we are considering the following issues emerge: What is the likelihood that any set of investigators, applying the stated principles of salience, would extract similar material from the original data set? Further, given any sample of extracted material, what is the likelihood that it will be transformed similarly by any set of data analysts? Thirdly, given any set of reduced or transformed material, what is the likelihood that similar consistent subject response patterns would be detected by different data analysts?

From the standpoint of desirable psychometric practice the answers to these questions are critical in order to assess the possible value of the methods. How to answer these questions fairly is in itself a weighty problem.

In the first instance, what must be considered is the background of the subjects to be used in interobserver reliability. How powerful a factor is training in the use of the methods in determining these sorts of reliability estimates? What level of proficiency need be demonstrated by observers before a fair test of reliability could be undertaken? From my experience of teaching personality assessment techniques to beginning graduate students in clinical psychology for more than two decades, the answers to these questions are not simple. The ability to detect salience sequences is learned easily and agreement is quite high. However, I have found considerable variability among intellectually gifted students in their ability to go beyond this step over the course of a two-semester exposure. Some few progress rapidly. Almost all demonstrate reasonable understanding of the basic principles by the end of the instructional period. What is clear to me in retrospect is that unusually high reliabilities, in the manner normally measured, would probably not be achieved in the transformation step. In contemplating what such a conclusion means, I have at various times had different reactions. One involves the science-art controversy with regard to interpretive material. Perhaps what we are talking about is largely art, and any attempt to codify it or lay down its structure is largely futile. Countering this view was the fact that reliability when assessed was seemingly moderate. Some people came out with a fair amount of agreement, and these were typically the ones who "took to the work" most easily and rapidly. What was even more striking was that after exposure to the method the products of reduction or transformation, even when different, could easily be seen as related to the original data.

I shall return to an earlier example to illustrate this point. Recall the incident involving the subject and his boss. It read in part, "My boss called me in to discuss a report which I had just finished after a week of productive and satisfying effort. He chose to dwell on a minor point which he thought might contain an error. This made me very angry and I sat there dumbfounded." It was diagrammed: Independent effort → productivity and satisfaction (+ affect); unwarranted criticism by authority ($\delta$) → anger and inactivity (− affect). Were I to imagine a family of student-diagrammed reductions to this descriptive incident, they might include: (a) good things for petty reasons → bad things, (b) lack of recognition → negative affect, (c) self-evaluation → positive affect; evaluation by other → negative affect, (d) being alone → positive affect; interaction with another → negative affect, (e) exercise of power by authority → unexpressed anger → depression. How one would establish a reliability coefficient from the data I have just supplied is beyond my methodological sophistication. Yet upon inspection, one can see that a reasonable degree of relationship exists. In trying to conceptualize the problem encountered, I have imagined asking people to look out my office window and then asking them to describe what they see. The actual scene involves a lawn, massive trees, bushes, a hewn-stone building, and people, all of these in some dynamic mix. The answers I imagine to be forthcoming would rarely be complete unless the instructions included the direction to specify all or everything one could see, and even then there would not be perfect agreement. Each one would see accurately some part or parts of all that is possible to see, but agreement in the sense we think of as reliability would not be all that high. The solutions then to the interobserver reliability problem seem to me to lie not in the measurement of independent interpretive agreement but rather in what I would call congruent interpretive agreement. In our examples, it might take the form of offering a number of alternative answers to the window scene and asking the rater to judge them in terms of overall descriptive suitability. Or in the incident with the boss, the experimenter's diagram (in this case my own) could be embedded among the alternatives presented and others even more remote to assess its descriptive power.

What I have done thus far in grappling with the various facets of the reliability problem is to focus on the first two issues, the reduction of the initial data pool and the transformation of the times selected into a similar diagrammatic form. I have suggested that these issues may be manageable. With regard to the third problem, whether the diagrammed data, when intuitively factored, will lead to the same scripts, deductions, or hypotheses in different observers, I shall adopt another stance, redirecting it as a validity problem rather than one of reliability. It is my thought that the most important aspects of the methodological search are those of identifying the critical bits of data and putting them in comparable form. The remaining task of then factoring for commonality, assessing specificity or limits of repeated means-end sequences, assigning power to emerging relationships in the data, while they could conceivably be handled in the suggested manner for reliability, might better be treated as validity issues to be resolved by the usual techniques of prediction and cross-validation. To extract consistent but differentiated imagery about affect resulting from being alone as opposed to being with others under various contextual conditions for solitude or company leads to all sorts of hypotheses about life as experienced by the possessor of such imagery and thus lends itself readily to validity study.

The question of validity is a variant of the one with which this inquiry was begun. How do we know with any certainty anything about the personality of another human being? Thus far we have dwelt on what materials to examine, what to look for in the materials, and how to deal with what is found. Once having done all of that, one is faced with the fundamental issue of whether what you think may be the case is in fact so. In clinical work the repetition of sequential patterns frequently serves as a validator of initial hypotheses drawn from the client's verbalizations, and I have certainly experienced this with the detection of nuclear scenes and their attendant scripts. In personality assessment, especially in the extended study of single individuals, one can extract all sorts of relative invariances from early material and predict their impact or appearance in later samples, and this has also been done with sufficiently encouraging regularity about aspects of the personality which were not easily available to the naked eye.

Recently Demorest (1987) presented the results of an inquiry based on the methodological stance I have elaborated. She extracted sequential "messages" from the imagery (autobiographies and TAT stories) of nine subjects. At a later time these same subjects were given a series of photographs depicting various emotions but no action or human interaction (from O'Sullivan, Ekman, and Friesen [1977]) to which they were asked to generate stories. The resultant sequential "messages" extracted from this source of data were then matched (in a blind comparison) to those produced from the earlier data set. Of the fifty-four "messages" extracted from the nine subjects in this latter task, roughly 80 percent were successfully attributed to their owners, based on the recurrence of message elements extracted from the imagery produced earlier and from different tasks.

In tracing the evolution of my methodological approach to data I have consistently referred to the areas of personality assessment and psychobiographical study, with an occasional hint at its relationship to psychotherapy. In what follows I should like to redirect attention to possible uses of various aspects of the methodology to the areas mentioned, uses which may not be immediately obvious.

### Applications of the Method to Personality Assessment

With regard to individual personality assessment, one might legitimately inquire about the various reasons for which such study is typically undertaken. If we put aside for the moment the limited number of research studies dealing with life cycle development that emanated from the Harvard Psychological Clinic and the relatively small investigative heritage it produced, much of what remains in personality assessment deals with problems of psychopathology, its diagnosis and remediation, and with occupational selection and advancement.

The typical ways of dealing with these problems are normative and comparatively based. To use a simple example, we might think of wishing to design an instrument which would allow us to discern whether an individual was neurotic, psychotic, or normal and what are the chief identifying features in that personality. Such an instrument has in fact been produced in the Minnesota Multiphasic Personality Inventory, probably the most widely used personality test in clinical settings. The massive research conducted with this instrument has made known its psychometric properties. We have good estimates of the likelihood of misdiagnosis, either of being classified as a member of a category when in fact no supporting evidence can be found or on the other hand the likelihood of not being identified as a member of a category when other evidence strongly suggests that this is the case. The test is refined to a point where such errors are as minimal as one can expect from the method employed. In addition when a personality profile is identified by the points of greatest deviancy from the responses that are most typically given on the variety of test scales, a general set of statements can be made about what people with these profiles are like. The description can include a variety of personality markers, such as traits, behaviors, social and interpersonal interactions, and indications of the affective life. The information derived from an MMPI profile is cost efficient, rich in a global fashion, and most helpful within a medical, biological framework where the identification of a particular disease syndrome leads to a prescriptive pharmacological solution. Somewhat facetiously it could be said that in such a setting it is not who you are but what you are that counts. Yet we know that any kind of illness or difficulty, no matter its presumed origin, does not manifest itself in the same way in all sufferers. The impact of suffering, whatever the symptoms, differs for different people, and the effect, psychological or physical, of any kind of treatment regimen is not uniform for all people identified as being members of any diagnostic category. The material that could result from the search for the critical scenes and scripts in a person's life may be used to make judgments about category inclusion, if this seemed important. More importantly, however, it might lead to insights about treatment, whether the pathology is judged to be psychologically or biologically based, mild or serious, long-term or transient. When we know the elements that constitute the critical positive and negative scenes in a person's existence and what scripts result in the attempt to cope with the negative ones or to retain or reestablish the positive ones, we have the grounds not only for making psychodiagnostic judgments but also for initiating relevant therapeutic intervention. By this I am referring not simply to whether the treatment should be psychological, biological, or both but also what might be important in maximizing the possibilities for success in treatment no matter which route is taken.

Recently, in line with what has just been presented, I had the occasion to listen to a lifelong friend and professional colleague describe some of his experiences and thoughts over an eighteen-month period following a serious myocardial infarction. While he had been exposed during part of this time to excellent programmatic attempts to teach him about heart functioning, exercise, diet, weight control, and even general knowledge about the effects of stress on personality, he lamented the lack of attention to the psychological and experiential aspects of the condition. In fact, his ruminations turned toward improvements that could be made in the program he attended to deal with this issue. Much of it involved the group format, in accordance with the general design of the program, and the ideas he presented about what people could discuss and become aware of excited me because of their soundness and promise. Yet, in consequent afterthoughts, I could conjecture how effectiveness might be improved if the major scene/script mix of the participants were known, especially insofar as they related to health, illness, dependency, and independence.

### Application to Psychotherapy

In a similar vein I would like to explore the added value of scenes and scripts and their detection to the field of psychotherapy from another point of view, that of training. For many years I have been intensively involved in preparing graduate students in clinical psychology for the various roles they may be called upon to assume as professionals. Clearly that of psychotherapist is highly valued by students. Yet in my own experience, which includes knowledge about not only my own institution but a considerable number of others as well, leads me to believe that training efforts in this regard leave much to be desired. My characterization of the existing situation is that there are some un-specified number of programs that adopt a very specific theoretical approach to the teaching of psychotherapy, most typically behavior modification, and their students are trained to think and work within this framework. In a fair number of other graduate programs, those typically with limited in-house facilities or unusually heavy emphasis on the research role, the training in psychotherapy is delegated to outside sources, beginning perhaps in the internship year, but it is mostly thought of as a postdoctoral phenomenon. The remaining institutions, which I would judge to be in the majority, are ones that are seen as "eclectic" in their treatment of psychotherapy training. By this I mean to convey that their staffs contain members who represent a variety of views on psychotherapy, and the student's training will be largely influenced by who happens to teach what at any particular time and who turns out to be the particular person from whom he/she will receive supervision. The latter system, although beneficial in many ways, certainly in breadth of exposure, also contains the greatest potential for confusion on the part of students. Many struggle with the questions of what to listen for and how to put together what they hear no less than what to do about whatever they see as the issues of the person with whom they are working. All too often the therapeutic work becomes confused with the problems encountered in supervision. How then to find an approach to the conduct of the therapeutic work which would be conducive to learning what one needs to know about the nature of another no matter in what systematic framework the critical data are then considered or what particular ideas are instituted in the interest of remediation or change?

The ideas which earlier in this presentation were used to elaborate an assessment methodology seem to be reasonably applicable to initial training in psychotherapy. The data, the retelling of personal experience, is ideal. The issues then become how to use the principles of salience to reduce the data, how to identify commonalities in the data, and how to ask the accumulated data bank existing in the memory of the therapist the relevant questions which provide confirmation, negation, or conditional limitations on the material extracted. All this, of course, unlike in the assessment situations earlier explored, must eventually take place during the therapeutic hour. How long this skill takes to acquire is not a simple matter to answer. It depends on almost all the same kinds of variables that would be involved in acquiring any kind of skill. With a sufficient grasp of the overall dimensions of the task and continued practice, speed in performance increases and consciousness concerning the various elements in the process is reduced. In an oversimplified sense I am comparing it with learning to type. The point, however, is that the method does focus attention on how to identify important but perhaps not obvious aspects of the individual personality, a necessary condition, I would hold, for psychotherapeutic intervention.

### Application to Personnel Issues

Earlier it was mentioned that assessment techniques have been increasingly employed in selection and advancement decisions found in business, industry, government, and even academia. One of the controversies that has surfaced with some prominence from time to time is how much attention to pay to the data emerging from normatively based comparative personality indicators, whether they deal with trait descriptions, values, ideological stances, or psychopathology, as opposed to material emerging from either personal interviews or the more idiosyncratic or idiographic personality indicators. Again, the resolution of this controversy involves the evaluation of a variety of factors too numerous to explore in depth here. The utility question must of course be considered. What are you spending for what degree of certainty? If anyone can do the job in question adequately except for those with low attention spans, and there is an adequate pool of applicants, then anything other than a reliable measure of attention span may not be necessary or economical. However, for many selection tasks for which psychological assessments play an important role one should only be looking secondarily for the limiting condition for elimination of candidates. Primarily one should hope to find, especially in a buyers' market, the most suitable person for the task. Frequently when the candidates have different but equally attractive features in trait configurations assessed by major standard paper-and-pencil tests, the search on the part of a selection committee turns toward finding some flaw, oftentimes minor, to magnify in order to come to a decision. The search then essentially turns to the discovery of alleged imperfection rather than a search for uniqueness which fosters the possibility or in the best instance the promise of unusual achievement. Under these conditions, selection committees are very likely to be drawn to the "safe" candidate. In examining this problem, both from the position of a selection committee member on numerous occasions and as a psychological consultant to selection boards, I have thought seriously about the possible value that material extracted by the methods I have been discussing could have in this realm.

The issues pertaining to selection are indeed complex and clearly dependent, perhaps at base, on the accuracy of the analysis of what it takes to do the task in question. In an instance in which the personality of the candidate is seen to be a factor in the ultimate selection equation, it behooves us to seek ways to tease out the scenes and scripts which characterize an individual and apply them against the criterial demands.

In searching for an example of the position I am advocating, I am reminded of an experience in consultation that I had just a few years ago. While abroad, serving in a visiting capacity to a department of psychology, I was asked to consult with the members of the medical school admissions committee on methods of selection, especially as they related to personality variables. The procedure used in this institution had been in place for many years. They initially selected a short list of candidates on the basis of prior academic achievement and recommendations. Each candidate then appeared for a personal interview with the full complement of selection committee members. There was no fixed procedure for the session. Any member could ask any question of the candidate. In viewing one such session, I found that a rather large amount of the time was spent on questions pertaining to the intensity, range, and duration of the candidate's medical interest, and questions relating to what the candidate might do in a medical emergency. The first set of questions were so apparent in their objective that they seemed to demand stereotyped socially acceptable responses. The second set of questions left me puzzled as to what they were supposed to measure and what each committee member was taking away from the responses.

In their meeting with me the group was initially concerned with whether the interview should be retained as a part of the selection procedure. They had been advised by distinguished senior members of the psychology department to abandon the exercise for the following reasons: (a) The interview did nothing to enhance the success ratio in selection over the usual data sources (academic record, recommendations). They also intimated that evidence existed which showed that the interview could lower the success ratio.[3] (b) The interview was costly and time consuming, and could maximize irrelevant factors (impression management, subtle social influence). From what I could detect, the only reasons that prompted them to consider retaining the interview as part of the selection procedure were: (a) the fact that it had always been part of the process, which probably translated into a respect for tradition and a faith that each of the members had in his/her ability to detect potential through personal interaction and (b) some residual dissatisfaction with the candidates ultimately selected and trained, as though, somehow or another, not enough of them lived up to the faculty's initial expectations, and that this could be remedied by closer personal scrutiny of the candidates. My response to their concerns dealt mainly with this last issue, which will return us to the question about personality with which we have been concerned throughout this paper: what is important to know (what is salient about the data), what do you need to know (ask the data a question), in order to make a considered judgment.

I had no quarrel with the analysis offered the committee previously. There was no way that the interview, representing individual personality data, could improve the selection ratio, given the conditions under which the system operated. The applicant pool was so highly qualified by previous academic performance measures that I would have wagered that random selection would have produced as high success ratios as any other method, especially when typical criterion measures are employed. In most instances they are either completion of the first year of training in good standing or the achievement of the M.D. degree. The modern medical academic climate almost guarantees meeting these criteria as long as their highly selected students retain the motivation to be trained.

The big issue that then remained was how to deal with the faculty's feeling that they were not selecting the "best" with regard to ultimate benefit to medicine. When the issue was raised as to what each of the committee members thought was critical or essential to becoming a highly regarded, important contributor to medical science and/or practice, certain personality features began to emerge, not so much in a trait-like sense but in a more dynamic fashion. "One must be able to put one's work above all else, no matter the cost." "One must be able to persist even when results are discouraging." "One must have the kind of confidence to take calculated risks and face the possibility of failure." "One must be able to enjoy the excitement of challenge." "One must be able to profit from experience both positive and negative and not be caught up in the affective consequences." These were the kinds of statements which resulted from the ensuing discussions of criteria. Without too much difficulty they lend themselves quite readily to assessment by the methodology presented. In this instance the interview can be directed toward description of life experiences relevant to the particular issues in question (enduring interests, hobbies, school work, participation in competitive activity) and it can be assessed to what extent and in what fashion the candidate meets the criterial standard. This is possible whether the committee has decided on a set of common criteria or whether each member is using his/her own, or whether in the instance of common criteria different weights are being assigned to different criteria in coming to the overall judgment about the candidate. Either or both of the suggested strategies, extracting by salience or by putting the question to the data, might well lead to the identifiable dynamic consistencies from which the ultimate judgments could be made. Of course, in all of this there exists implicitly the assumption that what one has already done in the past is the best indicator of what one is likely to do in the future. It is, however, not an assumption unique to this methodology. It pervades much of psychology.

I chose a rather complex example to illustrate the possible value of the methods under discussion. It involved a number of complicating factors in the selection process which were necessary to present in order to make the consulting issues clear, e.g., the relevance of the data of personal experience for improving selection ratios, the use or misuse by judges of personal data, the problems of implicit and explicit criterial standards. In many instances for which assessment techniques are utilized, these kinds of problems may be minimal. In the employment or advancement of professional or managerial personnel, issues of general competence or particular features of the technical aspects of job performance may be quite clear and the outstanding issues remaining are those relating to the personal "qualities" of the applicant, or "what he/she is like" and what impact that is likely to have on desired job performance. If such is the case it would be my contention that the more personalistic, specific, detailed, dynamic end products of the methods described are likely to be better indicators of performance outcome than those derived from nomothetic or comparative data for any particular applicant.

Earlier in this chapter I made reference to the fact that I had used the basic methodological ideas I have presented in several psychobiographical studies (see chapters 3–6). In the papers themselves, as is generally the case in psychobiographical work, there is little explication of the methods through which the essential ideas of the narrative were discovered. There are, of course, notable exceptions, Allport (1942, 1965), Baldwin (1942), McCurdy (1961, chap. 12), Rosenberg and Jones (1972) to name a few, but these are rare. I should like now to turn to the implications of the approach I have presented for psychobiographical analysis.

## Applications to Psychobiography

One of the major problems faced by psychobiographers is the massive amount of data usually available on people who appear worthy of study. If one is addicted in any sense to a prevalent but perhaps covert belief among personologists that any product of an individual bears some relationship to the personality of that individual, the problem becomes formidable. How then to reduce by selection or organizing principles the original mass? How can this be done with an eye toward retaining that which is critical or that which with further manipulation will yield something of importance psychologically? I am not attempting to approach the problem of how to do biography but rather to deal with what to do with the data the biographer gathers in order to make it psychobiography. In one sense I have already suggested the answer to this question several times over in the preceding material. Processing whatever is selected as the data by extracting the salient aspects and factoring them into common or unique sequential patterns is one technique. The other puts a question to the data whose answer is deemed relevant for the psychological understanding of the subject, extracts all material bearing on the question, and processes the extracted material by the same factor technique. One might then study data samples from different points in the life history and estimate pattern stability and/or change and try to relate them to factors extant in the life history of those different times. Once sequential means-ends patterns are established as clear and defensible, one may then direct inquiry along the path of their origin and development, enlarging upon the continuity of the story. Although these seem like straightforward methodological paths, they are not frequently utilized in psychobiographical study. The more typical procedures employed are those of demonstrating the "fit" between various aspects of the data and either Freudian or Eriksonian theoretical views.

It is my contention that psychobiographers for the most part get interested in trying to explain through appeal to psychological means the controversial or unexplained aspects of a subject's life experience. Why did Van Gogh cut off his ear (Runyan, 1981)? Why did William James suffer from prolonged melancholia, or abandon art (Anderson, 1981)? What led Sullivan to his startlingly new therapeutic techniques with schizophrenia when he had little or no prior relevant training experiences (see chapter 6)? Why did Freud faint (Rosenberg, 1978)? These are some recent attempts to deal with circumscribed problems, only sometimes emphasizing the importance of methodological issues (Runyan, 1984).

As a departure point I would like to use the life of Sigmund Freud to illustrate what I have in mind in expanding the uses of these methods for psychobiographical study. This giant figure in twentieth-century thought probably has had as much written about his personal life, his scholarly work, and their interaction as any other single figure in recent history. For my purposes this is important in that it seems somewhat unlikely that anyone interested in the subject matter to which this book is devoted would be unaware of the major details of that life, reducing the need for extensive background and relational descriptions.

From all that exists on Freud, the data that would appeal to me most would be the voluminous correspondence that remains, because the material was personal, private, and likely to be spontaneous. From an analysis of these materials one could undoubtedly arrive at consistent sequential patterns which would pertain to the general "other" and yet others that would be gender specific, role specific, situational, or condition specific, and so on. Another obvious source of value would be the autobiographic study Freud wrote in 1925. However, applying the principles of salience, I might immediately be led to those inquiries that were most unique in some way, clear departures from the main body of the work. Several examples come to mind, all having a variety of things in common. If we dwell for a moment on *Totem and Taboo* (Freud, 1914/1938), "The Moses of Michelangelo" (Freud, 1914/1959), and *Moses and Monotheism* (Freud, 1914/1964), a set spanning more than thirty years, it becomes apparent that they have a variety of salient things in common. In the first instance they were all outside the pale of typical analytic works. They were written to demonstrate the power of psychoanalytic ideas to areas beyond the immediate medical concerns of psychotherapy. They were addressed to problems of interest to other fields, cultural anthropology, art history, and theology. They also shared a rather consistent negative response from scholars in those respective fields and were not even prized among those faithful to psychoanalysis. To follow this line of reasoning a bit further we may become aware of two additional points of similarity. They all deal with heroic leaders, father-like figures whose ultimate fate is contained in two major scenes, one positive ("The Moses of Michelangelo"), the other negative (*Totem and Taboo,* and *Moses and Monotheism*). In the Michelangelo story, Moses successfully contains his anger toward the idolators in the interest of preserving the law, the "perfect" Moses. In the other two, the father is displaced, actually killed by the faithful (sons, followers) only to arise in another form (in one a totem, in the other a substitute Moses). They also deal with the theme of origins (the origins of culture and of the intent of Moses and of Michelangelo) and they convey the common message that things are not what they seem on the surface. The latter is a consistent message that pervades the most important of all of Freud's writings reiterating consistently the power of what resides in the unconscious.

In this brief extension of the use of extraction by salience and simple combinatorial and difference principles I have already outlined leads to important relationships between Freud's life (read personality) and his work which can be analyzed and assessed by asking the biographical data particular questions. The importance of origins was already seen and discussed by Jones, who related it to Freud's early history, the age differential of the father and mother, and the ages of his half-brothers who stemmed from the father's earlier marriage or marriages. He did not, however, recognize the lack of internal resolution of the origins problem and its impact on various of Freud's later writings even as late as his last few years. Jones's sensitivity to the issues of origins is interesting in this regard. It is the title of the opening section of his own autobiography, which is one of the most impressive illustrations of the principle of primacy in the detection of salient data.

What also is brought into sharp focus is the importance of the Moses figure in Freud's life, the analysis of which I have attempted in a separate study found in this volume (see chapter 4). It deals with the use of the figure of Moses as a positive identification upon whom Freud could project his own unconscious conflicts of the time. Considering that the first reference to Moses appears in Freud following his first visit to Rome after the turn of the century, the second (an anonymous paper) some thirteen years later, and the third twenty to twenty-five years beyond that, we are treated to the possibility of discovering the dynamic conflicts he endured at particular moments in time, their fate over time, his particular solution to them in fantasy, and their reality consequences.

Still another psychobiographical lead that may be followed from the more esoteric writings relates to the importance of the father-son relationship in Freud's life and how it influenced his own psychological development. I am referring here to what emerges particularly to Freud in the search for the ideal father image from the standpoint of the son and what happens to the son when he in fact moves into the role of father, a specific issue dealt with in detail in a later chapter (see chapter 3). From the works in question, however, we can extract the following summary material relevant to the questions we have raised:

(1) The sons are shamed and/or made fearful for either wishing to replace the father, or demanding a clear-cut share of what belongs to the father, or committing an act counter to father's expectations. These sequences are easily located in *Totem and Taboo*, the two treatises on Moses, and Freud's comments after first viewing Michelangelo's statue in Rome in 1901. Suppose we diagram it in a very general form as: displeasing authority by any manifestation of the power issue → expectation of or actuality of wrath (−affect) by authority → shame and/or fear (−affect) by recipient. In Tomkins's script language such a sequence would constitute an important negative scene.

(2) A second formulation relating to authority can be derived from "The Moses of Michelangelo" and can be related to the first. Its message is that the authority was more intent after seeing the transgressions of the followers in preserving the law (tablets) than punishing the people and thus followed a path of self-restraint, isolation, and attention to the abstract, nonpersonal task. This may be identified as an important positive scene and after slight rearrangement diagrammed thusly: displeasing authority (♂) by violating authority expectations → calmness and withdrawal on the part of authority → no clear affective consequences for the initial instigators. A further positive sequence from these works is: authority is supportive and protective, both in a noncoercive way. The scenes then might be further reduced to (a) fear of shame and anger for errors of commission as the negative scene, and (b) support and protection in an uncritical manner from a distant authority as the positive scene. How enduring and pervasive these scenes were in his life may be pointed to by a variety of bits of evidence from the biographical material. Recall the early incident of Freud's display of incontinence in which his memory is of being shamed by the father. Recall as well the general characterization given of father as a protective, supportive, noncritical admirer of his son, who received all sorts of privileges and financial benefits from his father

(Freud did not become concerned with earning his livelihood until age thirty), a father who allowed him freely to select his own life's occupational path no matter the hardships imposed by the choice.

Without carrying the analysis further, anyone acquainted with the major aspects of Freud's life and his work will immediately recognize the ramifications of these scenes and the attendant scripts developed to promote the positive and avoid, overcome, or repair the negative scenes described. The problems related to shame, anger, humiliation and their relationship to strength and weakness in the authority role were major issues in Freud's life, ones commonly treated by the various biographers. Their importance was pointed to by even a superficial analysis of the major contents of a few of the more esoteric works he had published.

In the introduction to this section on psychobiography, I referred to the fact that people working in this area frequently set a question for investigation that is much more circumscribed, one that relates to a specific aspect or incident in the life of the subject. An example of how an extension of the methodological stance I have been presenting might be used in such an instance may be borrowed from a longer psychobiographical study of Harry Stack Sullivan (see chapter 6). One of the major questions raised in this work is how Sullivan, with little or no formal training in psychiatry, began a program almost immediately in his first psychiatric post which used methods hitherto unknown in the psychiatric community. These early efforts were seen as landmark changes in the psychological treatment of schizophrenia. Since in those days, the 1920s, the ideas of psychoanalysis were beginning to permeate upper-echelon psychiatric circles, especially those related to the importance of unconscious factors in psychological illness, it was fascinating to consider the various elements which could have contributed to what Sullivan himself sometimes referred to as "social engineering," a very different approach. The study of Sullivan deals with a variety of elements contributing some piece of the answer to this puzzle. At this time I would like to deal with a single one for its illustrative value.

In all of Sullivan's published work, there are very few dreams reported and only one that I can recall that he acknowledged as his own. It appeared in a chapter on sleep, dreams, and myths, in his *Interpersonal Theory of Psychiatry*, at a point where he is attempting to illustrate the intrusion of dreamlike material into waking life in schizo-phrenia (Sullivan, 1953, p. 335). Its salience is accounted for in a variety of ways other than uniqueness. He pooh-poohs the idea of ever really understanding its meaning and yet hints at the idea that he really did, with assistance, understand its essence (emphasis, nega-tion). He rejects either simple or symbolic explanations for the dream and reduces it to its illustrative value in recognizing symptoms of schizophrenic process (misplaced emphasis, negation).

In leading up to the dream report, he indicates that as a child he was afraid of spiders, which were used to discourage him from the danger of exploring the basement of the farmhouse in which he lived. His grand-mother would place a dead spider on the top step leading down. He also points out that this fear of spiders is somewhat unique in that he is not generally fearful, and that his attitude toward spiders has not changed as a function of age. He also places the dream at a time when he first had the opportunity to intensively study schizophrenia, al-though the imagery he describes surrounding the dream would place it as occurring a bit earlier, when he was still in Washington, before he began his work with patients. It was, perhaps, a dream in anticipation of the role he was to take on shortly in which he would have to assume responsibility for both treatment and research for a condition about which he had limited formal knowledge by training and medical expe-rience. Given the conditions described (the times, his fear, schizo-phrenia), the decoding of the dream contained the promise of provid-ing valuable material relating to our original question concerning the unique path he followed in his work with schizophrenics.

He introduces the dream imagery by recalling for the reader the "geometric designs that spiders weave on grass . . . when the dew is on the ground." He then follows with:

> My dream started with a great series of these beautiful geometric patterns, each strand being very nicely midway between the one in front of it and the one behind it, and so on—quite a remarkable textile, and incidentally I am noticeably interested in textiles. Then the textile pattern became a tunnel reaching backward after the fashion of the tunnel-net spiders, and then the spider began to approach. And as the spider approached, it grew and grew into truly stupendous and utterly horrendous proportions.

Thus the dream ends and he goes on to tell us that he awoke from it shaken, unable to rid himself of the spider image until he "got up and smoked a cigarette, and looked out the window and one thing and another." He feared going back to bed, seeing the image of the spider on the sheet. After partaking in simple reality testing, looking and smoking, he looked on the bed for the spider image, which by this time had disappeared, and he concluded that it was again safe to sleep. His description of the dream incident then ends with the statements, "Fortunately, with some assistance, I guessed what might be the case, and thus escaped certain handicaps for the study of schizophrenia. I might add that spiders thereupon disappeared forever from my sleep— so far as I know."

What was it that Sullivan might have guessed from the dream imagery which allowed him to avoid pitfalls and set a fruitful direction in his study and treatment of schizophrenics? Let us assume a symbolic equivalence between spider and schizophrenia, despite the obvious difference that one is an object and the other is a mental state or condition. The assumption of equivalence is based on the fact that for Sullivan both were sources of terror, and their products were sources of great interest. In the dream we are told that the geometric patterns of the spider are like textiles, in which Sullivan claims "noticeable interest." With regard to schizophrenia we are reminded by Perry (1982) that at Sheppard he sought recording equipment in order to record the utterances of patients. It was the product of the patient which would allow him to study the patterns of schizophrenic thought.

If we follow the dream imagery literally, what we see is that if one begins to follow the interest object back to its origin, one will be confronted with terror. The implication that follows from his behavior upon awakening is that one must remain anchored in reality and not seek to understand the source of the terror, a solution quite opposite to that taken by Jung, for example, in attempting to deal therapeutically with schizophrenia. Sullivan's ultimate therapeutic path follows the direction suggested in the dream. Reduce the patient's panic by anchoring him in reality, indicating to him that these fears (homosexual panic, for example) were not unique but acceptable to like-minded peers and ultimately manageable. He may have thus, on some level, decoded the dream message as, "Don't go where you cannot go, no matter its lure or intrinsic fascination. Stay anchored." This certainly was the treatment path he followed with schizophrenic patients.

In attempting to present a methodological stance for dealing with personal data, I have indicated all too briefly at various junctures the chief sources of influence on my work, Tomkins, Murray, Freud, Allport, Lewin. What I have borrowed and utilized from each of these giant figures is no longer clearly evident to me. The resultant, while undoubtedly my own conglomerate for which I assume full responsibility, often seems to me to be nothing more than obvious extensions of the seminal ideas which they presented.

While explicating my own manner of working with assessment or psychobiographical material, I have followed the path of the introverted personologist, essentially by-passing the relationship of my efforts to those of others similarly embarked on trying to understand the individual in his/her world. But why this is the case seems to me to go far beyond personal predilections. On the most positive side, the recent publication of Runyan's *Life History and Psychobiography* (1982), makes extended discussion and comparison of recent efforts in the study of individual lives somewhat superfluous. His is a most comprehensive piece of work which will likely take its place as a standard in the field.

While Runyan has summarized various methodological advances in single case study from the statistical point of view and more comprehensive approaches to data gathering in a taxonomic sense, we are still left with a variety of interesting approaches, a veritable smorgasbord whose continued power of attraction and ultimate nutritional value have not yet been decided. From my own point of view I have resonated to some aspects of the recent work of Bromley (1977), Horowitz (1979), Carlson (1981), Stolorow and Atwood (1979), and Elms (1972), noticing some points of agreement in some of the ways in which we conceptualize either the task or the underlying theoretical importance of the task of understanding an individual life either in part or more wholistically. Work in this field, while undoubtedly influenced by the work of countless others, does not yet seem to have the systematic, cumulative quality found in the more established bodies of knowledge. Perhaps this awaits a more established methodology for personology.

How one solves the epistemological question of how one knows anything about self or another with any degree of security has been the focus of this chapter. One resolution offered by nomotheticists is to question the scientific legitimacy of the study of the individual which has led to critical outcomes in training new generations of people interested in the basic issues of personality development and personality functioning. The present training scene reflects a massive nomothetic bias. People are generally taught research design in a manner which in a sense dictates how they will study the problems they become concerned with in their areas of content interest. Within this framework the individual is reduced to the status of error variance. What we want to know, according to this view, is the weight or power of any variable we think important in contributing to some outcome as it is reflected in some sample of the population. What people do is the legitimate concern. Why any individual does not conform to the pattern of the group outcome is a matter assigned to error or uncontrolled factors. The usual resultant of this kind of training, whether intended or not, is to make a real distinction between "research" as opposed to "clinical" knowledge, the former, in this instance, being related to communicable estimates of certainty, the latter to "intuitions," or "hunches." What I hope I have been able to communicate in this essay is that I believe this to be a false, artificial distinction which may be demonstrated by the use of the position I have just explicated.

But what is the alternative or more reasonably the methodological concomitant in the training of future scholars, researchers, and clinicians to offset this nomothetic bias? How can we train future personologists whether their ultimate interests turn to personality assessment, personnel selection, psychotherapy, psychobiography, or the study of any personality process or attribute? This is a matter which I have been concerned with for the better part of three decades and to whose explication I would like to turn my attention next.

# CHAPTER 2

## A Format for Teaching
## Personological Inquiry

In the preceding chapter I have raised the question of how we know with any certainty anything about the personality of a human being. It was, in part, a critique of an exclusive use of a nomothetic way of knowing, a knowing by comparison with the performance of others. The investigative position adopted was personalistic and a methodology for extracting important data about a single other was described. The preferred source of material was designated as that emerging from the memory of lived experience and the imagery involved in the retelling of one's own story or bits of it. This kind of material abounds in all sorts of personal documents (autobiography, correspondence, speeches, creative productions) and in the end product of life history interviews. The methodology focused on a set of guidelines for extracting salient units from the total data set and called attention to some principles for analyzing that which emerged. An issue raised at the end concerned how one can teach or impart a personalistic stance to incipient investigators, scholars, and clinicians—a matter which I would now like to address.

Over a period of many years, more than two decades, I have enjoyed the relatively rare opportunity of developing the above-mentioned ideas largely through the medium of a two-semester graduate seminar on personality assessment. The basic format of the course was modeled on the investigative work on individual personality structure characteristic of the Harvard Psychological Clinic in the 1930s and early 1940s under Henry Murray's direction[1] and later carried on in the teaching and writing of Robert W. White (1952, 1966, 1975). Two essential elements in that model involve the multiplicity of data sources used to study the personality and the group council format for coming to grips with the analysis of the data. These elements, as we shall see, are invaluable for examining the critical problems of reliability and validity. Other important features of the model were the *long-term* study of single individuals (which translated in my work to a year of investigation), and the selection of subjects who were devoid of serious psychopathology. A minor modification of the latter condition in the people we studied was to seek those who, on all obvious selection criteria, seemed to function well.

### Background: The Princeton Experience

My own introduction to this kind of experience occurred while I was a graduate student at Princeton in the late 1940s, in a seminar on personality assessment conducted by Silvan Tomkins and Dan Horn, who had been members of the Harvard group and who in 1942 had collaborated in producing a modified projective technique called the "Picture Arrangement Test," or PAT (Tomkins, 1952; Tomkins and Miner, 1957). Since only a small number of students, six to eight, were annually admitted to the graduate program during those years regardless of field of interest, the course was given for all students. The major emphasis in the course was on the inferential process as it relates to personality description and analysis, and not on the more particular problems of clinical diagnostic evaluation. We were encouraged to comb life-history and test data to find the dynamic processes characteristic of the individual being studied. No particular theory of personality was advocated as the basis for understanding a person, nor was any special data source lionized. In many ways the seminar paralleled the one later summarized by White (1974).

For me the experience was a profound one. I was engaged at the time in a series of studies related to the question of how we hear, particularly the relationship of anatomical structure to physiological and behavioral function. There was a kind of implicit order to this work that gave me the feeling that one could "know" with a reasonable degree of confidence the relationships sought. The variables were limited and the techniques for investigation, although not free of error, known and mostly agreed upon by investigators. Until this time I had thought of knowing about the personality of another as being sort of an intuitive process which some people were good at while others were not. Listening to Tomkins examine the data of a TAT record made me aware that the process of "knowing" was not all that different for the data of personality than for the data of audition, despite the obvious disparities in complexity and control. Observations led to hypotheses, which led to the search for feedback about the "power" of the formulation.

In the years immediately following, I found little opportunity to consolidate the insights I had gained in the work with Tomkins and Horn in assessment. Nor was I able to explore unresolved residual questions involved with knowing about the personality of an individual in a manner that might satisfy me. When I turned to the study of clinical psychology my work in assessment, especially on internship, was mostly involved with answering diagnostic questions with little emphasis on extended discussion of personality dynamics. Therapeutic supervision seemed much more involved with either issues of technique or the supervisor's evaluations of my own contributions to the therapeutic mix, leaving me with less opportunity to formulate and validate what the verbal data produced in any hour were telling me about the personality of the person with whom I was working.

Some seven or eight years after my initial introduction to assessment, the chance to resume this kind of inquiry occurred when I was asked to give a seminar in personality to Princeton seniors. The format I worked out grew out of my knowledge of the earlier Harvard Clinic model. It was a one-semester course during which we studied a single subject through the analysis of a written autobiography and a series of interviews on various aspects of the life history suggested to be of special importance by a reading of the autobiography. The subject studied was a university freshman whose psychological path through life thus far had not been marred by undue psychological difficulty, a person who was judged by the selection interviewer to be functioning well in the world. The choice of a freshman was dictated by the increased lack of likelihood that the subject would be known to the members of the seminar, and since the course members were seniors, no continuing interaction with the subject during the college years was likely.

In looking back on the two consecutive years in which the course was given, I am struck by a number of thoughts. One relates to the enthusiasm of the participating students and their highly positive estimation of the experience in their course evaluations. When I think of their limited preparation for the work and mine for leading the seminar, I am led to wonder what were the critical ingredients? They were not instructed in any systematic fashion on how to deal with the analysis of personal material nor were they given extended instruction on how to interview. They were left largely to their own devices to extract from the material that which they found to be important, to tell why they found it important, to search for stable features of personality structure, and to find reliable principles as to how that personality functioned. "What's he like," and "How did he get to be that way," were the guiding questions under which they worked.[2]

Part of their enthusiasm, I would suggest, stemmed from the fact that the work was directed toward examining questions with which a great many people enter the study of psychology—namely, how can I "know" what other people are like and either its antecedent or derivative, how can I "know" about myself? A second source of gratification resulted from the purely creative aspects of this complex task. There were in fact no predetermined answers known by the instructor or absolutely identifiable templates known to experts. The outcome for each member and for the group was an emergent which had to be fashioned in part by each individual and ultimately bear the critical scrutiny of the group. One had to argue from the data in order to be convincing. The independence and responsibility demanded by the task was quite in keeping with the institution's educational ethos.

While this experience served as one of the highlights of my early teaching career, I was also impressed by some of the problems encountered during the progress of the work. The lack of preparation of the students, no matter their inherent brightness, made much of the data suspect. This was especially true in the material gathered in interview sessions in which the interaction of the examiner and subject was an obvious variable or in the extraction of delicate personal material. On another level it became clear that what people "saw" or became attuned to was not always independent of their own particular ways of viewing the world, and this became a sensitive matter when it came to establishing group consensus. What also became evident was that all discussions pertaining to the life of the subject were not without their repercussions in the self-awareness of the participants, and this had both its positive and negative emotional consequences as conveyed to me personally by different members of the seminar group. Certainly at the end of the two-year period during which the seminar was given, I knew that I was fascinated by the issues involved in personological study, and committed to exploring them further within the teaching framework which I had experienced. I also knew that there were many unsolved problems in how to transmit to students a personological approach. During a brief respite from academic life, I gained a bit of perspective on some of these problems, at least in deciding what not to do.

During the ensuing five years, as a member of the Training Branch of the National Institute of Mental Health, I enjoyed the rare opportunity of becoming familiar with graduate education as it existed generally in psychology and especially in clinical psychology. It fell to my lot to consult with and evaluate for support graduate training programs in most of the major institutions in this country. As part of that experience, I became intimately acquainted with the manner in which personality assessment was taught in clinical psychology programs. In those years, the late fifties and early sixties, the largely exclusive format was to offer courses in the variety of techniques or methods used to investigate or assess personality. Thus in any description of a course of study in clinical psychology one would find individual courses on intelligence testing, projective and objective testing, and in many instances, especially in the fifties, special courses devoted to specific tests (Rorschach, TAT, MMPI, WAIS, and the Stanford-Binet). This latter situation changed somewhat as a function of increased requirements in research skills and the increasing disappointment resulting from the research evidence on the reliability and validity of personality testing. In fact, it was not uncommon during the period in question for assessment courses to be given by people essentially opposed to the use of tests not normatively derived or for which conventional validational data was difficult to amass. Furthermore, the typical emphasis in such courses was on the use of these instruments for answering the diagnostic questions likely to be imposed in clinical settings. In those years the study of personality in the personological sense, except at Harvard where Robert White still offered his "life histories" course, was not easily found.

### The Duke Experience

When in 1962 I was asked by Karl Zener to come to Duke to direct graduate study in clinical psychology, I saw this as a marvelous opportunity to build a program with a personological underpinning. The program prior to this time, an excellent one, intimately connected with the psychiatry department in the medical school, had its major emphasis on psychopathology. This arrangement had grown cumbersome administratively over the years and its modification was hastened by the departure of several of its chief architects to enticing, new opportunities.

At that particular time it was largely the custom in graduate programs to fill the first year of study with general course requirements, which kept clinical students from beginning work in their area of interest until the second year. Aware of the growing multiplicity of hurdles imposed in clinical study and the increasing length of time such study was consuming, I decided that the foundations for clinical training would be laid in the first year. They were introduced formally by a two-semester sequence in personality theory and, simultaneously, another of equal length in personality assessment. The logic was simple, straightforward, and a bit naive. If our students were armed with the tools for data gathering and the various theoretical positions which could help to "explain" the data, they would undoubtedly be well prepared to begin their professional lives as scientists and/or practitioners.

The assessment sequence was designed with a variety of goals in mind. In the larger sense it was aimed toward the identification and understanding of the chief features involved in how the subject under study experienced his or her world. To accomplish such an undertaking it was necessary to: (1) introduce the major sources of data for the study of personality, (2) practice the inferential processes involved in hypothesis formulation from limited bits of data, (3) learn how to assess the value of an hypothesis by prediction to as yet unanalyzed data, and (4) learn to relate present data to likely historical antecedents. The entire experience was also planned as an indirect introduction to knowledge about the self. The expansion of this simple summary, within the confines of a two-semester course, will occupy a large part of what follows.

## First Semester: Background of the Course

In its most typical form, the student population for the seminar was kept within the range of six to fourteen. With nine or more participants, the group was divided into two subgroups, each studying one of two paid subjects over the period of a semester. During the first semester the materials used for study were: (1) an autobiography written by our subject expressly for the course, and (2) a series of life history interviews, twelve to twenty, conducted by the seminar participants. In the second semester the subgroups exchanged subjects and gathered formal test data on them. Each of the subjects was given the WAIS (Wechsler, 1958), Rorschach (1942), TAT (Morgan and Murray, 1935), and MMPI (Hathaway and McKinley, 1943). Both subjects were further exposed to a variety of tests chosen by the members of the subgroups. Typical selections were made from the following group of tests: California Psychological Inventory (CPI) (Gough, 1957, 1964, 1988), 16-PF (Cattell and Stice, 1957), Myers-Briggs Type Indicator (Myers, 1962), Sentence Completion (Rotter and Rafferty, 1950), Interpersonal Checklist (Leary, 1957), Q-Sort (Block, 1961), Kelly's Role Construct Repertory Test (Fransella and Bannister, 1977), Adjective Checklist (Gough and Heilbrun, 1965), House-Tree-Person (Buck, 1966), Study of Values (Allport, Vernon, and Lindzey, 1960), and the Picture Frustration Test (Rosenzweig, 1978). The central instructional tasks involved preparing the students to: (1) gather the necessary information, (2) extract from it that which it can yield, (3) assess the adequacy of the formulations, (4) transmit the product in a clear, communicable form.

The operational logistics for group meetings were a bit complex and bear describing. The seminar was scheduled for two three-hour meetings each week, usually spaced three days apart. When sessions were scheduled for general instructional purposes, e.g., principles of interviewing, test administration and interpretation, analysis of personal documents, etc., all students attended. When sessions were devoted to presentation and discussion of subject data, the three-hour sessions were divided and each group met separately for half the time. With fewer than nine participants, the seminar met twice weekly for a total of six hours. Separate subjects were studied in each of the two semesters.

In the early meetings when the overall plan of the year's work was revealed, a fair amount of time was spent in dealing with the interpersonal conditions that attended the seminar experience. At first the position of the subject to be studied was explored. Reviewed carefully were the steps by which the subjects were chosen, what arrangements were made with them financially, socially, instructionally, therapeutically, and ethically. The basic intent of these discussions was to impress upon the seminar participants the rare privilege it was to be able to share, for study, another person's existence and the ethical responsibilities the privilege engendered. The group was reminded of the importance of confidentiality for the protection of the subject, and a set of procedures concerning discussion about the subject outside the confines of the group meeting time was instituted. Such discussions were restricted to the members of the investigating subgroup and could include no one else, not *even* members of the other subgroup. The reason for this latter restriction was to avoid contamination of the data to be gathered in the second semester. Each subgroup at that point approached a new subject whose history was unknown to its members but entirely open and explored by the other group. We sought ultimately to establish the similarities and differences in the personality pictures that would emerge as a function of the methods used for data gathering. What is it that is learned about the functioning of the personality from the analysis of personal documents and life history interviews and what from responses to a variety of standard tests both objective and projective? Further, with regard to the subject, seminar members were asked to avoid establishing any sort of social contact with the subject in order to minimize the possibilities of confounding factors in the work. They were also asked not to give feedback on any of the material produced by the subject nor to act in any manner relating to a therapeutic role. All requests by the subject involving any of these issues were to be referred to the instructor. The core of the extended discussion on the treatment of subjects related to the concern about maintaining the subject's feeling of dignity while sharing with others intimate and important details of his/her life. Having witnessed, all too often, in professional discussions the depersonalization of a human being into a "case" or a member of a diagnostic category and all it might implicitly involve, I attempted to make sure that the participants maintained empathy with the subject's increased vulnerability and to respect the sacrifice which that entailed.

The subject population resulted from an ad in the campus newspaper inviting seniors to apply for a full year part-time job, with hours to be arranged, to act as a subject in a graduate seminar in personality assessment. Remuneration was set at an hourly level slightly above minimum campus standards. Seniors were sought since the overlap between them and the seminar members was unlikely to last beyond the target year. Each candidate was interviewed by the instructional staff for suitability as a subject. We sought well-functioning people without psychiatric histories, or academic backgrounds in psychology, who communicated without difficulty and seemed interested in participating. The task was described to the candidates as involving a written autobiography and a series of interviews on various aspects of their life histories in the first semester and a battery of psychological tests in the second semester. They were told that the seminar participants were novices who were in the process of learning the techniques involved in personality assessment and thus would not be capable of providing the subject with feedback about any aspects of the work. The subject was invited to a weekly session with the instructor to deal with any part of the experience as it unfolded. In this way the subject's concerns could be continually monitored. Over the many years the seminar has been given it has been a rare occasion when a subject showed unusual distress, and these were usually connected to ongoing life history events, e.g., the break-up of a romance, difficulty in finding a job, anxiety about admission to graduate or professional school. Most subjects reported the experience as a positive one in which they learned, by exposure to their own material, a fair amount about themselves. During the entire period no subject withdrew from participation at any point in the proceedings.

The instructional aspects of the first semester's work involved two major parts. The first concerned the interview as a source of data about the personality and all that was implied therein. The second centered on personal documents, in this instance the autobiography, in similar fashion. I shall discuss each in turn.

### The Interview

The interview can be a very deceptive source of information about personality. Perhaps that is the case because all of us maintain at some level the naive idea that if you want to know something about some-one else—just step up and ask that person. On further reflection, we know that this is not quite so. Some things are easily shared, some not. Some are more easily shared with some people but not with others. Some things flow easily in certain contexts yet not in others. Some things about self are known by the subject, not others. The number of factors that can impede or distort communication about the self in a personal interview are multiple, yet many people who aspire to the role of a clinical interviewer seem initially oblivious to its complex-ities. This may partly be so because the interview is frequently and mistakenly confused with its social counterpart, an intimate conver-sation with a friend. While success in both is clearly dependent on the establishment of rapport or trust, the similarity largely ends there. One is a give-and-take situation usually involving people known to one another who have shared personal experiences and assume mutual acceptance. The other, at least at the beginning, may be described in almost antithetical terms.

To teach bright, articulate, people-oriented people how to speak to another person can be a delicate matter. There often exists in the stu-dents' thinking a tacit assumption that they know implicitly how to interview, which makes instruction superfluous, or that they *should* know, which makes the contemplation of error debilitating. The work sessions devoted to interviewing are designed to dispel both of these notions early. We begin with some working assumptions most clearly related to personal data or life history interviewing but which may also be reasonably entertained for most kinds of interviews. The first involves the subject and states that people who volunteer to "tell their stories" likely derive gratification from such activity. The task then is to direct the interview unobtrusively, guided in large part by the mate-rial produced by the subject, and interfere minimally. The set of the interviewer is on getting the subject's closure on that which he or she is relating and not on what the interviewer needs or thinks is needed for his or her own purposes. The interviewer's major goal is to extract personal data, influenced as little as possible by the interview process, which will ultimately become the basis for personality assessment. In this model the interviewer is urged to abandon a well-practiced habit developed in social interaction, namely to hypothesize, interpret, and seek meaning immediately in the communication of the other. In such instances questions are very likely directed toward the verification process. Our attempt is to turn the interviewer toward helping the subject communicate more fully those aspects of lived experience which remain unclear in verbal expression. To illustrate this point one might conceive a subject describing in some detail an enjoyable family outing as an example of typical family interaction. Embedded in this content is a brief mention of a conflict between the brother and the subject, almost an aside, then the exposition continues until completion. At this juncture an interviewer, perceiving the salience of the abridged conflict, has a choice of how to proceed. One could move to an exploration of the subject's relationship to the brother. Our preference would be to move the subject toward an expansion of the cryptic incident from which inferences about the relationship could later be made. This expansion could then instigate similar associations which would further bear on the brother-brother mix. We seek to inhibit the subject least by mystifying questions posed by the interviewer, e.g., at the point of the aside to ask, "How did you and your brother get along"? Other assumptions with which we begin are that people tell their stories better when they find an apparently interested listener who seems to comprehend; one who responds to implicit cues for expansion. We also assume that people are less willing to impart their tales if they must be translated into the language or experience of the listener.

Our format for instruction in interviewing is designed to accomplish a variety of purposes at this early stage of overall skill development on the part of seminar members. In order to prepare them for work with the subject, much has to be done rapidly over and above imparting the technical aspects of successful interviewing. What also must be introduced is the treatment of the data once gathered. How does one begin to approach the issue of what is revealed about the personality in the interview material? Part of the task at this juncture also involves setting an atmosphere in which productive work can take place. Although this may appear as an obvious and widely shared goal among academicians everywhere, special circumstances surrounding our work make this issue worth examining further.

While we are ultimately concerned with trying to understand the psychological functioning of a single other, a paid subject, our initial data sources are seminar members who begin their practice by interviewing each other in the presence of the group. This procedure introduces a number of hazards which we feel are important to expose and to try to overcome in order to work with the subject most effectively. These relate primarily to increased feelings of personal vulnerability as a result of the procedure followed. Although the interviews concern seemingly nonthreatening aspects of personal experience selected by the interviewee (what you did last summer, jobs you've held, hobbies, your home town, or any other topic suggested by the interviewee), the observers are asked in the postinterview critique to select from the data that which impressed them as possibly being indicative of stable aspects of the personality and to offer as many hypotheses as they can as to its meaning. While no attempt is made to verify any of the hypotheses with the person who produced the interview material, the exploration of what further data might be examined in order to verify can extend the period of subject unease.

From another standpoint, each of the participants is exposed to increased vulnerability. All of these interviews are spontaneous, take place in full view of all the other members, and are followed by an analysis of various aspects of performance. Since typically these are all first-year graduate students, newly gathered, as yet largely unknown to each other, the situation is usually experienced with anxiety.

One could ask at this point whether some of these hazards could be overcome by supplying practice interview subjects other than members of the group. The answer is undoubtedly yes, but we choose not to do it for several reasons of importance to the conceptualization of the overall learning experience. The intention is to avoid setting up artificial distinctions between subject and examiner as the basic model for investigation. If the examiner is going to attempt to find out about the experience of another, we feel it enhances the sensitivity of the interviewer to know what it feels like to be in the position of the subject. When one multiplies these expressions, explored in the postinterview session, by the number of seminar participants, increased sensitivity is very likely to result. This is all encapsulated in exploring interview technique and thus has value over and above the issue of empathy for the position of the other. For example, in a postinterview critique, the subject, in response to an open-ended question probing the experience of being interviewed, may focus on a particular moment in which what the interviewer did created distress in the subject. One part of the ensuing discussion could then focus on matters of technique. Was it possible to accomplish the purpose intended by the interviewer without creating the distress, and if so, how? Was the distress produced by the interviewer (assessed by how likely what the interviewer did would distress anyone), or was it largely subject centered? If the latter was obviously so, what could the interviewer do when the discomfort was recognized?

Still another goal of this interview procedure is to instill a helpful, noncompetitive attitude within the group's ambience. Although everyone experiences the increased feelings of vulnerability, we hope that this takes place under a supportive umbrella induced through instructional preparation. The students are told about the experience of others who have preceded them and both the goals and means clearly set for the task.

The basic interviewing instruction and practice is completed within the first four weeks of the semester. Each participant serves as an interviewer on three occasions and is interviewed on three others. The first two interviews are conducted on topics suggested by the person being interviewed. These are submitted in advance and one is drawn by the designated interviewer. A brief period of three to five minutes is allowed for the interviewer to plan the beginning stage of the work. The observers are then subdivided to carry out two specific tasks. One group attempts to capture verbatim the question and answer interchange. This provides practice in listening and writing in a self-devised shorthand script, essential for analyzing the developmental structure of the interview, a task of the postsession critique. It is also important to learn such a technique for later work in Rorschach and TAT testing. The other group is assigned the task of observing and recording notable aspects of the nonverbal communication of the interview participants.

With regard to the formal instruction given prior to interview practice, we try to keep it simple, fundamental, and relevant to aiding the subject to tell his/her story with a feeling of being appreciated and understood. As background the seminar members are assigned readings in standard sources on interviewing procedures. Instructional emphasis highlights that which we feel most important for beginners to assimilate. These can be conveniently separated into matters related to interview procedure and those related to the demeanor of the interviewer.

We urge the interviewer to begin with a clear, simple statement about the purpose of the interview to set the subject for what lies ahead. Any deviation from this purpose must then be brought to the attention of the subject and its intention explained. Even in the instance in which the subject is suggesting the interview topic, as in our beginning work, we advocate this procedure. Thus for the suggested topic "jobs I've held," the interviewer might begin with "I would like to explore with you your recollection of various jobs you've had to get some idea about how your work experiences have influenced your life." That which follows, the first question, is important in establishing the tone of the interview. We advocate a meaningful, open-ended question, clearly within the repertoire of the subject's ability to answer. The choices for the interviewer are usually multiple. In our job example, one could move historically either forward or backward. "Tell me about the most recent job you've held," or "What do you recall about the first job you had." One could use pleasure or interest as the variable on which the subject might be asked to respond, or indeed a variety of others. No matter the choice of the question by the interviewer, it should be designed to elicit material easily from the subject about matters that clearly relate to the purpose of the interview. To be avoided particularly at this point is any question that would likely institute a defensive posture on the part of the subject, e.g., questions relating to success or failure.

If the first question accomplishes its purpose, it should engender in the subject the feeling that there will be sufficient opportunity to tell what he/she knows and wishes to share. The material elicited is apt to be more than ample and likely to suggest appropriate questions with which to follow. For example, we could imagine a male subject responding to a question asking for a description of the experience of the most recent job held. In the response which tells about duties, responsibilities, salary, working conditions, and memorable instances during his tenure, he also says, "I'll never forget that job because it was instrumental in the break-up of my marriage," and at the end he says, "But it was not the worst job I ever had." Both are statements that invite expansion. They are summaries which the subject can and is likely willing to expand but may not be sure if they are relevant to the purpose of the interview. At this juncture the interviewer has a choice of which issues, introduced by the subject, should be pursued. If one wishes to stay within the stated purpose of the interview, the path is clear. If the marriage question is followed up and the worst job held in reserve, that question should focus on the role of the job in the fate of the marriage and not on the marriage per se. If one travels the latter course, the interview will quickly resolve itself into something other than that contracted. If one moves to explore the worst job held, some mention could be made of the unfinished aspects of the job-marriage relationship to be revisited at a later time.

In discussing the importance of the beginning of the interview in the above manner, it is not unlikely that one of the seminar members will raise the question as to whether it is the marriage issue which is foremost in the mind of the subject and thus, in order to be true to letting the subject tell his story, pursue that avenue. Our response is that if it is a burning issue, excluding all else, necessary to be cleared before any other information can be gathered, it will return in salient fashion which will then demand attention and resolution. What is important to avoid is confusion on the part of subject and/or interviewer as to what they are trying to accomplish.

Along with some emphasis on the launching of an interview, attention is paid to the manner in which questions are asked, a frequent pitfall for beginners. Simplicity, brevity, clarity, and directness in question posing are stressed. To be avoided are multiple-claused inquiries like, "Tell me how you got the job, how you got along with the boss, what you did, you know—what was good about it and. . . ." Although probably intended to help the subject organize a response, it has the possibility of either increasing confusion or directing the subject toward aspects of the experience not at all salient for him or her. A more productive possibility might be, "Tell me the things that you readily recall about that job." Anything of importance obviously omitted in the response could then be queried specifically. What is important is that the subject is free to compose a response, a condition much more likely to reflect the particular cast of that subject's experience.

Not infrequently beginning interviewers will pose a question offering the subject alternative response possibilities when these may not cover the gist of the subject's experience. Cooperative or compliant subjects may then force this experience into an artificial summary demanded by the nature of the question. An illustration of this point is contained in the question "Did you feel that your boss treated you well or did you feel that he treated you poorly?" A more desirable question strategy dealing with the boss's treatment might be an open-ended question, "What are some incidents typical or highly indicative of the way you felt the boss treated you?" Such a question more likely avoids the difficulty of either a yes/no response or a presuggested unexpandable summary. It rather forces the subject to bring from memory real experiences which can serve as the basis for further analysis. If in this situation all the instances reported are positive, one could then inquire whether any negative instances come to mind. We are primarily interested in extracting imagery related to the subject's life experience. Only after this is done are we concerned with the subject's reflected opinion or evaluation of that happening if it has not been given spontaneously in the response to the open-ended question.

Another early instructional point about question posing involves sequence or order. The admonition given is to avoid mystifying the subject by introducing a question that has no clear relationship to material which has preceded it, at least not without an appropriate transitional statement. The subject should not be put in the position of wondering why a particular question is asked, because this could very well influence the content of the response and also jeopardize whatever trust has been built up in the interview thus far. To illustrate, we may return to the example given earlier in which the subject responded to an opening question about his last job with a reference to his defunct marriage. A mystifying question might be one in which the subject is then asked to reflect on whether he has generally experienced difficulty in intimate relations with women. While that possibility might arise in the mind of an interviewer hearing the subject's reference to his divorce, to investigate that remote prospect by resorting to a direct question at this point would risk a smooth continuation of the work.

With regard to interviewer demeanor, we advocate common sense rules that pertain to early stages of new human interactions, e.g., be friendly but not effusive, be accommodating but not timid, be understanding but not overly empathic. Our advice is to be natural and avoid an artificial professional mask, also to avoid being insensitive and intrusive. Finally we dwell on the value of listening attentively to what the subject is saying as a guide to appropriate use of language and affect in the communication process. Frequently beginning interviewers have difficulty in maintaining their attention on the subject. They are typically led astray by the anxiety of preparing a question in reserve to be asked at the next pause. We try to emphasize that the most natural source for that next question lies directly in what the subject is saying.

Practice interviewing usually begins in the second week of the semester and much of the instruction then takes place through the medium of the critique. Starting high intellectual achievers at a task like this in a group format can produce undue anxiety about performance. To minimize this possibility we try to set a context for the work. The image imparted to the initiates is that learning to interview is akin to the learning of any motor skill and thus follows similar principles. We hold that with instruction and practice any motivated person can become comfortably adept as an interviewer. We tell them that although there are individual differences in the pace of acquisition of this skill, all who persist reach acceptable levels of performance. The comparison is made between learning to hit a golf ball and learning to interview. It looks easy, as though any coordinated person ought to be able to strike the ball. The parallel here is that anyone who knows how to speak and has decent social skills ought to know how to interview. But the golf swing is not a natural movement, it has to be learned, just as one has to learn to interview. At the beginning in both instances there seems to be so much to be remembered about so much that one ordinarily takes for granted. In golf there is hand placement, foot placement, hip movement, shoulder movement, wrist movement, head movement, etc. In interviewing it will include what you say, how you say it, when you say it, as well as who you appear to be. Yet with awareness of the variables and continued practice in melding the parts, it becomes second nature, a smooth skill. As with all skills, though, unrealistic expectations as to rapidity of acquisition, fear of error, and overemphasis on shame avoidance can be the greatest barriers to progress.

The length of any practice interview varies between five and fifteen minutes. A halt is called when either the interviewer is stymied in moving the proceedings along a productive path or the interview is running smoothly and its direction is clear. The postinterview critique follows a standard procedure. Both subject and interviewer in turn are invited to share with the group that which they experienced in their roles and what about the behavior of the other was significant in what they experienced. These exchanges are particularly helpful because consensual validation about person perceptions are possible in that several observers were party to the interaction. For example, one can picture a situation in which the subject reports feeling that the interviewer's manner was somewhat harsh and this over time had an inhibiting effect. The interviewer, on the other hand, reports feeling warmly toward the subject at the start but less and less so as a function of the subject's increasing lack of cooperation. The observers may then choose to comment on how they perceived the actors and the interaction. Furthermore, having focused on different aspects of the interview, verbal and nonverbal, they may be able to pinpoint various places in the interchange that could have fostered the behaviors identified by the actors—an intonation, a particular form of question wording, a look, a body posture, a phrase, or a unique combination of words. The observers have the possibility of making the participants more aware of themselves as interviewers and as people. The task is not designed to be therapeutic but instructive. The observers are required to seek and share the evidence on which their conclusions are based. Or, in the absence of any clear evidence, must state their positions as a "hunch" or conjecture. The interviewers have the opportunity to check their perception of how they appear to others in an interview situation and how they evaluate various aspects of their performance against the perceptions of others.

When the interviewer and subject have reported, the scene shifts to the primary notations of the observers. They are asked to assess those features of verbal and nonverbal behavior which seemed to influence the course of the interview either positively or negatively. Each observer, in turn, is asked to share what he/she perceived. The comments are helpful, not only in the ways we have indicated vis-à-vis the interviewer, but also in stimulating discussion about more general features of interview practice, e.g., the value of self-disclosure, empathy, affective responsiveness, admission of error or difficulty, summarization, and interpretation by the interviewer, along with the circumstances or conditions under which they may or may not be practicable.

Observer reports are then followed by a point-by-point analysis, led by the instructor, of the interchange between subject and interviewer. Each question is gone over with regard to its value in the development of the interview. From whence does it flow, how is it posed, what did it produce, and what follows from that which it produced, are all questions that are asked. Critical points in the development of the interview are identified and discussed. General principles are sought to explain what enhances the possibility of smooth exchange and what inhibits that possibility. Choice points are revisited and alternative strategies are developed. It is often extremely revealing to follow the sequence of questions and answers. Here lies the actual data upon which the impressions are based. Often new material emerges about the process not clearly seen initially by observers or participants.

The next stage in the critique involves summarizing those aspects of performance to which the interviewer might turn attention in order to improve skill. These generally include such things as voice quality, facial expression, posture, question-wording, pace of speech, disturbing mannerisms, and nonproductive stylistic aspects (premature summarization, impatience, frequent interruption, fortuitous interpretation).

The final step in the postinterview discussion turns attention toward the information produced by the subject and how we can detect what it can possibly tell us about his/her personality. Early discussions are directed toward what in the material stood out in any way as being important or promising in this regard. Whenever anything said by the subject is selected for consideration we seek then to identify the basis for selection. Within a few such experiences there begins to emerge a group of "principal identifiers of salience." These generally include those concepts already visited in chapter 1 (primacy, frequency, uniqueness, negation, emphasis, omission, error, distortion, isolation, incompletion) and more. Illustrative comments would be, "Of all the things he could tell you about that job, he *started* by pointing out the *importance* of his role" (primacy stressing importance), or "Despite *all* the *detail*, he *never* mentioned *salary*" (omission regarding reward or perhaps value), or "His voice grew *louder* and *deeper* as he described how he ran his department" (emphasis and frequency regarding importance), or "The one thing, he said, that *never bothered* him *at all* was that he was *clearly* and *obviously* bypassed for *promotion*" (negation + emphasis + frequency regarding value). These examples were deliberately chosen not only to point out a working method for reducing the data for further analysis but also to call attention to the search for commonalities in the data, in this instance value or importance. At this point in the training, when a bit of salient data is identified, the finder is asked to hypothesize with regard to what it may be telling us about the subject. The request is then expanded to that of generating as many reasonable hypotheses as can be extracted from that particular data source. When all possibilities are exhausted by the person reporting, and they turn out at the beginning to be surprisingly few, the other members of the group are invited to add whatever possibilities they are able to see. This exercise is an important one which serves different purposes. A significant impediment to understanding another's experience lies in the width of the band of one's own experience. Thus our hypotheses are likely at first to come from the meaning any bit of data might have for us. The exercise moves people to think beyond a self-oriented baseline. When this is coupled with the efforts of other group members, the impact can be exciting and often eye opening.

A second purpose for which the exercise is designed relates to an educational set with which many students enter graduate training. In a loose fashion it may be described as a tendency to assimilate, reproduce, and utilize effectively that which is known. While these are necessary and admirable assets, clearly fostered in elementary and secondary education, they are not always helpful in dealing with that which is not yet known, the task which we have set for ourselves by exploring the life history of another for what it can tell us about the personality. Not infrequently when the question of what the data could mean is posed, the response by extremely bright, highly motivated people is "I don't know," accompanied by a look of puzzlement or embarrassment. When encountering this situation I have frequently thought of how a champion speller would respond given a word in a foreign language whose sounds are totally unfamiliar. If the search is for the known or familiar, the answer would likely affirm a lack of knowledge. If the search is for the possible, given what one knows, an answer in the form of "it may be" or "could it be" is likely to ensue. Our attempt in this exercise is to turn the search toward the possible and to expand one's skill in doing that. In the beginning we reinforce any attempt, no matter how remote the hypothesis seems at face value. It is difficult enough to get people to tune in on what they are thinking without immediately adding a well-practiced and well-learned inhibitor, namely whether what they are thinking is correct, acceptable, desired, or valued. What is done at this point is to ask whether one is able to specify the connection between the elements of the data and the resulting hypothesis. When these elements are not clear to the formulator, the question is opened to the rest of the group to try to locate the connecting link.

When hypothesis formulation becomes a familiar and comfortable part of the work regimen, further questions are introduced that relate to the power of any hypothesis. Issues of centrality, remoteness, inclusiveness, specificity, clarity, and testability are raised and discussed. This leads naturally to the inclusion of the questions, "What sort of data would you seek?" or "What expectations would you have about as yet unexplored aspects of data already gathered in order to evaluate your hypotheses?" or "What kind of evidence would negate your hypothesis?" when new hypotheses are offered.

As mentioned previously, each seminar member participates equally as interviewer or subject in six practice interviews. For the remaining interviews (6 × n/2) the role changes to that of observer and analyst of the interchange. Of the three assignments as interviewer, the format for the first two interviews follows that just described. The third interview is set up with a different goal in mind. The focus turns to what the subject may be doing to impede the flow of the interview, whether and how soon this is detected (by the interviewer and by the observers), and what is done by the interviewer to accommodate to this set of conditions. A number of prearranged roles are written by the instructor and selected randomly by those in the subject role. One role might include, "Be hesitant and suspicious. Inquire whenever possible, without appearing bizarre, why any particular question is asked of you. Continue this practice any time the interviewer's answer seems unsatisfactory or the question you are asked does not have a reasonable relationship to the answers you are giving." Another might state, "Be especially compliant and overaccommodating, give long, full, detailed responses bordering on the irrelevant. Continue this practice as long as the interviewer accepts it. If you are asked in some fashion by the interviewer to modify your behavior, do so, but return to your former practice once or twice after complying with the interviewer's request." A third might instruct, "Be cold and noncommunicative. Answer any question as economically or frugally as possible without being hostile. Follow this practice until the interviewer does something which would make its continuation appear pathological." The exercise is designed to accent awareness of the subject, a matter which could escape attention in earlier practice interviews in which the subjects are cooperative colleagues who will be in a similar position as interviewer shortly. As in the previous interviews, the session is followed by a critique.

### The Study of Personal Documents

Sometime within the third or fourth week of the semester, the group begins its study of the analysis of personal documents. After an introductory reading assignment (Allport, 1942, 1965; Baldwin, 1942), works begins with a series of preliminary exercises. An early one, carried out in class, is to examine the first paragraph of an autobiographical statement formulating as many hypotheses as one is led to about any aspect of personality of the writer, identifying the elements of the narrative that led to each hypothesis. Most instructive in this regard is the beginning of Ernest Jones's autobiography (1959), *Free Associations: Memories of a Psychoanalyst*. The first paragraph has only two sentences, each of which is pregnant with leads about what Jones was like. He says,

> I was born the first child and only son of my parents, on the first of January 1879, in the parish of Llwchwr, in a village called Rhosfelyn; the Great Western Railway had in 1852 rechristened it Gower Road, a name my father later got changed to the hybrid Gowerton. It is situate in the centre of Gwyr (Gower), the ancient kingdom between Swansea Bay and Caermarthen Bay, and is about six miles away from both Swansea and Llanelly, though the direct road between these towns does not pass through it.

Interestingly enough, in the next paragraph he introduces the psychoanalytic emphasis on the importance of primacy and says, "I know that the essential story of my life lies hidden in those sentences, though they need a minute examination to decipher it or even to discern its elements." He then begins to tell his story as though it is an elaboration, without conscious intention, of the opening two sentences.

Most students when asked to focus on that material will conjecture on one or another of the themes of importance, power, uniqueness, grandiosity, precision, detail, economy (of expression), and control, with varying ability at first to point to the elements leading to the conjecture. Less prominently mentioned are the themes of being involved in or around something important but being essentially bypassed, or that of being between two important and thriving objects but in some sense not fundamentally connected to either—being a part of and apart from two separate attractions. Jones himself offers some immediate feedback by the sentence following the two-paragraph prelude. It reads, "Much of life consists in the gradual taming of the grandiloquent hopes and fantasies of infancy." The narrative then unfolds, providing ample material for the evaluation of any hypothesis formulated from the opening sentences. The method that we have introduced at this point involves "letting the data reveal itself" by focusing on the identification of salience with special attention to the importance of primacy. A more extensive and detailed description of this method is to be found in chapter 1.

After the class exercise is completed, each of the participants is assigned an individual autobiography selected from those written by subjects studied in prior years. They are in the first instance assigned the task of examining only the opening paragraph of the work, formulating as many hypotheses as seem practicable from the data, identifying the narrative sources of the hypotheses, and indicating the degree of likelihood with which each hypothesis is invested. When this work is completed and discussed, they are further assigned to select one or two of the hypotheses generated, indicate what in the remaining data they could assess in order to support or cast doubt on the hypotheses in question, and then to carry out the evaluation. The results of this effort are typically mixed. Some attempts turn out unusually well, others are dismal failures. In all cases much is learned in the analysis of the effort, which includes examining the clarity of the hypothesis, the basis upon which it is formulated, and the representativeness of the criterion measure or measures. By this time, having read through the entire autobiography assigned, much is learned about criterion selection in hindsight. This actually turns out to be an important lesson, in that any personality characteristic can be manifested in a variety of human expressions singly or in combination, and the reliance on a single one places an undue burden on the process of verification. The model for personality investigation is not likely to be satisfied by a single variable, single outcome approach as in agricultural research, and thus should not be fostered.

When this exercise is concluded, the practice autobiographies are exchanged and a new task illustrating a different method of dealing with the data is introduced. Now the seminar members are asked to construct a question which each thinks might be relevant to the study of individual personality. These could be generated by a reading of the beginning sections or felt more generally to be things critical to know about anyone. While the number of such questions that could be asked may seem endless, the queries that are initially posed turn out to be reasonably limited. Mostly they pertain to attitudinal sets about gender, sex, power, aggression, family members (individually or as a group), work, and aspirations. The method of "asking the data a question" (described more fully in chapter 1) is then elaborated. Essentially it consists of extracting every bit of data relating to the question from the total sample and factoring it by use of a single set of similarity and difference procedures originally suggested by J. S. Mill and adopted for TAT analysis by S. S. Tomkins (1947).

For illustrative purposes one could imagine asking about a male subject's particular conglomeration of expectations from women. Suppose then that upon examination a limited number of specific references to or about women can be extracted from the data. In the simplest instance one could diagram each example as means-end or what-led-to-what sequences. Let us generate a few greatly simplified possibilities and examine them: (1) Expression of positive regard for ♀ → increased demand for attention by ♀ → unhappiness in the subject → dissolution of the relationship, instigated by subject, (2) inhibition of expression of positive regard for ♀ → lack of interest on part of ♀ → dissolution of the relationship by the ♀, (3) expression of positive regard for ♀ → return of positive regard by ♀ → continuation of a mutually supportive and gratifying relationship. In working with these abstracted summaries of incident description in the autobiography, one can readily see a number of things. Two of the three instances result in a negative outcome, the dissolution of the relationship. The third results in a positive outcome. For the negative outcome the behavior of the subject varies with regard to affective expression, the only variable he mentions, but outcome is the same. However, in situation (3) expression of positive regard by the subject leads to a positive outcome. What then constitutes the difference between situations (1) and (3)? A search for the differentiator in the original data provides the answer. Situation (1) involves an age-equal female, while situation (3) concerns a much older female. From these bits one might conjecture that an expectation of positive regard from the female exists when positive regard is offered by the subject. This expectation may originate in the early and continuing relationship with the mother or a mother-like figure. However, experience with contemporaries does not seem to follow the expected pattern; in fact the problem seems on-going and without solution at the moment. One could however imagine a more extensive data pool consisting of more than the three examples given in which solutions are either reached or conjectured and thus a more complex and rounded attitude toward women uncovered.

When the basic ideas involved in "asking the data" a question are assimilated, the students return to the new practice autobiography, pose one or more questions, and employ what they have learned to explore what the data reveals. The use of this method is frequently preferred by beginning students because it demands no manipulation or hypothesis formulation at early stages of the work. The steps are much more clearly spelled out, starkly empirical in nature, and little concerned as yet with problems of adequate criterion measures for validation. In contrast, the first method to which they are exposed makes great demands on the data analyst once salient bits of data are identified. What turns out to be impressive about sorting the accumulated relevant data when asking a question are the patterns of response that emerge which are usually hidden or masked in a contextual reading of the personal document. When this happens there is a real feeling of discovery due to the employment of a method rather than to the experience or ingenuity of the observer. Success in either method is highly gratifying but of a different order of experience.

By this time, usually the sixth week of the semester, the employed subject's autobiography has been completed, reproduced, and distributed to the members of the groups. The subjects are then called in to meet the members of the examining group in order to set up mutually agreeable dates and times in which to work. Since it is required that group members be present as observers (in a visually screened room) for each interview, scheduling becomes an important matter.

This first meeting with the group subject also becomes the basis for discussion at the next seminar session of the data involved in the formation of "first impressions." Each of the participants is asked to report on what he/she came away with concerning the subject's personality and the cues, verbal or nonverbal, on which the impressions were based. Again, seminar members are urged to share their ideas even when the cues are not identifiable. Others in the group may prove to be helpful in the location of relevant data.

In this same session, the group must come to agreement about the general structure which the interview schedule will take. Preparation for this discussion is provided by a set of reading assignments in which life history study is central (White, 1975). The interview topics selected come from a predictable list of those important in human experience: family, friendships, school experiences, work experiences, hobbies and interests, love relationships, attitudes toward love, sex, and marriage, religious and political attitudes, aspirations and goals, greatest success and failures or disappointments, reflections on things past, present, and future, etc. Topic selections and interview assignments are agreed upon. At this point each group is ready to turn attention toward the study of the subject.

When the subject's autobiography is first distributed, each group member is asked to read the document and prepare a personality sketch of the writer. Since this assignment precedes the intensive involvement with methods of data analysis, it is as close as we can come to establishing a base level for each of the participants in the assessment work to be done. They are asked, in the prevailing spirit of the seminar, to disclose what they surmise and to identify the data leading to those conclusions. The products, read and critiqued by the instructional staff, are examined mostly with regard to the fit between data and conclusions, strongly reinforcing successful efforts and correcting or improving, where possible, weaker efforts. As is the case with all seminar performance, written and oral, during the ongoing, instructional life of the course, no grades are assigned to the work.

Students are told that overall performance markers assigned at the end of the year will depend largely on the progress of each from initial baselines and only secondarily on the absolute level of final performance. This initial personality sketch based on the subject's autobiography is assigned in large part for each seminar member to gauge his/her own progress in dealing with the narrative description and explanation of the personality of another.

### Interviewing the Class Subject and Integrating the Material

When subject interviewing begins, still another instructional format presents itself. Since now, for the first time, the observers are separated from the interview participants, unlike the conditions prevailing in the practice interview sessions, ongoing analysis and critique of the proceedings can take place. The observers and instructor in another room are free to comment on or question any aspect of what is evolving within their view. As was the custom in their practice interviews, a postinterview session is held in which feedback on technical aspects is offered to the interviewer and a discussion of the salient aspects of that interview's content ensues. The verbatim record of the interview, logged by the observers in ten-minute assignment stretches, is then duplicated and kept for further and more considered analysis by group members. This obviates the need for having the material transcribed, a time-consuming and costly process for a series of interviews, each of an hour's length, numbering from twelve to twenty depending on the size of the group. For individual study or interview supervisory sessions, each interview is videotaped. The interviewer's impact on the subject is also gathered in the instructor's weekly meeting with the subject and the information filtered and fed back constructively to each interviewer.

Seminar material from the eighth through the twelfth or thirteenth week of the semester consists largely of reports by the interviewers on the analysis of the subject's data. Since all seminar members are usually present at each of the interview sessions, various conjectures and impressions can be checked by consensual agreement or strength of logical persuasion. The analysis of the interview material by the interviewer and consequently by the group is geared toward establishing new hypotheses or factual material about stable aspects of personality functioning or verifications or modifications of previously derived indications. The discussions that surround these reports inevitably relate to matters of personality theory, and different theoretical views are brought into play as possible elucidators of the material in question. The effort, however, is not directed toward a comparative evaluation of existing personality theories. The emphasis remains personological—how to construct a theory about the personality of these particular subjects.

When all interviewing has been completed and the reports discussed in class, the work focus is directed toward the synthesis of what has been learned. Two formats are used. One calls attention to the problems of interobserver reliability and attempts to determine what degree of agreement exists among the group's members as to what the subject is like. In order to provide a set of ready quantitative statements about observer agreement, it becomes necessary to resort to a common language in which the summarizations or conclusions of their observations can be cast. For this purpose we use the Q-Sort technique, Block (1961). By having each observer do a "sort" of the subject we are able to establish the level of agreement between all observer pairs, and by going back to the Q-Sort data analyze the strongest points of disagreement and discuss their bases. This exercise not only introduces the more general problems of assessing interobserver reliability with the data of personality, but also calls particular attention to what is gained and what is lost when the observer's particular perception of the data must be translated into a summary language which may or may not do justice to the essence of what he/she has derived from a study of the material.[3]

A partial antidote to the restrictions provided by an already established set of descriptive statements emerges from the final assignment given the participants. Each member is asked to write a personality assessment of the subject highlighting the most central aspects, their possible origins, and to use the material to make predictions about the future of the subject under specifiable conditions, e.g., if she marries, then . . . , or she will marry if. . . . These papers are carefully read and later commented upon by the instructor in an individual meeting with each seminar member. More qualitative estimates of group agreement on a number of dimensions can be made by the instructor and discussed with each group.

Earlier in this exposition the various goals of the seminar were identified. They included the establishment of a personological viewpoint toward the study of individual personality and the acquisition of necessary techniques to make that study possible. Additionally it was mentioned that the experience was designed in part to increase knowledge about the self outside of the therapeutic framework. Much of the attention thus far has been placed on the steps taken to accomplish the first two goals. Let us examine the various experiences which related to self-awareness and how they were treated.

For many years during the period when outside financial support for graduate training in clinical psychology was readily obtainable, we made an important experience available to our students entering the assessment sequence. We employed a senior clinician from a neighboring institution, a person who would have no continuing educational interaction with our students, to give each of them a standard battery of psychological tests, including the Wechsler-Bellevue, the Rorschach, the Thematic Apperception Test, and the Minnesota Multiphasic Inventory, among a few others. The material once gathered was then sealed and safely kept until returned to the students when their assessment seminar work was completed. They then could, if they wished, work on their own material either alone or in consultation with the person who originally gave them the tests. Some advantages of this practice were that early on they were exposed to how an experienced clinician worked both in interview and with standard personality materials. It also provided them with their own material extracted at a time prior to when it could be influenced by what they were learning. We were of course aware of possible dangers in this practice, but a variety of safeguards were available, including the observations of the outside clinician and our own observations during the year of assessment work. In no instance were we aware of any negative consequences of this procedure. A further advantage from our point of view was that it provided for each student the experience of being tested, a matter which was explored in seminar sessions. We wanted them to know firsthand something about the variety of reactions people can have to this situation, so that these things could be taken into account more easily when establishing their own roles as psychological investigators using test material. Outside testing unfortunately had to be discontinued when supporting funds became scarce.

Throughout the history of this seminar students have been asked at the very beginning to write an autobiography largely in accord with the instructions given to the subjects. These too have been sealed, unread by any person other than the writer, and returned at the end of the year. The work carried out through the year provides the tools to analyze the material they created, if they wish. No data exists with regard to how many worked seriously at this task.

Other sources of learning about self are more directly related to the work that takes place during postinterview critiques, both in the practice sessions and in those which follow interviews with the subject. Much of the feedback that is given at that time concerns consistent behaviors, both verbal and nonverbal, on the part of the interviewer that tend to influence the course of the interview and what particular ends these behaviors might serve. There is little doubt that the person whose work is being discussed has ample opportunity to see how he/she is viewed by others in this situation, with what consistency these views are held by colleagues, and how these pictures match one's image of self. The atmosphere is positive and the critique is realistically embedded in the context of how to improve one's interviewing technique. Yet, without serious question, based in large part of postseminar reflections of students in advanced stages of graduate training, there is a considerable personal impact derived from the feedback offered by confreres and the instructional staff.

A less direct but nevertheless important source of learning about self results from the early practice of isolating salient bits of interview material and hypothesizing as to its possible meaning. This interview material is produced by each of the seminar members when they act in the role of a practice subject early in the semester. To hear one's own experiences discussed and probed for meaning frequently begins that process independently by the practice subject. While at this point there is no serious attempt to deal either with the validity or power of any formulated hypothesis, the discussion usually turns not only to the basis for the hypothesis but also to any immediately apparent evidence regarding its credibility. What turns out to be important about these exercises is not solely what one can learn about self from some other's reflection on one's experience but rather that it moves the subject toward increased reflection on his/her own experience with an expanded set of analytic tools.

The final paper summarizing each participant's view of the personality of the subject studied has over the years been treated in a variety of ways. The mass of data accumulated, the multitude of hypotheses entertained, the frequent and often lively discussions of alternative explanations entertained, summate to make this a forbidding task for many. Early on there were no restrictions placed on time to be spent on the task. Students usually began the work in the thirteenth or fourteenth week and were generally required to submit the completed copy at the end of the examination period. Since this was a fall semester offering in a required two-semester sequence, for which a final grade was not assigned until completion in the spring, the instructor had ample time over the year and during the break between semesters to read and critique the papers carefully. The system worked as long as the students were able to complete the assignment on time. However, the press of other papers and examinations plus the importance attached to this effort made the meeting of the deadline problematic for too many of the students. In response a number of alternative solutions have been tried over time, none with unequivocal success. To reduce the magnitude of the task a group product was attempted with each member writing a particular section. This worked fairly well but was highly dependent on each group's ability to function cooperatively. Individual complaints about lack of coherence and closure in the final product made the continuation of this alternative less attractive.

During one period when time constraints for the students were particularly pressing, the final paper was treated as examination performance whose execution was limited to a three-hour period no matter the length of preparation. Student response to this format was unusually negative, claiming that outcome was little related to what they had assimilated and felt they were capable of expressing without such prohibitive restraints.

Our most frequent solution has turned out to be a specified length of time for the writing, decided upon by the participants, and left to the honor and good will of each for compliance. The limit selected is likely to vary between ten and twenty hours.

The meeting of the instructor with each member of the seminar prior to the beginning of the new semester serves both as an opportunity to go over the content of the final paper and as an occasion to assess general progress in the various aspects of seminar performance. Since there is no official grade given at this point, it becomes the chief source of summary information relating to individual achievement and the elements upon which the judgment is based.

## Second Semester: Preparatory Work

The work of the second semester is carried out in quite a different context than that previously established. Whereas earlier the autobiography, distributed and read prior to the initial face-to-face meeting with the subject, provided a fund of information upon which further data gathering could be based, the group now approaches the new subject with no biographical or historical data as background. Everything to be learned about the subject must come from performance on test instruments designed specifically for the study of personality. Since the seminar participants have rarely had previous exposure to test administration or analysis, a period of training in the use of personality instruments lasting seven to eight weeks is initiated before work with the new subject begins.

Since, for multiple reasons, it is not really desirable for seminar members to test one another, especially because as graduate students they remain part of an ongoing group with continuing social and intellectual interactions beyond this course, a format different from that used in the first semester training is employed. Undergraduate students from either the introductory psychology course (where each student is required to participate as a subject in research studies) or from the first course in personality (where interest in assessment procedures is high) are solicited on a volunteer basis. They are informed that seminar members are beginners who need practice in assessment techniques that they are just learning. For participation volunteers are offered a group session at the close of their period of service in which they have the opportunity to ask whatever questions they want about personality assessment in general and the tests they took in particular. Volunteers typically exceed by far the numbers needed as practice subjects. Each member of the seminar then locates from the volunteer list a practice subject with whom he/she works for the entire training period.

As a prelude to the work with tests, readings dealing with psychometric issues, test construction, reliability, validity, are assigned and discussed in class (Wiggins, 1973). For those with limited undergraduate preparation tutorial sessions with a graduate assistant assigned to the seminar are sometimes arranged. During the ensuing eight to ten weeks, four specific instruments in turn become the object of focus, the Wechsler Adult Intelligence Scale (WAIS) (Wechsler, 1972), the Rorschach Ink Blot Test (1942), the Thematic Apperception Test (TAT) (Morgan and Murray, 1935), and the Minnesota Multiphasic Personality Inventory (MMPI) (Hathaway and McKinley, 1943). While so brief an initiation may seem minuscule for the magnitude of the task, especially in light of teaching practices in earlier eras of clinical training when single courses were devoted to many of these instruments, it is possible to impart the critical features of administration, scoring, and analysis rapidly enough to provide the students with the basis for their practice work. Actually ten to twenty hours of seminar time are given to each test. Administration is demonstrated by the instructional staff, and practice protocols are examined to illustrate major scoring problems when they exist, as well as critical principles of interpretation for each test. After the introductory session on any test, each participant administers the instrument to the practice subject, then scores and analyzes the material with the help of the course assistant in extra class sessions. The results are presented to the rest of the group. Further instruction about the test then takes place around the material offered in class.

In our scheme of things each seminar member works with a single practice subject. This is in preference to assigning a different subject for each test or several subjects for any test, in order to maximize exposure. The procedure is considerably different from earlier general models of training in assessment where number criteria were usually set as indicators of familiarity or competence with a tool. In those schemes the student had to test a specified number of subjects before satisfying requirements. Our departure from this custom is based on several factors. The fundamental attitude we are attempting to impart is that tests are *means* to the *end* of knowing about a person and not to be treated primarily as ends in themselves. We do not aim for expertise in the Rorschach, TAT, etc. If for no other reason, the time devoted to each instrument is too limited for that purpose. Instead we stress a personological approach to the test material to extract that which is particular to the individual tested over and above that which the test is designed to tell us from nomothetic comparison. To follow a single subject through a number of different testing experiences allows for the assessment of hypotheses formulated from the responses to one instrument by prediction to the responses of others. One begins to see the variety of ways in which any stable characteristic of personality may be manifested in different performance contexts. Let us, for example, imagine a subject who in her responses on several of the WAIS verbal tests always gives multiple answers whose content is generally correct but at different levels of criterion satisfaction. Thus in response to the way in which an orange and a banana are alike, she responds, "You eat them, they grow on trees, they are recommended as healthy foods, they are fruit, they both have skins, and the color of the skins with which they are covered are both at the long end of the visible spectrum." When asked to select a single response from among the many, the subject finds this difficult and is only moderately successful in deciding upon the one which best meets the criterion. From consistent data of this sort on the WAIS, a rather sizable number of plausible hypotheses relating to various aspects of the subject's personality can be formulated. These could relate to such issues as rigidity-flexibility of the thought processes, poverty or richness of the intellect, degree of reality testing, security of judgment, ability to discriminate importance from trivia, among others. It then becomes possible to follow the fate of these various hypotheses by conjecturing on how they might be manifested on succeeding tests. Let us simply follow through some ideas which stay close to the manifest data: that the subject is of high intellectual potential, with good reality testing, clearly in touch with her imagery, not terribly discriminative about the centrality of what she sees, and thus not able to easily detect incipient conflict nor resolve it easily or successfully when conflict is presented to her by others. Think then of how these conjectures might be used to predict various aspects of performance on Rorschach, TAT, and MMPI. Without laboring the issue, confine the task to such criteria as number and quality of responses on Rorschach, multiplicity of story possibilities to any TAT card, ease or difficulty of decision making on

TAT outcomes, or use of the ? response on the MMPI. The work then becomes, in addition to the learning of the formal properties of what any test is designed to reveal, an extension and continuation of the analytic practices begun in the first semester. Our procedure affords us not only the opportunity of predicting (from limited information) from one test to another without additional knowledge about the subject, but also how information about personality characteristics extracted from one instrument may be represented on any other instrument. As an exercise, when each new test is introduced and discussed, each seminar member is asked to predict the performance of the subject studied the first semester using the data from the first semester as a base. In this way one begins to appreciate the complexities that attend the validity issues in the study of personality, how widely the net must be spread in order to satisfy the quest for secure knowledge, e.g., how many different ways the rigidity-flexibility dimension could be represented in the variety of instruments in question and which criteria selected will indicate congruence with the hypothesis.

### Work with the WAIS

When examining the properties of the WAIS we begin with a discussion of each of the subtests and what they are intended to measure, move to an analysis of the face sheet scored data including pattern analysis, and then focus on the analysis of salient data revealed by a return to each subtest, item by item. We are concerned with locating responses that meet salience criteria (see chapter 1) and examining them further. One extremely fruitful source is the analysis of error. What is revealed in what the subject does or says when in fact the response falls short of criterial standards? Which items provide difficulty for the subject on various subtests and do they cluster into any informative dynamic pattern or patterns? Which items even when answered correctly contain something in the response which attracts attention?

To illustrate these ideas let us examine a hypothetical group of responses extracted by salience criteria from two of the verbal subtests of the WAIS, Information and Comprehension. The first, an information item, "Who wrote *Hamlet?*", draws the response, "A play by Shakespeare in which *murder* is a *central theme*" (the explanatory clause calls attention by uniqueness). The response is of course factually correct in terms of the scoring schema. Yet it promises the possibility of revealing more than the subject's knowledge about commonly shared information, something special about the way the subject experiences the world. Three further items from the Comprehension subtest then fall out by inspection. One which asks why we should avoid bad company is answered, "Because they can influence you to do bad things like beat up on other people" (uniqueness by virtue of the particular example). A second item dealing with what to do if one detects smoke or fire in a theater draws the response, "Get out quickly so you won't be hurt in the rush of the crowd" (selected by error). The third item asks why child labor laws are necessary, and is responded to by, "To avoid the *pain* caused by putting a child to work too early" (error, incompletion, frequency).

One can readily see from these few responses that the subject indicates some preoccupation with aggression and pain, perhaps even a concern with hurting or being hurt. At this point one could work with the material in various ways. It is possible to formulate hypotheses and seek to test them in the rest of the material. Or one could pay special attention to any further material dealing with aggression and pain and seek to construct the underlying patterns from the total extracted data pool. To illustrate we might hypothesize an experiential maxim derived from the subject's imagery as revealed thus far in the four salient bits extracted as, "You could be hurt by others but you dare not hurt others." One could then specify the operations under which that hypothesis could be evaluated for credibility and perhaps even for power. In this instance the operations could include (1) the extraction of all material related to aggression and pain whether or not they meet the salience criteria, and (2) examine particularly those items within the test material and those aspects of the subject's test performance that are likely to reflect the dimension in question. Let us go further by identifying likely candidate items on two of the remaining verbal subtests, Similarities and Vocabulary. The items chosen by inspection on Similarities are those which ask in what way an axe and saw are alike and also for the common element between praise and punishment. A perusal of the Vocabulary items reveals the following words as having possible relevance for our inquiry: sentence, cavern, consume, and remorse.

Extracting the subject's responses to these particular items reveals the following information:

*Similarities*

| | |
|---|---|
| axe-saw | useful cutting instruments which must be used with caution because they are potentially dangerous |
| praise-punishment | they are not alike, the first you get when you do well, the second when you hurt others |

*Vocabulary*

| | |
|---|---|
| sentence | a jail term—like a life sentence for murder |
| cavern | a place to hide from danger or harm |
| consume | to eat—or be eaten like he was consumed by his anger |
| remorse | regret for hurting people you love |

To see the responses to these six items embedded in their normal context of fifty-three items on two subtests or to read all ten scattered among ninety-six responses is quite different from examining them in juxtaposition to one another. No matter whether you derive a hypothesis from four and try to evaluate it against the data from the other six, or you comb the data for all ten from which to formulate a testable dynamic pattern, personological consistencies have much greater possibilities of standing out in bold relief even to the naked eye when the data is factored by procedures that make psychological sense. From the responses we have just created for illustrative purposes it is not too difficult to approximate some aspects of an internally summarized life story which includes fear of being hurt for a variety of possible reasons, including that of retaliation for expressing aggressive impulses. The struggle involved in how to deal with this backed up anger which can be activated by any instance of being hurt (and is more likely to be activated because of the lack of acceptance of one's own aggressive impulses) and its consequent projection onto the object world may be a significant aspect of the personality structure of our hypothetical subject. At this point one could be led toward the kinds of socialization scenes that could produce this story.

The treatment of the personological data on the wais takes on a special importance in the seminar work because it is the first instance in which we are dealing with material that does not directly deal with the life story. To translate the methods explored in the first semester's work with personal documents and life history interviews takes a bit of doing. This is the case partly because the task is conjoint, adding to its complexity. On the one hand there is the necessity of imparting the basic elements of what about personality can be derived from the test instruments as they were originally intended. From the test's very inception David Wechsler was aware of the "clinical and practical" uses of the material, and the lore expanded with consequent revisions of the book. Additional uses for clinicians were introduced for many of the instruments designed to assess human characteristics.

Thus the student at the beginning is faced with a seemingly massive task which gets sorted only over time. There are the problems of test administration and scoring, evaluation of intelligence as revealed by the pattern of results, the uses of the test data for the assessment of psychopathology, and additionally the individual's responses as indicators of prominent features of his/her personality. However, once the novelty of the mysterious or unknown instrument which will "introduce one to the secrets" of professional life reduces, the techniques practiced with life history data reassert themselves and are readily adapted to the new data set.

One of the important balancing exercises introduced toward the close of the time spent on the WAIS is the discussion of the prediction made by each of the seminar members as to how their last semester's subject will perform on this test. They are asked to predict that performance at any level from the full-scale IQ score down to responses to individual tests or items. The task also involves specifying the basis for the prediction and the degree of security with which it is held. The purposes intended for this assignment are multiple and partially explained in what has previously been discussed with regard to ease of hypothesis formulation and the identification of the data upon which any hypothesis is based. The additional value implied in designating this as a balancing exercise is that, ordinarily, tests are almost exclusively approached (when dealing with an individual) in a revelatory rather than in a criterial sense. It is much more likely that a test will be used to tell us about what an unknown person is like than to verify our conjectures about one well known to us. The exercise then serves the purpose of introducing the problems of prediction of individual performance from relatively stable personality data. The model is extended to include not only the former subject's performance for each new test introduced but also the present subject's performance from one test to another. What have we learned about how the subject's intellect is manifested on the WAIS and how might that be expressed on the Rorschach, TAT, etc.? The attempt is to instill the attitude to search for stability in any data set, establish its limits or conditionality, and explore its manifestations in other data sets.

### Working with Rorschach Ink Blots

Toward the end of the third week or the beginning of the fourth week, formal instruction on the Rorschach begins. It is preceded by the assigned reading of the translation of Rorschach's original monograph (1942) and either Beck's volume one (1944) or more recently Exner's book (1974). As with the WAIS, initial attention is paid to the analysis of face sheet or summary data based on a fully scored record. Since scoring problems are formidable for beginning students, they are aided in this endeavor by the seminar assistant. Following this introduction, instructional time is spent on content and sequence analysis using the general principles of "letting the data reveal itself" or "asking the data a question" as applied to this kind of material. The terms *content* and *sequence analysis* are used here in their more general sense and not as they typically apply in Rorschach language. We are not particularly concerned with Rorschach's categories of content (such as human, animal, landscape, etc.) but the image or percept itself and what it may connote in the mind of the perceiver. By the same token, we are not particularly concerned at this stage of analysis or interpretation with sequence in the sense of the relationship of whole to part responses and what that might reveal, but rather the succession of content as associative material and what that succession could imply in light of the stimulus conditions prevailing, i.e., the qualities of the particular card in question. Some illustrative materials may help to clarify these distinctions and make more apparent what we attempt to do.

We begin by focusing on the task posed to our subjects. It may be characterized as reporting all you see or can make of a more or less ambiguous stimulus, knowing that the examiner believes that your responses reveal something about your personality but you know not what. It is a new situation whose properties are generally unknown to the subject and whose outcome cannot be foreseen by the subject. How then does this subject-task interaction influence the initial response and what immediately follows to card 1? What can we infer about the subject's set to novel and uncertain experience?

There are a number of variables, inherent in the situation, which must be taken into account before one can suggest an answer to the question posed and the particular cues that led to that surmise. Briefly stated they include the time it took to respond, the portion of the blot identified, the quality of the form identified, the degree of mental activity required to form such a percept, and the nature of the particular response given.

Imagine then an initial response from an undergraduate subject of "The whole thing is a cloud" given after a lengthy, active, serious perusal of the card. The response might suggest a cautious, conforming, noncommital approach to the unexplored. One could then invoke primacy and consider the possibility, to be further examined, that this approach may be indicative of a more general characteristic of this personality structure. Were this hypothesis offered for the response in question by a student in the seminar, he/she would be asked to supply the cues upon which the resultant is based. In this instance "cautious" would be derived from the preresponse activity of the subject (lengthy, active, serious), "conforming" from the attempt to satisfy the instructions by encompassing them in a single percept of vague form quality (the whole thing is a cloud), and noncommital because of the variety of clearly identifiable percepts which are frequently and easily seen by subjects yet not offered by this one.

Another conjecture concerning this particular initial response could be that the subject was extremely anxious, which then affected the normal perceptual processes. The cues upon which such an hypothesis might be based include the determinant of the stimulus upon which the subject reportedly based his percept, "The shading reminded me of a billowing cloud." In Rorschach lore the use of shading has been associated with the internal state of anxious stirrings. Beyond that one could invoke the symbolic use of the term "cloud" in the language and its relationship to anxiety. "It hung over him like a cloud," "It was cloudy, not clear," are images of impending doom or vagueness which are not at all uncommon in anxiety states.

Consider now the difference in examining a rapidly given initial response of "two costumed figures dancing around a maypole," a percept whose content can be sustained by the form quality of the card. Certainly spontaneity, active mental involvement, and positive affect would suggest themselves as concomitants of exposure to this new experience and could be used as the basis of a more general hypothesis about this subject's response to the new and unknown.

These examples chosen to illustrate some elements of an approach to the data were deliberately oversimplified by making them extreme and limiting them to single responses. In sequence analysis, matters quickly become more complicated and interesting. Let us return to our first example and instead of limiting the subject's performance on card I to a single response, we shall follow that response with a variety of different possibilities. For ease in exposition, then, let us subdivide subject A's performance into $A_1$, $A_2$, $A_3$, each starting with a cloud.

$A_1$ follows that response with two more clear, frequently seen percepts. The second response is "a mask," the third, "a dress mannequin." Now the initial vagueness (a cloud) disappears and is displaced by a willingness to commit, to identify an object. However, the content itself, a mask, still suggests caution, reserve, cover-up. The third response continues in the same vein, a humanlike form, without life, representing in this instance a body rather than a face. If these opening responses are being scrutinized as possible stable, stylistic imprints, we may then hypothesize that the initial caution is slightly modified as a result of increasing experience but still far from spontaneity. With regard to the particular question we are asking, the succeeding responses to new cards with different properties may continue to be revealing. Does the introduction of color, a symbolic concomitant of affect, modify the stance? Do obvious human forms have an effect, or suggested sexual forms?

Contrast the further responses of $A_1$ with those of $A_2$, who follows the cloud by saying, "It clears and now I see two birds soaring on high," and then "a monk in solitary prayer." For ease in explication, I have chosen to hold the parts of the card in which these percepts are seen constant with the parts used by $A_1$. While the images presented are rich in hypothesis-generating power, let us remain fixed at the level of the question we are considering. Here the initial reserve is almost literally thrown to the wind by resort to soaring birds, animals, and then replaced by a more somber, solitary, but nevertheless communal human activity. The responses certainly speak to the possibility that initial hesitation and uncertainty are replaced by affectivity and increased spontaneity and participation, all with good, clear outcomes as revealed in the quality of the form perceived and the reasonableness of the activity in which they are engaged. Even more may be suggested in the progression from the inanimate to animal to human.

For the responses of $A_3$ I have chosen to follow the cloud with "a dead bird," and "a squashed bug." In this instance the caution and hesitation are replaced by lifeless, crushed, once-living forms. Whether such a set is indicative of a more general and massive psychological state or confined to the issue of response to new and uncertain experience could only be determined by further analysis of sequence in the remaining responses as well as the more established route of formal scoring and analysis of the summary record. With regard to the response to new experience we could hypothesize that the subject continues to try but expects negative outcome for the effort. What this subject will see or do will not be good, enjoyable, or reassuring.

In presenting these examples I again became aware of the response of some students when content and sequence analysis is introduced with Rorschach material. They indicate that their hypotheses would differ from mine, or that they would be led to different aspects of the data than those upon which I chose to focus. At this point I generally return to the purpose of the exercise, which is that of organizing the data of observation so that it may reveal consistent aspects of its form. Once such order is suspected, it remains incumbent on the discoverer to demonstrate its generality or power by all the usual means employed by those concerned with settling epistemological issues. Data, however, is typically rich and thus conducive to all sorts of ordering depending on personal disposition, theoretical stance (implicit and explicit), and breadth of experience. Thus it is not unlikely that different observers may see different things. Of importance at this point is that the observer is free enough to organize his or her experience into some logically explainable form which can be further examined to establish its value. Students all too frequently do not have the freedom to engage in such exercises. For the most part they have been expected "to know" what is known rather than to create knowledge or verify what they think they know.

When discussions on such issues ensue it is likely that the question of what is important to know will arise and the place of explicit theory will come to the fore. For heuristic purposes, despite my great attraction to and formal study of a variety of personality theories, I have advocated a personological view of constructing a theory of each individual from whatever building blocks one can reliably and with some reasonable degree of certainty extract from the data. My own preference continues to be to know what I can know about a person, no matter how restricted it may be in the total scheme that constitutes that person's psychological essence, rather than to accrue a ready-made knowledge about a person from the concordance of a limited number of cues to the contours of a general theory about the psychological nature of humankind.

Additional analysis of the Rorschach record includes the use of the techniques we have already introduced earlier. The content of all poor-form responses might be extracted and examined for what they might reveal. Or one might ask what the data reveals about the subject's human interactions and focus on those responses in which human figures are perceived and/or those in which they are ordinarily perceived but omitted by this subject. While the number and kinds of questions that may be put to the data may seem endless, in reality this is not the case. Two general circumstances will likely influence this procedure. One results from the material itself. Questions tend to be generated by some salient aspect of the data. The quality of the subject's human interactions may be suggested by a response to card 1 reported as "two figures in mortal combat" and another of "a head with hostile looking eyes." One might then be especially tuned to examining the responses to cards 2 and 3, where human figures are frequently seen in some sort of interaction with each other, to see whether this negative image prevails. The second circumstance arises from the predilections of the examiner. What does one feel is needed to be known about another in order to assess the way in which the personality functions? To ask the data a question for which the test is not specifically designed does not guarantee that the data will contain sufficient bits of information to be able to approximate an answer, or that those bits that it does contain will reveal clear-cut patterns. One must be ever mindful of these limitations. The structure of the Rorschach test and the way it can be administered offers some possibility of overcoming a natural paucity of data needed to answer any sort of question. It is contained in the sometimes used practice of "testing the limits" after the original protocol has been completed. Basically the technique calls attention to frequently seen percepts in certain areas of the cards when they are in fact not reported by the subject. To return to our earlier example probing the subject's human interactions, the examiner could try to elicit such responses if they were not spontaneously given or, if given, the examiner could continue his quest by probing elements of the interaction not originally included in the recorded response.

After the instructional period each seminar member administers the Rorschach to his/her practice subject and reports on the findings in a class session. Problems of scoring and interpretation then arise from the practical exercise and provide much of the basis for discussion. One part of the report usually deals with the correspondence or lack thereof of the Rorschach and previously acquired WAIS data.

## Working with the TAT

It is usually seven to eight weeks into the semester before the TAT is introduced. The preliminary reading assignments include sections from the work of Henry (1956) and Tomkins (1947). Already established in our work with the WAIS and the Rorschach is the experiential fashion in which instruction is begun. What we try to do is to have the seminar participants create responses to the material under conditions which are not the standard ones for administering and taking the test. In this way we can create a pool of responses with which we can work—live material, so to speak—and avoid the implication that the responses are necessarily indicative of what would emerge if the seminar members were responding under usual testing conditions. Thus in dealing with the WAIS we might begin with the seminar assistant illustrating the technique of administration by testing the instructor, who tends to respond heuristically. We then substitute members in the two roles for various of the subtests, stressing the various points of atypicality in the testing conditions that may influence the results, e.g., the group situation, the comments on various responses while the test is in progress, questions raised by observers, the lack of experience of the examiner, etc. The material gathered, however, even though it is composite material—different subjects for the various subtests—is treated as though it was produced by a single subject. In this way each of the participants retains interest in the material gathered since some of it is personal and the rest given by others with whom there has been a fair amount of interaction.

With Rorschach we have done similarly, having the entire group record individually their responses to card 1, held at different distances from each participant by the instructor at the head of the seminar table. This is followed by individual volunteers from the group to serve as subject for each succeeding card. The composite protocol is then treated as though it were the product of a single subject. The same format then obtains for the first ten cards of the TAT. On both Rorschach and TAT the observers during any particular subpart of the test will record their own material prior to discussion of the designated subject's responses.

From a variety of standpoints one might think that little more need be done when the TAT as an analytic tool becomes the center of focus. The principles and techniques of working with data have already been explicated many times over and with a variety of data sources. Besides, the particular techniques we are discussing were essentially derived from work with the TAT and thus one might expect them to be adopted rather rapidly. This, however, is not necessarily the case. Each test instrument employed lends itself in its own particular way to the ideas of analysis we are considering and thus each demands its special due. For example, salience by uniqueness in TAT story themes cannot be seriously considered without taking into account the demand characteristics produced by each card as a stimulus. On card 1, where a boy and a violin are pictured, stories of achievement or coercion are common. Thus a coercion story to this card might be of little value in assessing the importance of this variable in the life of the subject, although how such scenes are structured and resolved may be informative about how the subject deals with coercion. Should a story deal with an unexpected theme, one should be immediately alerted to the possibility of personal meaning in the life of the subject. Imagine a story to card 1 in which the boy is depicted as mourning the loss of a loved one and consequently is unaware of the violin even being present, or one in which the boy's infirmity makes it impossible for him to consider learning to play. To detect this form of salience is however only a beginning step in the analytic process. One must have a strategy with which to proceed. Unlike the situation that prevails in personal documents, where one is usually dealing with a description of real-life events or some modified versions of them, TAT stories are products of fantasy guided in part by the stimulus configuration. Therefore to take the stories literally, as though they were directly converted descriptions of actual experience, may turn out to be quite misleading despite the fact that it occasionally happens to be so. To return to our first salient story involving mourning, we might entertain a number of different possibilities as to what it may be telling us. We might consider the idea (the direct relationship) that this is a subject who is at present handicapped by negative affect due to loss. This would be easy enough to evaluate in light of the remaining data. Massive affective states are not easily dissipated and thus we should expect a continuation, a stereotypy, of this kind of imagery in consequent responses. Alternatively, we might conjecture that this is a rather creative person who wishes to break the set of the obvious (coercion, or achievement) and thus charts a new and personally *non*-relevant theme. This is also relatively simple to explore for consistency and limits in the remaining data. One could ask how frequently the subject ignores the apparent stimulus demands, with what success, and at what cost. The number of hypotheses one could entertain are multiple although not as unlimited as one might like to believe.

Our strategy beyond that of hypothesis formulation to explain salient data is to reduce each story to its elemental core and retain it as a transformed unit representing the original data, a technique introduced earlier in the analysis of personal documents. In this instance the loss story could be rewritten as: negative affect (sadness over loss) leads to indwelling (unawareness of the outside world) for which no relieving solution is offered (lack of outcome), or more briefly, loss → − aff → inactivity. Such a shorthand procedure makes possible comparison with other sequences containing related elements. For illustrative purposes, let us imagine two further sequences that emerge from the stories of this imagined subject. In the first the derived sequence is: sadness over loss is followed by withdrawal of interest in others, then sympathy from best friends results in immersion in work. Shortened it would appear as loss → − aff and inactivity, sympathy (from intimate other) → activity. The second sequence is that loss is followed by shame and anger, which results in self-absorption and practiced absence from work or, loss → − aff (2) → inactivity. What becomes apparent in comparing these sequences is the consistency with which negative affect of different quality and produced by different stimuli leads to indwelling and withdrawal from the outside world (work and/or people), and the particular condition (sympathy from another) which can lead to a change in the sequence, at least as far as work is concerned. Whether the critical feature leading to change must be sympathy rather than any form of attention or positive regard, or whether it must come from an intimate or any kind of other are matters still to be investigated. Were we to add a sequence in which positive affect from success leads to indwelling and withdrawal such as could result from a story that might be given to card 3BM (a human figure lying on the floor), new hypothetical possibilities would emerge. The story tells of an author who has written a best seller which has given him great pleasure, who lies on the floor in despair because he feels devoid of ideas and fears not being able to write again. This sequence is much like the first we introduced except for the fact that positive affect led to indwelling rather than negative affect. The outcome, however, is the same. We might now consider that any kind of strong affect, positive or negative, can lead to indwelling and withdrawal from activity with only one known (thus far) modifier, sympathy from a best friend.

To be able to engage in this sort of analysis of TAT data demands practice in reducing stories or sequences to summary form. We have used two different exercises to increase skill. One involves the shorthand reduction to basic elements which we have been discussing. Students are asked to do this with the stories they get from their subjects and to present their results to the group. The value of this exercise is to check one's own reductions or summaries against consensus. The search for the most acceptable general form in which to summarize the particular content turns out to be interesting and instructive. Everyone seems to know when the outcome is "right," although it is not always easy to pinpoint the reason or reasons why a transformation does not attract a positive consensus.

A second exercise involves a less formal and painstaking reduction of the data. Instead of reducing the story to its sequential elements, the task is to extract from the story its meaning or meanings, trying to transform it into a one-liner or as many one-liners as it can sustain. If we return to the story of the prostrate author, we might characterize it as (1) success is no royal road to continued happiness, or (2) if you once have it you could lose it, or (3) you never have it made, or (4) you are afraid that you can never replace what you lose; and these examples are not exhaustive. A data pool of such items derived from a set of ten or more TAT stories may reveal underlying sets reflecting important aspects of the way the subject experiences the world. As an exercise it forces one to focus on implied meanings without getting lost in the detail of specific content.

TAT stories provide a rich source of data to which specific questions relevant to the assessment of personality may be posed. If one wished, for example, to ponder the affective life of the subject, one could extract all sequences where affect is exhibited and supplement those with sequences in which affect would be expected but is not expressed. From the material that results it is possible to gain entry into the affective repertoire of the subject, as it is represented in imagery. One could become aware of which affects the subject uses, the ease or difficulty of affective expression, the circumstances producing affect, the basal affective substratum with which the subject lives, the reaction of the subject to the affective expression of others, and so forth.

Suppose in such an inquiry positive affect expressed as joy was only experienced in cooperative activity with another and all other human interactions were embedded in either neutral or negative affect. Or suppose that in every situation where affect would be likely to be generated, either positive or negative, it happens, except in the case of anger. Or suppose the preponderance of positive affect is generated in solitary pursuit while little or no affect results from interaction with others. Each of these possibilities, made evident by salience indicators, would lead to formulations about the way the subject experiences the world.

The kinds of questions that can be put to the data are theoretically endless but, as I have already indicated, there are no guarantees that the data will contain sufficient material to approximate an answer. One could be concerned with the subject's ability and typical ways of responding to disappointment and failure only to find that no particular story includes elements of this aspect of life. What the absence of such concerns may indicate could mark the beginning of another data search, in the sense of whether it reflects defensiveness or unusually strong feelings of competence.

In extracting material out of context we run into dangerous ground and force an examination of some of the assumptions which may be implicit in the practice. Since we are making no distinctions at this point as to the characters involved in the sequences or the degree to which the subject identifies with each of the characters, are we not taking undue liberties with the data? The answer is undoubtedly yes, but not irretrievably so. The situation may be likened to some practices in dream analysis where some have assumed that the figures in the dream are all related at some level to aspects of the personality of the dreamer. Thus, we are holding that the story reflects the repertoire of the teller no matter the awareness or acceptance by the teller of any of its elements. To make this more concrete, let us imagine asking the question of the subject's view of peer relationships. In the data bearing on this question we find that regardless of gender one person always dominates the other and the reasons are multiple (strength, intelligence, attractiveness, position). Additionally, we find that when the story is told from the standpoint of the dominator, the attitude is always justified in terms of the behavior of the one dominated. When told by a dominated character, the other's behavior is assessed as unfair and unwarranted. From such a data set we could hypothesize that the dominance theme is an enduring aspect of the subject's peer relationships and that furthermore there is self-justification no matter which side of the dominance coin the subject finds himself or herself to be, and both are likely within the repertoire. It says, however, nothing directly about the subject's awareness of this state of events. On the basis of these responses alone it would be difficult to predict the subject's response to an open question like "How do you get along with your peers?" The answer could range from "Pretty well because I try to be fair with everyone," to "Sometimes good, sometimes not, it's variable," to "It's better when I lead because otherwise others try to take advantage of me." These responses are indicative of various levels of awareness of the peer-authority dominance problem. Yet no matter what degree of awareness exists, it is likely that the behaviors of the subject in peer relationships are predictable although variable, depending on the role in which he or she is cast. The point being made is that the subject's repertoire as represented in imagery is the best indicator of what the subject expects from others as well as what the subject would be likely to do if cast in the position of the other, whether or not that has yet occurred.

Since the TAT provides a data set rich in possibilities for exploration, we encourage the group members to pose questions and indicate what in the material they would seek and how they would evaluate it. We are particularly concerned at this point in setting questions that are answered by other materials given to the subject so that comparisons may be made. The questions may be quite general, like an overall assessment of intelligence, what in the stories would bear on this question (e.g., vocabulary, breadth of content, abstraction ability, indications of conceptual clarity, problem solution, etc.), to more specific ones like the punitive style of the subject (extrapunitive, intrapunitive, impunitive) and how that would be reflected. The questions could be designed to reflect on propositions stemming from established theory like the basic defenses used by the subject and the conditions that induce them, or the dominant attitude and first function of the subject as they would be reflected in the Jungian typology. The major purpose of this exercise is to increase skill in framing questions and in thinking through how they might be answered from the available data, whether the data has been originally gathered for these purposes or not.

### The End Phase: MMPI and What Follows

By the end of the tenth week of the semester we are usually finished with instruction on the four common test instruments covered in group, including the MMPI. Since administration and scoring problems are minimal with the MMPI, it is possible to go rather rapidly, after preliminary reading assignments (Cuadra and Reed, 1954; Carson, 1969), into profile analysis. Our major reasons for including the test relate to its extensive use in clinical settings especially as an indicator of psychological distress and psychopathology. It also serves as an important anchor for some of what we have been trying to do all along, namely predicting test performance from knowledge about an individual. The MMPI, because its scales are so well defined, affords the students the opportunity to translate what they know about the subject they studied the previous semester, as well as the practice subject they have been working with on testing, to predictions on the various MMPI scales. The exercise raises all sorts of interesting questions about the ease or difficulty of translating what it is you know or think you know into another language or into a comparative schema against other people (the normative sample). Thus we structure the task as one of selecting what the peaks and valleys are likely to be and any other prediction for which there exists a fair amount of certainty. When large discrepancies exist between prediction and performance, we have suggested an examination of the response to particular scale items to try to understand the differences. With the administration of the MMPI the work with the practice subjects is completed. Each seminar member is then required, within a two-week time period, to turn in a written personality assessment of the practice subject he or she has studied.

In the eleventh week primary attention is turned to the hired subject whose WAIS, Rorschach, TAT, and MMPI material, gathered earlier by assigned seminar members, is presented. The general format followed is that each participant is required to give the subject two tests. Since only the mentioned four are required, each person is free to choose from a suggested list those tests he/she particularly wishes to investigate. They then are required to present to the total group the basic information concerning the test's construction, validity, essential concepts, and uses. This is followed by an analysis of the subject's performance on the instrument. Depending on the number of members in the group, a rather large amount of personality data is examined in a two- or three-week period of time. Each student is required to turn in a written report of the results of the tests he or she has administered. Because of time constraints in the spring semester, no general write-up of the shared subject is required.

The last two weeks of the semester are spent in attempts to reflect on what we have done with the help of some comparative data. Again each student completes a Q-sort on the group subject studied in the second semester. We are then able to make several comparisons. One relates to *intragroup* agreement, and intragroup agreement as a function of the methods by which the subjects are studied (personal documents and interview as opposed to tests). Another involves *intergroup* agreement about the common subjects studied with the different methods. These exercises tend to raise all the issues inherent in validational studies—sampling, population size, the adequacy of the instruments used to represent what one knows, etc.

The final development occurs when the two groups come together to discuss their views of the two common subjects studied each semester. This situation generally produces a fair amount of agreement of the kind "Oh, yes, that was very evident on the Rorschach use of the *W* response, which was frequent, complex, and creative," or "We saw the power of the sibling rivalry immediately in the autobiography by the exclusion of the sister after naming her as a family member." More important, however, is that surprises are relatively rare and extreme disagreements even less frequent. For example, for one group to see the subject as socially adaptable and the other as socially isolated is not a very probable event.

What has been described thus far as a year-long seminar program is really a composite in the sense that not every step is taken every year, nor every exercise or assignment demanded. Different years with different groups demand flexibility in the program. In earlier years practice subjects for testing were not available for more than a single session. Thus it was impossible to have continuity for anyone other than the group subject. Occasionally, the entire seminar membership has been small enough (five to eight) for the group to remain intact and not be subdivided. When that has been the case the procedure has been modified somewhat. The group studies a different subject each of the two semesters in the manner previously described. The subject studied in the first semester through the analysis of autobiography and interview techniques is then tested in the second semester by an advanced graduate student, whose report of the test results and their analysis becomes the basis for comparison with the group's earlier findings. The task set for the group in the second semester's work is to relate various aspects of the personality uncovered in testing to possible life history and socialization factors that could have produced the testing picture. Such hypothesized relationships are then evaluated against the subject's actual autobiography, which is not revealed until all the testing and protocol analysis is completed.

The response to this kind of experience afforded in a year-long seminar is generally positive, with rare exceptions. The largest complaints involve the magnitude of the work load and what seems like an underemphasis on structure in the beginning phases of the work. They wish to be told what to seek, what is important. To attempt to let the data reveal prominent contours does not guarantee that what will be revealed will make you feel secure that you have uncovered the most important aspects of another. To ask the data a question without knowing what might be important to ask can also be a trying process. However, as the work progresses these issues tend not to remain paramount. The shared wisdom of the participants is of help in this regard.

While the continued positive response of students, both immediate and in retrospect, is rewarding, the best indications of the value of the seminar experience occur when one sees the attitudes, principles, and methods with which we worked successfully generalized to other relevant professional experiences. I have seen this happen frequently in my role as a clinical supervisor both in assessment and diagnostic work and also in psychotherapy. To listen to students sort a diagnostic or treatment question in terms of the immediate data presented by the patient, or to make any kind of inference and be able to point to the cues that led them in that direction is a satisfying experience. It tends to lead away from the jargon and mumbo-jumbo that all too frequently pervade clinical discussions. Perhaps my most satisfying experience with regard to the teaching of this kind of material occurred one year when I led the assessment seminar and also taught the course in personality theory. As a final exercise in the theory course I asked the participants, who were also members of the assessment seminar, to do a psychobiographical study of a personality theorist, relating the life to the work. The end products that I read gave me great pleasure. I felt reasonably secure that one could transmit these ideas to beginners in a relatively limited period of time (one year) and that the ideas could be generalized and used in various professional and scholarly endeavors.

# CHAPTER 3

## The Freud-Jung Relationship:
## The Other Side of Oedipus
## and Countertransference

This analysis begins with a case history, taken from history. It deals with a relationship between two colleagues that went awry. Since these colleagues were both therapists, and both responsible for important, seminal ideas about personality and about the psychotherapeutic process, one wonders why the outcome was so ill-fated. From an analysis of this relationship two theoretical speculations will be drawn which may illuminate their problems. The descriptive language used will be that of psychoanalysis, but hopefully the ideas will have more general value for personality theory and for dynamic psychotherapy. One speculation concerns the psychological effect of passage through the full life span. It deals more specifically with the fact that most Oedipal sons will one day be Oedipal fathers and most Oedipal daughters will be Oedipal mothers, and what impact this transition may have on individual psychological development. The other speaks more directly to the implicit effects this change may have on intimate human relationships.

Sufficient time has now elapsed since Freud and Jung were alive and enough of their personal material has been published to have encouraged a plethora of scholarly and popular efforts to understand the personality of each of the men and the dynamics of their intense, but relatively short-lived, relationship.[1] Most writers faced with the task of explaining the split between the two men tend to take one of two routes. The route of theory points to their differing views on the nature of libido, or to the importance of sexuality in the etiology of the neuroses. The route of personality dynamics usually leads to Jung's ambition or Freud's need to maintain authority and control. Freud traveled, at one time, the personality route and gave us one piece of the key to the underlying dynamic. According to Jung (Billinsky, 1969), Freud thought Jung's dissent, implied in his book *Psychology of the Unconscious* published in 1912, was an expression of Jung's unresolved Oedipal problem. This general statement, no matter what its explanatory possibilities, leaves much unsaid. Since the Freud-Jung relationship changed over time, what brought this transference issue to the fore? And how can we understand each man's particular contribution to the problem? In order to do this let us first examine what we know about the relationship between Jung and the members of his family. This may help to illuminate our path to the understanding of his side of the consequent relationship with Freud. We shall later follow a similar path for Freud.

The major source of material for Jung's early life is his dictated autobiography, *Memories, Dreams, Reflections,* recorded and edited by Aniela Jaffé (Jung, 1961). Central among all the descriptive characteristics ascribed to his father is that he saw his father as *dogmatic,* in that he was less interested in answering Jung's questions about the nature of religious belief than he was in maintaining authority. Jung's father, who was a minister, gave him in essence the message not to question but to believe. This message Jung found troublesome and a cause of constant and critical difficulty between himself and his father. On the positive side he saw his father as reliable in contrast to his mother. She is portrayed as having two distinct aspects to her personality, practical and mystical. In her mystical side, she is described as being very close to Jung and he to her. He felt that she could intuitively understand his innermost thoughts. In the relationship between father and mother, which is characterized as a stormy one, Jung as a child frequently played the role of the arbitrator. This role, played as a child, he later recognized as a precondition to an overinflated notion about oneself and one's powers.

In general it would not be too difficult to distill from Jung's recollections of childhood an Oedipal situation in which he thought that mother really preferred him to father. Father was not seen by Jung as particularly admirable, rather frightening in his dogmatic approach to things and thus not a figure to emulate. It is not unlikely that Jung was disappointed with him and harbored, in part, a wish for an adult male figure who would provide him with answers to his perplexing questions, but his early experience made him wary of such a possibility.

Further support for these conjectures abounds in the chapter on his student years (Jung, 1961).

In some fundamental ways Freud's Oedipal story is similar to Jung's despite clear differences in manifest content. They were both first-borns,[2] singularly prized by the mother. Each one's need for a male identification figure was not satisfied by the image of the real or biological father. In Jung's case the father's Achilles heel was the acceptance of dogma as a substitute for the search for truth.[3] In Freud's case the father's defect was characterized by his failure to succeed, which Freud attributed partially to father's lack of courage.[4]

Despite the similarity in assurance of favoritism by the mother, their reaction to the father as the male rival was quite different. In Jung's case there was anger generated toward a stubborn, dogmatic authority, followed by withdrawal.[5] For Freud there was contempt for weakness and a consequent search for a heroic figure[6] but at the same time a love for the weak but kind and supporting father. Thus, any thought of replacing him was followed by guilt, a theme he later projected in *Totem and Taboo* and in *Moses and Monotheism*. Jung for the most part avoided living male authorities although, using his language, the need for the archetypal or perfect father continued and was satisfied through a deep personal belief in a godhead. His claim was that he did not believe that God existed; he *knew* he existed (Jung, 1961, p. 62). His reaction to living male authorities was that sooner or later they would demand that you "believe" and the adherence to that demand would estrange you from self. Freud, on the other hand, not-withstanding his great gift for independent thought, for a long time as an adult persisted in a search for a heroic living male-identification figure. Brücke, Breuer, Charcot, even Fliess, whom he idealized in order to make him fit the image, were brief candidates. However, he finally settled, without awareness, on the historic figure of Moses.

Leaving family history and its impact on our two central figures, let us now turn to where they were in life when their relationship started and where they were by the time it was over. The position to be explicated is that the split in their relationship was inevitable, the result of incompatible overlapping features in their personalities aided and abetted by life-role differences between them. Jung's story has already been drawn in outline. While he could be intrigued by the possibility of a positive male model, his early experience had imprinted him with the idea that in the end such an identification would be at the expense of his own development. Thus, he came with the transference expectation that the authority would demand of him unquestioning belief in dogma and, further, that no amount of reasonable discussion could change the situation. Ultimately the authority would appeal to its time-honored allies: faith and greater experience. This expectation, as we shall see, Freud lived out for him. The case for Freud revolves around his adoption of a Mosaic, father-leader attitude toward his followers and his accompanying fear of displacement.

In tracing their relationship, Jung tells us that he first became aware of Freud in 1900 when he read the newly published *The Interpretation of Dreams* (Jung, 1961, p. 146). This was the year in which he finished his medical degree and took up his position as assistant at the cantonal psychiatric facility in Zurich, the Burghölzli. He had written his medical dissertation on a case of multiple personality, and already brewing in his head was the extension of the philosophical ideas of Nietzsche and Schopenhauer, of a "world behind a world" and its extension into the domain of mental disorder. His comment about Freud's book was that he knew he had read something very important but did not quite understand it nor its relationship to his thoughts and his work. He proceeded then to undertake his famous association studies which established his reputation in psychiatric circles as a person of great promise, a potential leader in the field. It was not until 1903 that he reread Freud's book and realized the link between Freud's ideas about repression and his idea of unconscious complexes. Repression was the mechanism by which complexes were formed. Despite his ensuing interest in psychoanalysis and his defense of Freud in local psychiatric circles, their known correspondence did not begin until 1906 and their first meeting did not take place until 1907, in Vienna. This delay is pointed out to support the earlier speculation regarding Jung's avoidance of the influence of a real, face-to-face authority (Jung, 1925).

Before returning to that historic first meeting in 1907 whose contents already foretold the future of the relationship, let us try to understand where Freud was psychologically at this time of his life. He had already published what he often referred to as his most important piece of work, the theory of dreams. Although with this work scientific recognition had still not been achieved, the next few years brought forth a spate of works whose origins were already contained in the book on dreams, *The Psychopathology of Everyday Life, Wit and Its Relationship to the Unconscious,* and the all important *Three Contributions to the Theory of Sexuality.* Libido theory was born, papers on technique were produced, and long case histories were offered. He had already in 1902 begun to gather a circle of disciples who afforded him a continuous forum for his ideas. He was a man, entering the sixth decade of life, who was bursting forth with original views on the understanding of fundamental human problems. However, he had not yet "arrived." He was still on his way. On the personal side he had gone through a series of disappointments with real authority images, Brücke and Breuer, and an idealized authority figure, Wilhelm Fliess.[7] The latter relationship ended badly during the first five years of the new century, just prior to his meeting Jung. It seems likely that the problem that could not be solved overtly through a real relationship, namely the search for a male identification figure, actually found its solution in the unconscious, and the outlines can be clearly traced.

It is commonplace among biographers to suggest that Freud unconsciously adopted Moses as his major identification figure.[8] I would further suggest that during the period from 1901 to 1913 he went from the role of the fearful Oedipal son vis-à-vis Moses to that of an equal, and that his own unconscious conflicts were continually played out or projected onto the figure of Moses. The evidence upon which this conjecture is based is contained in the Jones biography and has been used by many writers to analyze various aspects of the Freud-Moses relationship (Bakan, 1958; Jones, 1958; McLean, 1941; Oehlschlegel, 1943; Puner, 1947; Robert, 1976; Rosenberg, 1978; Sachs, 1941; Wallace, 1977, 1978). The essential elements can be seen in two separate experiences some twelve or thirteen years apart. The first involves Freud's initial visit to Rome in 1901, a story in itself. For many years prior to this visit he had expressed a great desire to view Michelangelo's statue of Moses but for some reason was not able to do so. It was not until thirteen years later that he indicated a recurring reaction of his when this wish was satisfied. He felt like one of the children of Israel who had been worshipping the golden calf and who was now feeling the wrath of Moses as a consequence (Freud Coll. Papers, vol. 4, pp. 259–60). One could speculate that the guilt he suffered at that time was a function of the publication of *The Interpretation of Dreams* one year before. It was as though that work heralded the dawn of a new religion, an act of heresy, akin to that of the Israelites worshipping a false idol.[9]

The second element concerns the publication in 1914 of the anonymous work "The Moses of Michelangelo," in *Imago*, a psychoanalytic journal, a work claimed some ten years later by Freud (1959). In it he analyzes Michelangelo's intention in producing the statue and concludes after a marvelously rational tour de force that Michelangelo was portraying the ideal Moses rather than the historic figure. Moses in this rendition is not about to smash the tablets but rather is attempting to protect them, since the "law" is more important than the idol-worshipping people. Jones pointed out that this projection made sense at a time when Jung's defection was final and had been preceded by that of Stekel and Adler (Jones, 1958). Freud attributed to Moses the solution he adopted in response to the defections. Aside from the brief critical evaluation of Jung's and Adler's work in the historical description of psychoanalysis published in 1914 as the *History of the Psychoanalytic Movement*, Freud chose the path he imputed to Michelangelo's Moses, that of explicating the law rather than spending his time in punishing the dissidents or engaging them in argumentative discourse. What is evident from these two incidents is that from 1901 on Freud was a fearful child in relation to the Moses figure and by 1913 when the essay was written he had become the Mosaic father dealing with errant children.

Although we can be reasonably certain that the transformation in Freud from Oedipal son to Oedipal father began in 1901 and was certainly completed by 1914, we have further bits of evidence that suggest the change really started when the Vienna circle of adherents, meeting on Wednesday nights, began in 1902. By 1909 the completed change was obvious when Freud openly took a paternal role toward Jung in a letter which after a few brief introductory sentences continued:

> It is strange that on the very same evening when I formally adopted you as eldest son and anointed you—*in partibus infidelium*—as my successor and crown prince, you should have divested me of my paternal dignity, which seems to have given you as much pleasure as I, on the contrary, derived from the investiture of your person. Now I am afraid of falling back into the

father role with you if I tell you how I feel about the poltergeist business. But I must, because my attitude is not what you might otherwise think. (McGuire, 1974, p. 218)

The entire correspondence from 1907 on is replete with the father-son reference and such a relationship is mentioned specifically in letters from Emma Jung to Freud (McGuire, 1974, p. 456).

Jung in his report on their first meeting in 1907 already attributes to Freud those aspects of his father that he found objectionable. Despite his overall awe of Freud this negative aspect is quite salient in what he wrote.

I had not met with much sympathy for the ideas expressed in *The Psychology of Dementia Praecox*. In fact, my colleagues laughed at me. But through this book I came to know Freud. He invited me to visit him, and our first meeting took place in Vienna in February 1907. We met at one o'clock in the afternoon and talked virtually without pause for thirteen hours. Freud was the first man of real importance I had encountered in my experience up to that time, no one else would compare with him. There was nothing the least trivial in his attitude. I found him extremely intelligent, shrewd, and altogether remarkable. And yet my first impressions of him remained somewhat tangled; I could not make him out.

What he said about his sexual theory impressed me. Nevertheless, his words could not remove my hesitations and doubts. I tried to advance these reservations of mine on several occasions, but each time he would attribute them to my *lack of experience* [italics mine]. Freud was right; in those days I had not enough experience to support my objections. I could see that his sexual theory was enormously important to him, both personally and philosophically. This impressed me, but I could not decide to what extent this strong emphasis on sexuality was connected with subjective prejudices of his, and to what extent it rested on verifiable experiences. (Jung, 1961, p. 149)

And a bit further on he describes that first meeting:

There was something else that seemed to me significant at that first meeting. It had to do with things which I was able to think out and understand only after our friendship was over. There was no mistaking the fact that Freud was emotionally involved in his sexual theory to an extraordinary degree. When he spoke of it his tone became urgent, almost anxious, and all signs of his normally critical and skeptical manner vanished. A strong, deeply moved expression came over his face, the cause of which I was at a loss to understand. I had a strong intuition that for him sexuality was a sort of numinosum. This was confirmed by a conversation which took place some three years later (in 1910) again in Vienna.

I can still recall vividly how Freud said to me, "My dear Jung, promise me never to abandon the sexual theory. That is the most essential thing of all. You see, we must make a *dogma* of it, an unshakeable bulwark." He said this to me in the tone of a father saying, "and promise me this one thing, my dear son: that you will go to church every Sunday.[10] In some astonishment I asked him, "A bulwark—against what?" To which he replied, "Against the black tide of mud"—and here he hesitated for a moment, then added—of "occultism." First of all, it was the words, "bulwark" and "dogma" that alarmed me; for a dogma, that is to say, an undisputable confession of faith, is set up only when the aim is to suppress doubts once and for all. But that no longer has anything to do with scientific judgment; only with a personal power drive. (Jung, 1961)

What I hope to have established in this brief review of old documents is (1) that the relationship between Freud and Jung was set up as a father-son relationship in a rather obvious way, (2) that Jung's sensitivity to some aspects of Freud's attitude toward psychoanalysis was on overreaction based on the revival of an often experienced "nuclear neurotic scene" with his real father concerning religion,[11] (3) that unless Freud was able to interfere with this process, Jung was very likely to repeat the solution he had adopted with his own father, namely a complete separation in the interest of being able to pursue his own destiny, (4) that the reason Freud had difficulty in interfering with Jung's path was that Freud at this time was experiencing the concomitants of the father role in the Oedipal drama which he manifested by a Mosaic attitude toward the flock in the interest of preserving the law, (5) and that as the archetypal Oedipal father, Freud unconsciously feared what he projected out in his description of the development of civilization in *Totem and Taboo*, and again in *Moses and Monotheism*, annihilation by the sons. The latter fear was exacerbated continuously in his lifetime by the defections of the once faithful. For him the relationship with Jung was even more painful and puzzling in that he was willing to give over the reins to Jung and had already proclaimed this publicly. It was as though Jung could not even wait for him to step aside graciously—he needed to kill him before his time. The dramatic theme of being killed by the sons appears not only in some of the most controversial of Freud's metapsychological works (what could be called his projection screens) but beclouded the manifest or overt relationship between Freud and Jung. On at least three different occasions during the relatively brief span of their friendship Freud accused Jung of expressing in covert fashion an unconscious death wish toward him. Two of these reported incidents took place in 1909 and were connected with the famous journey to Clark University, where both men were honored by invitations to lecture at the twenty-fifth anniversary of the founding of that institution. The other took place at a small psychoanalytic meeting in 1912 in Munich just prior to the ultimate dissolution of the friendship. In two of the incidents Freud fainted when he thought he detected the wish but did not express this directly to Jung until after he had recovered. In the other incident, an analysis of an important dream of Jung's, Freud attributed the death wish as the latent wish underlying the manifest content of the dream. In this instance, when the wish was exposed he did not faint. Incidentally, one might ask what else occurred in 1909 to stir this theme in Freud's psyche. One possible element of some significance might be the invitations both received to be honored at Clark University. Freud was thrilled with the invitation, especially after the time and financial conditions were modified to suit his needs. Jung was invited somewhat later in his own right for the association studies. This independent recognition of Jung could have exacerbated the displacement fear.

With an analysis of their attitudes toward authority as background, one can understand why this historic relationship might have been ill-fated from the start. Freud, as father, feared in others the death wish toward the father he had discovered in himself during a period of self-analysis some fifteen years before, shortly after the death of his father

(Freud, 1958; Grinstein, 1968). This wish he assigned universal significance. Perhaps this was an error.[12] Freud's exclusive path to mother
was literally blocked by any number of figures, his real father who was
an effective husband during Freud's early years, his half-brother who
was confused by Freud as mother's husband because of their similarity
in age, and the succession of siblings who followed Freud in short
order. All the male rivals, however, half-brother and real brother, disappeared in the first five years of Freud's life, leaving only father. Despite
mother's strong attachment to her first born, she was also strongly
attached to her husband. Real or potential rivals thus always existed.

Jung, on the other hand, lived out a somewhat different script. The
only barrier to his affective unity with mother was mother's number
one personality, the Swiss hausfrau. With her number two, mystical
personality he was highly compatible. The relationship between
mother and father was extremely poor; they slept in separate rooms,
and no sibling appeared until Jung was nine years of age. There was no
need to eliminate father even in unconscious fantasy because father
was not a serious rival for mother's attention. In fact, father was
initially seen as a potential ally to help solve a child's life problems. It
was only when father could not satisfy Jung's need for answers to his
provocative questions that Jung withdrew from him affectively to
follow his own path, the same solution he used many years later with
Freud.

In thinking through the eventual resolution of the relationship with
mother, one is of course led to the choice of women with whom each
man was intimate in later life. This is a complicated story, hinted at by
others, which I shall largely by-pass (Billinsky, 1969; Stern, 1976).
However, I am struck by the observation that each man's attitude
toward mother was similar to his attitude toward his theoretical work.

If we think of "the work" as being the symbolic representation of
mother, the two men differed rather markedly in their imagery as to
how to achieve and maintain relationship with the object. Freud's
imagery is that of sole possession and overcoming of obstacles. His
early heroes were conquerors. He attacked boldly with ideas in order
to achieve and then fully expected to be attacked when he had reached
a position of prominence. The object had to be fought for, there were
others in the way, and you were never safe when you possessed the
object because someone else would try to take it from you—either

directly or by modifying it or demeaning its value. The basic belief, though, was that he knew it was his but others would not let him have it.

Jung's imagery was not so much that of external obstacles threatening to keep you from the object or take it away from you, but much more that of the object being totally yours to explore but endlessly deep and, thus, never ultimately attainable. You could know its outlines, its intent, the way it works, but you never could really possess it—it rather possessed you. No one could really keep you from exploring that which was basically yours, and if they tried either by distracting you or trying to interest you in what was theirs, you must separate yourself from them. This story fits the early family situation with father and religion as opposed to mother and the mystical as well as the later situation with Freud and the sexual libido theory as opposed to self and the mystery of the collective unconscious.

In retracing and trying to understand the Freud-Jung relationship, I have used material mostly from our knowledge of their interactions with their parents, a rather standard practice in psychological assessment. What constitutes novelty in this analysis pertains to the understanding of how Freud's reaction to Jung is related to his own Oedipal story, for now he was cast in the role of the father and not of the son. Psychoanalysis as a theory tells us little about what changes, if any, to expect when the role shifts and the son later in life becomes a father. Nor does it tell us in any real sense how long the need to remain a son will persist, nor how extensive will be its manifestations, nor what conditions will activate the need if it is dormant. Jung was in his midthirties when he began his separation from Freud. Freud was in his middle to late forties when he clearly adopted the paternal attitude. As I have already indicated, less than ten years before in his interaction with Fliess, a younger man, he was still in the role of the son.

The psychoanalytic story of personality development is a deceptively attractive one. It is an outgrowth of libido theory and is tied particularly to the genetic unfolding of libidinal interests through the first six years or so of life. It is a story seen through the reconstructed eyes and mind of the developing child. There are the universal problems of feeding, weaning, toilet training, and the discovery of the genitals which leads, in turn, to the emergence of the family romance. The particular resolutions to these problems constitute the foundation stones for the creation of basic personality and character structure. Individual differences in these structures are achieved through the variety of ways in which the socializing agents force resolutions to these universal problems. The child is molded, for better or for worse, through a harsh compromise between fundamental biological expression and necessary cultural dictates. From the sixth or seventh year on it lives out its psychological destiny influenced somewhat, but not excessively, by the impact of external sources. Although it is tacitly acknowledged that one grows older and the demands on the person change as a function of age and role in life, there remains an implicit belief that the personality is fully formed early in life and is simply lived out in a form adapted to age, status, etc. The danger, of course, is that this formulation emphasizing trait characteristics appears so intuitively attractive that we may be lulled into simple settlements in the understanding of complex processes by the trait continuities in personality. The statements that a person was trusting, even as a child, or stubborn, or reckless, or competitive, or penurious, or orderly, or any of the personality characteristics derived from any of the developmental stages in analytic theory are statements frequently made by parents about their grown children or longtime friends about one another. Does life from a different vantage point, father instead of son, force a change in the organization of the personality and, if so, is there any way that we might have a lead as to what form that change might take? While classical analytic theory never really addressed itself to this greater problem of personality change over the full life span, an examination of Freud's more esoteric writings would lead one to the conclusion that he exemplified that change whether he was aware of it in any overt sense or not. In these works the struggle for succession is viewed from the position of one who has achieved, the father and not the son.

To be an Oedipal parent necessarily involves a whole new set of universal problems whose solution may dictate how life will be experienced in middle and later stages. For example, mothers must eventually learn to live without being the needed giver in a trusting, dependent relationship. Fathers must learn to share and finally to give up power and control in relationships which were once almost entirely dominated by them. The solutions to problems of parenting, like those of adolescence, are influenced by the experiences of childhood in the nuclear family. However, the vantage point is now that of the adult, and not of the child, and if the regressive solutions of childhood are reinstated, psychological development is likely to be impeded. Rangell (1955), in an interesting paper published some thirty-five years ago, pointed out various manifestations of reawakened unresolved Oedipal conflicts in later life brought on by parent-child interaction. However, Rangell, while recognizing the continued importance of the Oedipal conflict throughout life, follows the imagery of classical theory, a child's response in an adult body. Wallace, in a well-reasoned analysis of Freud's "father conflict" as it was manifested in his adult life, also invokes the classical psychoanalytic position (Wallace, 1978). What is proposed here is a different perspective, the view from the eyes of an Oedipal parent. If the solutions stem only from the adult point of view without recognizing the child's position in the Oedipal drama, they are likely to alienate the child and perpetuate as one-sided a view of the relationship as that held by the child.

In Freud's case I have tried to spell out his Oedipal parent solution and indicate what it meant for the relationship with Jung. In doing this I placed Freud's transition from the position of an Oedipal son to an Oedipal father at a time when he was in the *fifth and sixth decades* of life. If we take the change in Jung's behavior toward Freud as an indication of that transition for him, it took place in the *fourth decade* of his life. Thus, I would maintain that the typical analytic statement about the time of Oedipal resolution is somewhat misleading and in keeping only with a one-sided view of the life space, the view from the vantage point of a child. The resolution for the male may begin when he is forced to separate from the intense and extremely intimate contact with his mother, but it is not truly complete until the adult role of father is clearly adopted. The Freud-Jung relationship took place when Freud was already an Oedipal father and as such he re-awakened in Jung an Oedipal crisis which redintegrated Jung's earlier solution. Each saw in the other the realization of their worst fears about the father-son relationship, the fear of loss of independence by Jung and the fear of displacement by Freud.

Now, if I am identifying another important stage or phase in psycho-logical growth, what can be said about its connection to what has gone before in the life history? This is a fascinating question which imme-diately invites a whole new world of speculation. With Freud one aspect is clear. When his father died in 1895 there was consequently released, in his dream material, the death wish toward the father, which in turn led to Freud's speculation about the universality of the myth of Oedipus as a factor in psychic life. It should not be surprising that, having discovered this in himself and generalized it to mankind, Freud should have feared displacement and death by the sons that he assumed the role of ideological father toward.[13] Why this same state of affairs did not obtain in his nuclear family, or at least not blatantly or obviously, may be accounted for by a number of complicated circumstances in his relationship with his wife. I would conjecture that with the birth of their children the relationship with Martha lost its exclusivity, a repetition of his experience as a first-born. His interest in the "lost object," just as in childhood, was transferred to his intellectual work, but now in a highly personalized manner. There was a way in which psychoanalysis was exclusively his own possession, just as a wife might be to a husband in a childless marriage or a mother to a first-born child, and he guarded it against intrusion as one would a cherished love object.[14]

To what extent the resolution of the Oedipal parent problem can be predicted from the resolution made when that parent was an Oedipal child, I am not certain. In retrospect, for these particular cases the path seems clear. Freud sought a heroic father image, found it later in life through an unconscious identification with Moses, and lived out the role he assigned to the father in the development of civilization. The women (work) were all his, but he was envied by the sons who would plot to take away from him what was rightfully his. If they succeeded they would suffer eternal guilt, and never mind, he would arise again in similar or symbolic form. To know how pervasive this theme was in Freud's unconscious one need do nothing more than reread *Totem and Taboo* and *Moses and Monotheism*, books of his later life, conceived and written some twenty years apart. The wish as a child to eliminate the rival was succeeded by the fear as an adult of being eliminated.

Jung's position also seems clear-cut and consistent, although less written evidence for this exists. He, like Freud, expected that the women/work would belong to him. Unlike Freud, and perhaps as a function of the different sibling situation in the two families, his Oedipal resolution was a bit different. Jung was an only child for nine years until his sister, whom he professed he really never got to know, was born. Freud was the first-born of a second or perhaps even third marriage, surrounded by half-brothers of the same age as his mother and followed by a succession of seven siblings, five sisters and two brothers. Jung withdrew from any alliance with the father yet maintained a peculiar relationship with the mother, whose central theme seemed to be great propriety and formality on an overt level but an underlying understanding of their affinity for one another. In his adult life, he was surrounded by women followers, treated mostly women, recommended them as controls for a working therapist, and, in general, seemed indifferent toward males. The indifference is best captured in a quote from Jung found in the introduction to his autobiography:

> I have spoken with many famous men of my time, the great ones in science and politics, with explorers, artists and writers, princes and financial magnates; but if I am honest I must say that only a few such encounters have been significant experiences for me. Our meetings were like those of ships on the high seas, when they dip their flags to one another. Usually, too, these persons had something to ask of me which I am not at liberty to divulge. Thus I have retained no memories of them, however important these persons may be in the eyes of the world. Our meetings were without portent; they soon faded away and bore no deeper consequences. But of those relationships which were vital to me, and which came to me like memories of far-off times, I cannot speak, for they pertain not only to my innermost life but also to that of others. It is not for me to fling open to the public eye doors that are closed forever. (Jung, 1961)

An analysis of this quote may supply the clue we are seeking. As a child, Jung separated from the father because the father was unable to produce the secrets, the answers to the puzzle Jung was probing. As an adult, he characterized his relationship with men as distant. They wanted something from him which was secret, not public for the world to know. Thus, whatever the relationship, intimate or not, Jung was entrusted with a secret he could not divulge. He, as a child, wanted from the father something he could not get. He, as an adult, had something he could not give.

The last two sentences of this quotation are concerned with intimacy and seem somewhat more cryptic than the rest of the statement. It is my conjecture that at the end he was talking about his intimate relationship with women and the relationship with Freud. Aside from the coterie of adoring women around him, the patients, the "alte tantes," the collaborators, there were two major intimate female figures in his adult life, his wife Emma and his mistress Toni Wolff. Each could be identified differently as typical of mother's number one and number two personalities, and for some thirty years the two women had to learn to live in peace with each other, at his insistence (Stern, 1976). What I am suggesting by these examples is that both Jung and Freud emulated the feared aspects they attributed to father, and expected from the "sons" their own unconscious resolutions to their difficulties with father. Whether this is a more general solution to the progression from son to father awaits further evidence.

I should now like to turn to another facet of the Freud-Jung relationship which may have psychotherapeutic implications. The question may be raised that if Freud knew that Jung was involved in a transference relationship with him stemming from the earlier difficulties with the father, why was he not able in five years to break through it, or work around it, or suggest that Jung have it analyzed? On the conscious level, as is evident from correspondence with Abraham, he needed Jung to further the psychoanalytic movement and thus treated him with considerable understanding (Abraham, 1965, p. 62 ff). However, on a deeper level, I am suggesting that Freud's lack of awareness of what impact his position as an Oedipal father could engender in Jung constituted the barrier to solution. Freud's fear of displacement had to be dealt with by Jung no matter what transference dispositions he brought to the relationship. There was a so-called reality issue to be faced by Jung. This is exemplified by the several times during their friendship that Freud is reported to have attributed to Jung a death wish toward him. In one sense, Freud really acted in the role of a classical analyst in interpreting Jung's dissent as transference behavior and *nothing more*. Perhaps, however, it *was* something more, and therein lies the rub. Freud had no awareness of how his own particular resolution to life at that stage of his existence played into the possibility of reactivating Jung's nuclear Oedipal problem. In true Mosaic fashion Freud advocated *belief* for Jung, and the establishment of dogma, because he thought he had discovered *the truth* and as a great man his authority should not be questioned, especially since it was offered in Jung's best interest. Because he did not see what he could unintentionally generate in another toward whom he adopted a fatherly role, he could only attribute the problem to Jung's psyche. He thought it was Jung's problem, not his own. Undoubtedly he was correct in identifying it as Jung's problem. However, perhaps he erred by resorting solely to the concept of transference and not recognizing his contribution to the appearance of the problem in Jung and the power it could have at that time in Jung's life. I would say that fear of displacement, being overcome by the sons, was a subtle countertransference problem of which Freud was unaware. It resulted in an overconcern with authority and control which acted as an insurmountable barrier to a recognition of Jung's basic concerns.[15] If he had been aware of this early in his relationship with Jung, given the talent and experience of the two people involved, the actual outcome of the relationship might have been different.

Having attributed Freud's restricted analysis of Jung's defection to a subtle countertransference problem, I am fully aware, and with some trepidation, that I have entered a theoretical "no-man's land" since I am not using the term in its commonly accepted ways. In the classical psychoanalytic literature countertransference was looked upon as the therapist's reactions to the patient which derive from the unresolved or inadequately resolved problems of the therapist. In more recent times in the orthodox and neoanalytic literature the term has been expanded by some to include all that is engendered in the therapist by the patient. In both instances, however, there is the clear implication that the patient does something, or says something, or is something, which affects the therapist and he or she is likely to be aware of it through well-known internal cues. What I am referring to as a subtle form of countertransference is what the therapist unknowingly engenders in the patient by what he or she does or says or is whether it has transference implications for the patient or not. If transference responses are generated in the patient, therapeutic issues may become confounded in the same sense that Freud's analysis of Jung's defection may have been confounded. In the case of the friendship it led to failure, with each of the participants aware only of the negative contribution of the other. In psychotherapy the outcome may be similar if the patient's response to the therapist is treated exclusively in transference terms without examination of the possible contribution of the therapist to the mix. The task for the therapist will remain difficult if the present conceptions of countertransference are strictly maintained, largely because they derive from Freud's original notions of the therapist as a "blank screen." While we are all aware that therapists are not merely projection figures, our conceptual understanding of the therapist's role sometimes belies that knowledge. Some clues to our countertransference impact may be gleaned from any uniform, consistent feedback we receive from patients and from other intimate relationships. When the messages are similar we must face the countertransference possibilities. Only when the patient's input seems sufficiently unique can we feel more secure in following exclusively the transference trail. The questions concerning therapeutic technique in dealing with such countertransference issues are formidable and beyond the scope of the present exposition. They demand a hearing in their own right.

In this brief review of the history of an important relationship I have attempted to call attention to some heretofore neglected aspects which may help to account for its particular outcome. The fruit of that attempt, the neglected role of the Oedipal parent, and an undetected form of countertransference may have more general implications for personality theory and for psychotherapy.

# CHAPTER 4

## If Freud Were Moses

### Introduction: *Moses and Monotheism*

During the waning years of his life Freud was fervently involved in bringing to fruition a set of ideas that plagued him like "a ghost not laid" (Jones, 1957, p. 225). He was concerned with the ethnic origin of the historical figure Moses, his relationship to the doctrine of monotheism, and his relationship to the Jewish people.[1] If at this juncture you are aware of the vague referent "his" in the preceding sentence, you have already identified the central theme in what is to unfold. We shall explore the role of Moses in Freud's life, focusing on what is to be learned about Freud and his work through an examination of his conjectures about Moses.[2]

The path that I shall follow in doing this is one suggested in a paper on Freud's *Moses and Monotheism* by Wallace (1977). Recognizing the wealth of personal information about Freud contained in the book, he hopes for more detailed analysis by other investigators and subsequent correlation with known biographical work. My particular strategy will be to follow Freud's exposition, relate the content to its referent in Freud's life, and consequently to weave the individual pieces into a pattern which would sensibly reflect the relationship between his life and his work.

In the unfolding exposition a number of critical problems in Freud's life will be examined, especially as we are led to them by the salient features of his tale of Moses and the Mosaic doctrine. These will include the issues of his ethnic identity, his handling of the fundamental "instincts," sex and aggression, and his attributions about the role played in his own psychological development by the chief socializers, his mother and his father. For these central figures we shall search for the consistent features and the critical "scripts" that governed the relationships and their impact on his later life.[3]

In the previous chapter, in an attempt to understand the course of the Freud-Jung encounter, certain aspects of the Moses story were reviewed. In brief, it was asserted that (1) Freud's search for a heroic male identification figure was never satisfied in his real-life relationships, (2) the search for such a figure culminated in an identification with the historical, biblical Moses, (3) the identification began with Freud living out the role of the heretical son vis-à-vis the disapproving father, (4) the role changed in the course of time to one of identity so that what Freud wrote about Moses was a "via regia" to not so obvious aspects of Freud's psychological life. The data to support these assertions were derived from a review of the events in Freud's life from the publication of his dream theory in 1900 through the publication of his anonymous paper on Michelangelo's statue of Moses in 1914. Although the present discussion seeks to extend our knowledge by continuing the analysis of the relationship with Moses beyond 1914, the path will not always be chronologically consistent. We will frequently find that what is uncovered has obvious roots in the past and may help to make some of the more cryptic aspects of the past more understandable. Thus, from time to time I shall exercise the privilege of reversing time's arrow.

Despite the fact that Moses seems to figure prominently in Freud's existence from the turn of the century until the end of his life some thirty-nine years later, there are really only three points at which Moses comes to the foreground. The first is at the time of Freud's initial long-delayed visit to Rome in 1901 when he stood in fear of the statue. This was after the publication of the theory of dreams, the book which heralded the birth of psychoanalysis not only as a theory of human mental functioning but as a "movement" as well. The second occurs in the context of a threat to the continuation of these ideas and the movement itself in 1913 after the defections of Stekel, Adler, and Jung from the psychoanalytic fold. In a few short years interest had spread beyond the limitations of Austria's national borders to include an international network, which was now threatened by competing ideas. The third begins in a similar context of threat in 1933 with the rise to power of National Socialism in Germany. The chronology is highlighted to introduce the point that Moses became prominent in

Freud's life only when in his mind psychoanalysis was at a critical juncture with regard to its survival. This is in contrast to moments of personal hardship or crisis alone. Thus, for the most part, Moses does not seem to serve as a general projection figure.[4] During the most difficult of times in the more than twenty-year period between the two publications on Moses—the war years 1914 to 1918, the unexpected death of his daughter Sophie in 1920 at age twenty-six, the death of his four-and-one-half-year-old grandson in 1923, the discovery and painful treatment surrounding his cancer of the jaw and palate beginning in 1923—Moses nowhere appears. Interestingly enough, the identification seems to be rooted in their similarity not so much as discoverers but as propagators and guardians of the law, recipients of important revelations.[5] In short, they are both authoritative, competent patriarchs protecting something whose value they have appreciated and fostered.

The difference in the way Moses is seen by Freud in 1913 and then in 1934 is also indicative of interesting personal changes in Freud himself. In his treatment of Michelangelo's statue in 1913, speculating on what the sculptor really intended, he sees the depicted moment as one in which Moses calmed his anger toward the idol worshipers, an attitude Freud consciously adopted in dealing with the defectors from the psychoanalytic fold, Stekel, Adler, and Jung, during that same time. The task of Moses, according to Freud, was to protect the tablets, ignore the people, and explicate the law, in contrast to the historical tale.[6] Perhaps the solution he attributed to Moses at that time resulted from what Freud surmised would be the result of strongly expressed anger on his part in response to his own problematic situation. That outcome is offered in *Totem and Taboo*, written in the same year, 1913, where the sons kill the restrictive father, a theme to appear twenty years later in connection with Moses. In 1913 Freud at fifty-seven felt ready and able to carry on the work connected with insuring the survival of his ideas despite the uncomfortable barriers presented by dissenters and an impending war. He did not wish to risk the consequences he feared if he expressed his anger. Thus his solution was to avoid conflict. The situation in 1934, when he was nearing the end of the eighth decade of his life, long ridden with cancer and threatened by destruction of his life's work, was quite different and thus demanded a new solution. No longer could he stay his distress, since too much was at stake. His time was limited and his resources meager.[7] Perhaps an examination of his final excursion into the character of Moses will suggest the answer he evolved.

### The Time and Setting

The circumstances surrounding the development and appearance of Freud's last volume, *Moses and Monotheism*, are sufficiently unlike those associated with most of his other work to bear retelling. I am not simply calling to mind the external conditions of central Europe. In the period following Hitler's accession to leadership in 1933, Freud's books were burned in Germany. Although early on he and others were certain of the eventual demise of psychoanalysis in countries dominated by Germany, Freud at the beginning expressed no fear for his personal safety in Austria as a Jew.[8] He was by this time both world renowned and aged. His concern was and continued to be the perpetuation of his lifework and the safety of the people entrusted with that task. Despite the fact that he was aware that his life was approaching an end and psychoanalysis was endangered, he continued to work productively and had much to show for his effort. Yet, of all the things he wrote in those final six years of his life, none was surrounded with the affect that accrued to the essays on Moses. Over a four-year period, from 1934 to 1938, his letters to Arnold Zweig, Lou Andreas-Salomé, Ernest Jones, and Max Eitingon, who were among his most faithful correspondents, contained much reflection on the difficulties he was having in bringing that work to completion (Jones, 1957, chap. 5). The period of time involved in the work was unusually long for Freud. The doubts about the power of the arguments gave him pause, and at various moments he expressed despair both about finishing it and the impact it might have on the future of analytic practice in Vienna. Thus the book was special, as indicated by these various salience markers and, as many have remarked, contained material pertinent to Freud's own personal existence.[9]

Even the conditions of its publication were somewhat unusual. Freud indicated that he had written a draft of the work in 1934 but was not certain of the material in the third of the three parts. He continued to be concerned with the ideas and then revised it in 1936. In 1937 the first two essays were published separately in *Imago*, but the final one continued to engage him in a struggle.[10] As late as April of 1938 he wrote that he was doubtful, given the inner and outer circumstances, that he would ever finish the work (Jones, 1957, p. 224). However, by the end of June, safely delivered with his family in London largely through the efforts of his later biographer the British psychoanalyst Ernest Jones, his affect toward finishing changed markedly. In a letter to Zweig he indicated enjoyment in working on the book and sent it off to the printer in Holland shortly thereafter (E. Freud, 1970, p. 163). In early August his daughter Anna read the long-awaited third essay to the International Psychoanalytic Congress in Paris. Following this Freud expressed eagerness to see the work in print both in German and in the English translation which was entrusted to the wife of Ernest Jones (Gay, 1988, p. 643). In a letter to Hans Sachs, a trusted colleague, Freud characterized the work as "not an unworthy leavetaking" (Jones, 1957, p. 242).

The content of the book was startling, especially to those trained in biblical scholarship, arousing surprise, but this was a rather commonplace impact of Freud's writings.[11] The succession of unusual explanations began with his earliest forays into psychology with the tracing of the origins of hysteria to sexual trauma. They continued through his various discoveries on dreams, psychopathology, early development, sexuality, the origins of culture, and selected psychobiographical themes. With none of these, however, did he exhibit the magnitude of discomfort he experienced with *Moses and Monotheism*.

In examining that discomfort, we find that it was not equally distributed among all sections of the work. The first two sections he claimed to be sure of as early as 1934. Only the third portion held him up. This in itself is rather difficult to understand since, as we shall see, the first two sections contained what was new and possibly threatening to many, especially Jews. The third was the return to a theme dealing with the origin of religion already given to the world more than twenty years prior, now embellished by further explication related to particular religious forms, Judaism and Christianity, and a repetition of the material of the first two parts.[12] The differences in certainty he assigned to the various parts lead readily to the conjecture that, whatever personal relevance could be assigned to the material, that which attends the third essay is less understood by the writer and less satisfactory to him (in a solutional sense) than the material in the first two essays.

## The Content in Summary Form

The story in outline may be paraphrased as follows. The first essay is entitled "Moses an Egyptian" and asserts that the title is in fact true, drawing upon etymological evidence relating to the name and an analysis of the myth of the hero. After establishing the Egyptian origin of Moses, Freud continues in the second essay to inquire about the origin of the monotheistic doctrine, the law that Moses transmitted to the Jews. He traces it to the deceased pharoah Akhenaten, to the stamped out religion of Aten. He further assigns the rite of circumcision, which he claimed Moses gave to the Jews, to the Egyptians. Freud then points out that Moses, to perpetuate the beliefs of Akhenaten, led a slave tribe including Levites out of Egypt into the desert and forced upon them a doctrine eventually too restrictive and spiritual for them. During the course of their wanderings the Jews then killed Moses, for which they were imbued with an eternal sense of guilt. After a continued period of wandering of several generations, with the remnants of the religion carried by some faithful Levites, there is a union with a Yahwehistic Midianite tribe led by the son-in-law of Jethro, the biblical father-in-law of Moses. The resultant is a merger of the spiritualistic, monotheistic doctrine of Moses with the aggressive, Yahwehistic Midianite practice which became the early religion of the Jews in Canaan. This is later modified to a return to the more spiritual aspects of the religion. Thus, according to Freud, the murdered Moses is replaced by the Midianite "Moses," compressed into one by history to obliterate the constant reminder of the parricidal act.

In the third essay Freud returns to the origin of religion and compares the development of individual neuroses to what he sees as mankind's neurosis, religion. He traces a similarity in the process for both: trauma, defense, latency, and the return of the repressed. He then compares Judaism and Christianity from the standpoint of the parricidal act, the alleged killing of Moses and the killing of Christ. He sees the difference between the two resulting largely from the admission of the act, and assigns absolution to the confessing Christians, and lasting guilt accompanied by a continuing search for the messiah to the non-confessing Jews. In this section he also deals with the multiple origins of anti-Semitism and the positive derivatives of religious belief. At one point in the discourse he refers to the situation of his real world by indicating that those who are the most vociferous anti-Semites are thinly veneered Christians whose barbarous polytheistic origins continue to dominate them. He then points out that the two great monotheistic religions, Judaism and Christianity, are both treated with hostility by the Nazis. These occasional excursions into present time add credence to the conjecture that the work reflected his internal struggles at that time.

What one may see even in this brief, selected attempt at recapitulation is that the first two sections are new, rather simple, and clear, although highly controversial. The third is repetitious, rather complex, and not all that clear, especially about his stance toward religion.

In what follows I shall attempt to relate the story contained in *Moses and Monotheism* to what we know about Freud's life. Some of the justification for doing so has been implicit in what has already been pointed out but perhaps needs emphasis: (1) that Moses was the figure upon which Freud projected his fears about that which he held above all else: his life's work, the ideas of psychoanalysis; (2) that psychoanalysis, as a movement and as a set of ideas, had about it a religious aura in Freud's psychic economy, (3) that toward the end of his life his major concern was with the perpetuation of his doctrine, which was under severe threat, and (4) that the difficulties involved in producing the last part suggest that it contained much personally relevant and perhaps unresolved material.

### The Impact of Nazi Germany on Freud

There was something terribly ironic about being in Freud's position during his last six years. Despite his continued fears about his work's not really being appreciated in the world (Jones, 1957, p. 202), he had a great deal of evidence to counter this. From 1909 on his work became increasingly known in the highest intellectual circles and his central ideas influenced developments in many fields. He was sought out by and knew a variety of people who enjoyed world acclaim. It was rumored that as early as 1916 he was suggested as a nominee for a Nobel Prize (Jones, 1955, pp. 189–90). The efforts to procure such an award for him were renewed in 1927 and the possibility remained a constant one from then on (Jones, 1957, pp. 137, 233–34). In 1930, in the waning days of the Weimar Republic, he was awarded the distinguished Goethe Prize (Jones, 1957, p. 151). By this time he was a world-famous figure whose works were translated into numerous languages. Yet, despite all this fame and recognition, the brief period between the Nazis' rise to power in 1933 and the beginning of his treatment of Moses in 1934 brought enough realistic signals to rekindle those ever-present latent fears that he and the work would be depreciated or ignored and ultimately displaced. During that time he saw the flight of many of the most prominent psychoanalysts from Germany and he was made aware of the desecration of his work in that land. To have come this far, achieved so much, be so fervently identified with a set of ideas which he likened to truth, and to have their future existence seriously threatened was indeed a trying state of affairs. Beyond that, however, lies an even more important consideration, namely that which constituted the basis for the threat. It was, of course, the fact that psychoanalysis was seen by the Nazis as the product of a Jew. The value of its basic content could never even become an issue. It was doomed because it was associated with the intellectual achievements of a Jew and labeled a Jewish psychology—a matter of fate over which he felt he had no control or influence.

Consider then the impact this threat could have upon a man whose personal history contains the following: (1) an expressed distaste for religious belief and practice including that of Judaism, (2) a passive attitude toward his identity as a Jew, (3) a strong valuation of courage to resist oppression, (4) a resistance to and a distaste for coercive or expedient solutions.[13] Consider also the impact of such a threat on a person whose previous solution to a danger to the psychoanalytic movement, the vehicle for perpetuating his ideas, was couched in a negation or denial of what was believed and turned into its opposite. I am referring here to the interpretation Freud offered in 1913 of Michelangelo's statue—*not* the angry, biblical, historic Moses, but rather the calm, peaceful, visionary, perfect Moses, whose actions are taken in the interest of preserving the law. To what extent these mechanisms of negation or denial were basically repeated we shall have the opportunity to examine.

What I am suggesting by this brief highlighting of certain aspects of his personal history is how Kafkaesque Freud's position was. To have one's lifework in danger of extinction for what he saw as essentially irrelevant reasons, the content of which he could neither affirm nor deny in any simple fashion, would have to be the occasion for great mental effort at both conscious and unconscious levels. On a conscious level he engaged in a bit of denial, especially at the beginning, believing that Austria would not follow the same path as Germany in all respects, that psychoanalysis would remain intact (Jones, 1957, p. 181). In fact this belief led to some of the difficulties he had with the completion of the third part of the Moses, because somehow he felt that the material contained or anticipated therein would antagonize the Catholic church, which he saw as the major source of protection.[14] On a less conscious level he came to a different solution, which is contained in the material of the two earlier essays. It is a solution couched in the same negation or denial framework used earlier with Michelangelo's Moses of turning things into their opposites. In order to facilitate the translation of the story it is only necessary to introduce two simple substitutions as decoding aids, Freud = Moses and psychoanalysis = monotheism. Let us return to the text for a more detailed examination of what it reveals.

### I. "Moses an Egyptian": Psychoanalysis and Jewishness in Freud's Life

Psychoanalysis has certainly pointed up the importance of initial communications, primacy, in decoding latent or unobvious psychological intent. In chapter 1, I have reviewed additional markers of importance or salience and emphasized the increased significance of the communication when indicators of salience are multiple. Freud's opening paragraph in the first essay contains several. It begins with an apologia for depriving the Jewish people of their greatest figure, saying that he feels compelled to follow the path of truth rather than ethnic interests, all in the interest of advancing knowledge. To introduce one of his works in this manner is a rare event for Freud, although interestingly enough it also occurs in the opening paragraph of "The Moses of Michelangelo." If we apply one of the decoding aids, Freud = Moses, we are already alerted to the possibility that what is about to unfold is an unconscious parting of the way of Freud from his Jewish identity, all in the interest of perpetuating a doctrine.[15] Let us pose the question of what that doctrine, psychoanalysis, represented in his own psychological makeup. It is a question to which we will return from time to time.

The title assigned to the first essay is an assertion, "Moses an Egyptian," which carries along with it an implied negation—"and not a Jew as you were led to believe." It is the beginning of a systematic decimation of the possible reasons for the German rejection of psychoanalysis. The assertion Freud = Moses leads then to the translation, "I am not of these lowly people to whom you have assigned me," and, following the arguments elaborated in support of the origin of Moses, "but rather of noble birth."[16] This conjectured translation has many roots in Freud's life, pointed out in various biographical essays. I would call attention to one which has to do with the different bifurcations that existed in Jewish culture in central Europe during Freud's lifetime. The ones to which I refer are encapsulated in the characterizations of Eastern European Jews in contrast to those assigned to Jews from Western Europe. The picture of the easterners was one of "stetl" people, largely steeped in the ritual and traditions of the synagogue, mostly uninfluenced by advances in Western thought, timid and subservient as a result of a history of severe oppression in the lands in which they resided. The Jews of Western Europe were much more identified as urban dwellers who had recently been released from ghetto restrictions and invited to partake in the world of the enlightenment. Their numbers swelled in the universities, leading to increased opportunities in the arts, the professions, and in the world of business and industry. Vienna in many ways could be seen as a city which housed both groups. As the eastern outpost of the Western European world, it was a gathering point for Jews migrating westward, a city whose Jewish population swelled in the last half of the nineteenth century. Freud, hardly a generation removed from the migrant's path, clearly identified himself with the Western position (Sachs, 1944). His distaste for religious ceremony and practice is a matter of record (Jones, 1953, 110ff). His negative attitude toward "the ostjude" has been explored and documented in a recent book by Oring (1984) which analyzes Freud's use of humor.

What I am suggesting here is that this contrast in different forms of Jewish life, well recognized and operative in Freud's experience, was essentially represented in the arguments he used to support his thesis that Moses was an Egyptian.[17] Freud professed that Moses lived among the Jews but was not one of them, and that he *gave* them a set of laws that were far superior to their own. This may be nothing more than the expression of distaste at being identified with the negativity that in his mind attended the pious eastern Jew. Then his statement about Moses may be translated into, "Although I lived among them, I was not one of them; in fact I gave them a doctrine of truth, psychoanalysis, quite different from the neurotically devised one to which they were attached (Judaism)." We can further surmise that a group of them, almost exclusively Jews in the beginning, did buy his doctrine and become members of a priestly class. These were equivalent to the Levites, who he suggested surrounded Moses and served in the vanguard to educate the slave tribe. The assertion then that Moses was an Egyptian serves to announce, in a sort of unconscious lament, that he, Freud, is not a Jew in the uncomplimentary sense assigned to religious Eastern European Jews, uneducated by Western standards. Furthermore, he gave them (and all the world) a doctrine of belief far superior to their own illusion-based form of worship.

Despite the fact that Freud said he was certain of the theses presented in essays one and two as early as 1934, what he wrote at the conclusion of essay one does not support that stance. There he admits to the tenuous nature of the evidence he has addressed and questions the justification for continuing the inquiry. His answer to the query amounts to saying that there is even more involved in why he must go on than he can say (or perhaps was even aware of), and engages the reader to accept the speculation about the origin of Moses for the promise of what may be revealed thereby (Freud, *Standard Edition*, vol. 23, p. 10).

## II. "If Moses Was an Egyptian": On the Future of Psychoanalysis

The polarity between certainty and doubt seems to be reflected at several points in the second essay. The first instance is in the title, translated into English as "If Moses Was an Egyptian," later repeated in the opening sentence of the text after an introductory paragraph, "If, then, Moses was an Egyptian," and finally at a later point in an anticipated defense against the accusation that the writer has brought forth his "conjectures with too much positiveness" (pp. 31, 41). If, as he frequently proclaimed in letters, Freud was certain about the assertions in the first two essays, to what can we attribute the occasional return to doubt? Perhaps his need to resolve internally his concerns about the future of psychoanalysis was the unconscious problem to which his conjectures about Moses are directed.

The revelation in this second essay is that the monotheistic religion which Moses brought to the Jews was not a Jewish invention but rather stemmed from an Egyptian source. The translation now continues with the introduction of the second decoding aid, psychoanalysis = monotheism, and reads, "I am not a Jew and therefore psychoanalysis is not a Jewish doctrine." In fact we might repeat what we have earlier surmised, that psychoanalysis was the replacement in his own mind for the religion of his ancestors which he had abandoned as a young man (see note 15). This change was already felt by him on some level around the turn of the century when his theoretical position and his hopes for it were beginning to jell. The lament some thirty-five years later can be seen as being addressed to fate. How could it be that these ideas, the product of a life's work, could be under threat as a Jewish product, when in part they represented his personal antidote to religion, including that of the Jews?

The remainder of essay two may be considered as the moment beyond the lament, the resolution of the fear over the fate of psychoanalysis that seemed to be represented each time the figure of Moses appeared prominently in his writings. How would psychoanalysis survive in the face of the combined difficulties of the Nazi menace and his own fading life? Here he resorts to a modification of the basic story he had outlined in describing the critical features in the development of civilization. These ideas were arrived at during roughly the same time that he was dealing with the defectors through the analysis of Michelangelo's statue, 1913. This initial attempt, as we have already pointed out, took place when he was fifty-seven, when his star was still rising rapidly on the international scene and when, despite his basic pessimism about life and people, he had the energy to survive the difficult war years ahead and produce important additions to the literature of psychoanalysis. Among these was the first attempt at codification of the ideas, a Mosaic task, in the series of lectures he gave in 1915–16 and 1916–17, later published as *A General Introduction to Psychoanalysis* (Freud, *Standard Edition*, vols. 16 and 17). In 1934, at the first writing of essay two of *Moses and Monotheism*, he was seventy-eight, pain ridden, with recurring appearances of cancerous tissue, living in a country filled with civil strife and heading toward rule by repressive forces. In 1913 his resolution of the threat to psychoanalysis was to divide the problem. In "The Moses of Michelangelo" (1914), he solved one part by staying his anger and resolving to spend his time explicating the law, which he in fact did. The other side of the resolution, contained in the consequences of the parricidal act in *Totem and Taboo* (1913) may be read as, "And so what if they (kill) displace me (the father), it will offer them no solace; some form of me (a totem) will remain as a reminder of their deed and have impact on their future behavior." At this time, since he felt secure in being able to carry on, his emphasis is more on the fact that the displacement attempt will not ultimately satisfy or benefit the dissenters rather than on the perpetuation of the ideas.

Now in 1934 he returned to the theme of the parricide but with little assurance of his own presence to carry on the battle for the preservation of his life's work. He resolved the issue by a complex variation of a death-rebirth motif which resulted in a historical compression or fusion of disparate characters. In his consideration of the historical event Freud speculated that Moses was actually killed because of the hardships his superior set of ideas imposed on basically barbarous people who then disowned them. However, a small set of his followers, although powerless, remained faithful at least in memory to the ideas. This may be interpreted as his bow to reality. The triumph of fascism in central Europe was assured and threatened a much wider world circle. Psychoanalysis as a movement was rapidly coming to a close in what had served as its intellectual and spiritual centers for many years, Vienna and Berlin. Psychoanalysts from Germany and Austria were fleeing to all parts of the world, not really knowing what ultimately awaited them and the theoretical position they represented.

The narrative then goes on to describe what happened after the carrying out of the most dastardly of acts (parricide) in order for the doctrine to survive. This time, unlike the resolution in the 1913 essay, the doctrine survives after a period of discomfort on the part of the unfaithful and a reassertion of the ideas by those who had kept them alive in memory. The mechanism by which this takes place is the fusion of two sets of ideas, those promulgated by Moses, stemming from Egyptians, and those promulgated by the son-in-law of Jethro, stemming from the Midianites (in neither case from Jews). The first consists of values associated with the spiritual, the good, the true; the second is more clearly associated with power. These differences, however, are embodied in figures who in their appearance represent values opposite to those represented in their doctrines. Moses, the carrier of a spiritualistic doctrine, is represented as harsh, unforgiving, angry, and powerful, whereas the son-in-law of Jethro, the carrier of the vengeful Yahwehistic tradition and the leader of the new fused movement, is seen as a simple, perhaps gentle, shepherd boy. To these antinomies we shall return shortly. At the moment it is important to try to understand what this resolution may have represented in the mind of the writer. In translation it could be read as, "So, suppose the worst actually does come to pass; the barbarians take over, my books are burned, my followers are scattered, and I die. Never mind, the ideas will not die. They are too valuable and will be perpetuated." But the manner conceived for their continuation is the most unusual and salient part of the story and invites further consideration. After all, it is not unknown in human history for a set of ideas to be discarded only to be revived in some altered form later on. In this instance it appears as though the reappearance of the ideas would not be enough. They had to be clearly connected to their champion. Thus a new leader would arise, not one who rediscovered the ideas but one who was given the doctrine by the remnants of the faithful following of the original leader. Even in fantasy Freud found it difficult to relinquish the thought of his connection to the ideas. While he had already indicated that in his mind the law was more important than the people, we can now add the conjecture that the law could not be separated from him.

### Freud's Conflict: Anger and Its Control

That we are dealing with extended aspects of Freud's own character structure in his portrayal of Moses is evident from the pieces written two decades apart. In a significant paragraph from "The Moses of Michelangelo" describing selected views of the character features assigned to the Moses statue by previous writers, Freud points out the strong, seemingly antithetical differences. The contrast seems to be between the angry, pained leader whose law is endangered by a return of the people to the regressive (barbaric) practice of idolatry and a proud, simple, calm leader who looks toward the "lasting survival of his people, the immortality of his law" (Freud, *Standard Edition*, vol. 13, p. 215). Jones has already pointed out the impetus for Freud's interpretation in the constant stream of defections that plagued psychoanalysis up to that time (Jones, 1955, pp. 366–67). He also commented on the struggle for control of the emotions that Freud experienced in the face of threat to his life's work. This contrast of emotions, between an outer calm and inner fire, mentioned over and again in various places in this anonymous paper of Freud's, seems to be characteristic of Freud's own personality makeup. He frequently experienced the "wrath, pain and contempt" that was assigned to the face of the Moses statue by Thode, with which Freud agreed (*Standard Edition*, vol. 13, p. 215). Earlier and under limited conditions his overt affective posture in the face of personal threat was to express the anger. This was certainly true in the various reports of his reaction to anti-Semitic incidents involving himself and his children (E. Freud, 1960, p. 77; Jones, 1953, chaps. 7 and 8). However, this was not always the case. When it came to the future of psychoanalysis he strove for an outer calm no matter what he may have felt on the inside. His pacification of Karl Abraham during the faithful Abraham's difficult encounter with Jung may be recalled in support of this contention (Jones, 1955, pp. 47–51). Anger for Freud, as well as for most socialized human beings, was not an easy affect with which to deal. In its most dangerous form it could lead to murder, a theme which he explored many times and under various guises: the family romance, the development of civilization, and the development of the Jewish religion. In the ideal situation he saw the anger being controlled by a rational ego interested in the ultimate goals of safety and security. However, he also saw that repressed anger had to find its outlet somewhere or else it would result in psychic discomfort. Thus in the analysis of Michelangelo's statue Freud found ways of reducing that discomfort by assigning not only the anger but also its control to Moses, a departure from the biblical tale.

The return to the theme of anger and its vicissitudes occurs in essay two of *Moses and Monotheism*. In this section Freud tells us that Moses met with a violent end at the hands of the people. He also tells us that this figure, the Egyptian Moses, probably had one set of the characteristics assigned to Moses in the Bible: domineering, hot-tempered, and violent. It is not difficult to take away from these two statements the implication that anger released in action is violence—and violence begets violence. With regard to the justification for postulating a second Moses who replaced the original, Freud points to the discrepancies in character description in the Bible where Moses is also pictured as the mildest and most patient of men. He then assigns these characteristics to the son-in-law of Jethro, who he claims history compressed along with the Egyptian original into a single Moses. To complete this treatment of the opposite sides of this critical affective dimension in Freud's life, we see it variously represented in the form of love-hate, trust-distrust, explosiveness-calm, resistance-compliance, in his life experiences and ultimately in Eros-Thanatos in psychoanalytic theory. In this regard Jones discloses that Freud once told Jung that should he suffer a neurosis it would be of the obsessional type, which Jones then interprets, following Freud's teachings, as signifying a deep ambivalence between the emotions of love and hate (Jones, 1955, p. 423).

Returning to the material in this essay, in addition to the bipolarity in personal characteristics assigned the newly separated Moses figures, Freud makes a similar bifurcation in the doctrines with which he identifies them. Thus the original explosive, angry Moses is connected to what he sees as the spiritual, more desirable (ego dominated) monotheistic doctrine of Aten adopted originally by Akhenaten, while the new, gentle Moses stems from the warlike, aggressive, vindictive (id dominated) doctrines emanating from Yahweh. So each of the Moses figures was complete in the fusion of his own character with the doctrine he espoused, and the two figures plus the two doctrines constitute the ultimate two-by-two balance between the poles of anger (aggression and violence) and its control. What seems to be represented here is the difference between the hero figure and the doctrine, just as it existed in Freud's life. His doctrine was bold; it aimed at breaking down resistance, conquering the irrational, giving vent to the biological urgencies in appropriate ways. His demeanor and face to the world was modest, conventional, proper, entirely unaggressive, and forbearing.

That aggression and its control were prominent in Freud's personality makeup is attested to in the extensive attempt that Jones makes to give an objective picture of Freud's "Character and Personality," the title of chapter 16 in volume two of the biographical trilogy. The predominant description calls upon such phrases as "soul of honor," "always kindly, considerate, generous," "a completely civilized being, to whom the idea of violence and cruelty was abhorrent," "essence of nobility" (Jones, 1955, pp. 403 ff). He further goes on to say that Freud only reared up when his creation, psychoanalysis, was in jeopardy. When commenting on others' views of Freud as a pessimist, an arrogant, disagreeable person who always had to quarrel with friends (the other side of the coin), he explains these features away as either not being typical, grossly exaggerated, or treated out of context. It is not important here to judge the accuracy of Jones's interpretation of the data. What is critical is to see that the dimension in question is a prominent one and that Freud's overt or conscious demeanor was more likely to be that of the simple, humble, dignified, kindly, concerned person, especially in his later years. The fires of anger could burn inside but had to be controlled. This was also his theoretical resolution, deeply embedded in the warp of psychoanalysis, as well as the one he adopted personally.

Joan Riviere, in her description of Freud's personality given by Jones in the same chapter, is much more balanced with regard to the dimension we are considering. While clearly stressing the positive pole, she seems always aware of its opposite in Freud. Thus we find the descriptive adjectives "tolerant" and "philosophical," yet also "impatient" and "intolerant," "witty" and "humorous" along with "choleric," "resentful," and "unforgiving." However, both she and Anna Freud stress his simplicity and dignity as being paramount in his appearance in the world. Jones's effort to bring together all he knew and thought about Freud's personality is a rich source of information. It is filled with examples of the same kind of description that Freud gave to Moses in 1913 and to the two Moses figures in 1934, a contrast between fire and calm. Freud's view of himself, however, is clearly consonant with the one he largely presented to others, one side of the contrast. In a letter to Putnam, quoted in full in Jones, Freud speaks to the issue of morality. On the personal level he says, "I believe that in a sense of justice and consideration for others, in disliking making others suffer or taking advantage of them, I can measure myself with the best people I have known. I have never done anything mean or malicious and cannot trace any attempt to do so" (Jones, 1955, p. 417). While this may be an accurate description of the values guiding his interpersonal behavior, we must recognize that for the man who led us to consider the primitivity of the id and its representations in psychic life—a man who studied himself constantly—couching his statement about meanness and malicious behavior or intent in an absolute negative has all the earmarks of a defensive statement. It is as though, for the variety of reasons already examined, the *direct* expression of anger was exceedingly difficult, especially when the fear of the consequences could threaten the things which grew to be of utmost value to him.[18] Perhaps the only incidents reported that would appear to contradict this line of reasoning refer to matters not concerned with psychoanalysis. There are reports of two incidents in which Freud responded with anger to anti-Semitic threats: in one instance his children were involved (Jones, 1955, p. 15), in the other he was alone facing a threat of violence (E. Freud, 1964, p. 77). These, however, took place much earlier in his life (1901 and in the mid-1880s), when anger seemed much closer to the surface and found easier direct expression. Certainly during the days of his courtship he was able to express anger about members of Martha's family and also in response to the demands for an orthodox Jewish wedding ceremony (Jones, 1953, chaps. 7 and 8). His most violent imagery, however, surrounded jealousy—the feared loss of the beloved Martha (Jones, 1953, pp. 110ff).

In the review of the first two essays of *Moses and Monotheism* I have considered the content of the text in light of the problems faced by Freud at that time of his life. It was my intent to relate the uniqueness of the story told, to explore his unconscious resolutions of those problems, and further to relate those resolutions to what we know about him from his prior history. In summary I have suggested that essay one, "Moses an Egyptian," could be seen as an unconscious attempt to refute the ostensible reason for the rejection and impending larger threat to psychoanalysis, namely the Jewish origin of its leader. The threat resulting from this connection was never really absent from Freud's mind but was now considerably exacerbated.[19] In essay two he extended the story to indicate that if the premise in part one was granted, then clearly he could conceive of how all was not ultimately lost. This priceless, universal set of ideas—in no manner connected to a Jewish heritage—by their inherent value would be kept alive no matter their immediate fate or that of their leader. After a brief interval the doctrine would be reinstated and its message carried on by a reincarnated leader whose image would remain as an heroic model for a permanent but constantly beleaguered people. Like most fantasy solutions, it has almost a fairy-tale quality about it. You cannot take away from the hero that which he values most.

### The Background for Essay Three

Why the story did not end here is an interesting question. We have pointed out earlier that from the inception of the work Freud seemed to indicate that the first two parts were clear in his mind but that the third gave him trouble. What more was really left to say? The ostensible reason that he gave for his difficulty in completing the third part had to do with real-world, practical issues. He was concerned that the content of this last section would sever the remaining threads of support from a religiously affiliated political government and put into jeopardy the earning capacity of Viennese psychoanalysts (*Standard Edition*, vol. 23, pp. 54–55). While this may indeed have been a realistic fear, it seems in retrospect not to have taken into account the larger picture. The material for the first two parts was completed in 1934, revised in 1936, and published in 1937. The content already published could certainly have been inflammatory for anyone seeking to victimize the Jewish people, whose dire plight was beginning to be recognized worldwide. Yet Freud seemed little concerned about this possibility. In responding to the pleas from others about his thesis, he claimed that the work would likely have little impact on the faithful (its impact in robbing the Jews of a hero figure in those perilous times), or on the world-at-large (Jones, 1957, pp. 234, 237–38). His central inhibiting concern was with the material he was elaborating in the third essay and what it could mean for the practice of psychoanalysis. It was as though, as already represented in essays one and two, his identification was solely with psychoanalysis and not with Judaism. One might here reiterate that Judaism as a set of religious precepts, especially as embodied in ritual, had strong negative valence for him. It was seen as an irrelevant but unmoveable barrier to the greater acceptance of his ideas and had long been replaced in the deeper recesses of his mind by psychoanalysis. Thus, the possible negative impact of the work in the first two parts for the fate of Jews could be overlooked if the connection between Judaism and psychoanalysis could somehow be isolated, negated, or denied, no matter how strongly it was held by others.

The reasons that he gave for the difficulty involved in completing the last essay went beyond external ones. He claimed, in letters to Arnold Zweig, uncertainty about the foundation upon which the arguments were based. He did not wish to suffer refutation by fools and he even found it difficult to satisfy himself that he knew all that he needed to know to make the story complete (E. Freud, 1970, pp. 97–98). The whole picture surrounding the production of this essay sounds quite out of character for Freud. While one might be able to understand what he felt about the major external constraint, the inner doubts were not typically present in a man whose conjectures about human nature were filled with novelty and surprise and almost always ran counter to accepted doctrine. Besides, the concern about publishing the third essay should have had little to do with his ability to finish it. That seems to be an independent matter. After all, he finished the first two parts in 1934 and sat on them for two years before deciding to share them with the world. Clearly the final essay had another cast to it which he recognized on several levels.

Extracting what was different about it presents some problems in that what turned out to be the content of the third essay was an elaboration of much that he had presented before in the two earlier sections, and in two books, *Totem and Taboo*, published in 1913, and *The Future of an Illusion*, published in 1927. The structure of the new essay is very much in keeping with so much of Freud's work in which he is constantly stating that things are *not* what they seem. In this instance the startlingly novel revelations of the first two essays (about Moses and his doctrine) came quickly and easily to him, while the ones he had already elaborated earlier (about religion and its origin) gave him continuing and unrelenting trouble. It is as though negation was his unconscious way of keeping others away from decoding his messages. This has an ironic ring to it in that he specifically called attention in 1925 to the importance of this particular mechanism (*Standard Edition*, vol. 19, p. 235). Perhaps then the major message concerning his fear about the survival of psychoanalysis and the resolution of this fear was contained in the already published sections, and the remaining work, while related, was of a different order. It is to this possibility that we shall turn our attention in our examination of the last essay.

To introduce the analysis of the material in the final essay it should be pointed out that the two earlier ones were basically concerned with the perpetuation of an important doctrine while the third primarily concerns the fate of humans. This is reflected in such questions in the first two essays as to how monotheism survived as a *Jewish* doctrine despite the fact that it was (a) of Egyptian origin, (b) given to the Jews by the Egyptian Moses, (c) so intimately connected with a man whom the Jews had murdered, (d) threatened by a fusion with Yahwehistic doctrine. The focus here is obviously on the fate of the doctrine, despite titles emphasizing the importance of the man (Moses). The basic question in the third essay is how to account for the suffering of the Jews in human history. In order to do this Freud found it necessary to review his ideas about the development of civilization and religion and relate these ideas to ones he had proposed as fundamental to the development of individual neurosis. What I shall propose from this delineation is that in these essays, so central to the core of his psychological being in this final stage of his life, he dealt with the issues in fashion typical for him. As he had already indicated in his paper on Michelangelo's Moses, the law was more important than the people, and this he took care of in the fantasies of essays one and two. The more unsettling problem had to do with the suffering of the people, which I shall try to relate to an unconscious attempt to come to grips with his own core conflict. This I shall maintain constitutes the heart of the third essay. Here the identification extends beyond the figure of Moses. Various aspects of Freud's own psychological development are portrayed in his particular formulation of the historical fate of the Jewish people. Moreover, the text contains so much of interest concerning what was important to Freud that it may be of value to review it in more than a cursory fashion.

### III. Anger and Aggression: The Role of the Father, the Omission of the Mother

Essay three is entitled "Moses, His People, and Monotheist Religion." It is preceded by two separate introductions, one written in Vienna before March 1938, the second dated June 1938, after Freud had arrived in London. The earlier one is an apology for why the essay will not see the light of day. In it he describes the incongruity of living in a time when "progress has allied itself with barbarism," and he describes the necessity of holding on to the tenuous protection of the Catholic power structure, which means suppressing the content of the work (*Standard Edition*, vol. 23, p. 54). Just a few months later, in a free atmosphere, he rejoices in being able to release the work but is still not free of his internal doubts. He relies finally on thin threads for his security. He says, "To my critical sense this book, which takes its start from the man Moses, appears like a dancer balancing on the tip of one toe. If I could not find support in an analytic interpretation of the exposure myth and could not pass from there to Sellin's suspicion about the end of Moses, the whole thing would have had to remain unwritten. In any case let us now take the plunge" (*Standard Edition*, vol. 23, p. 58). Why these statements about Moses's origin are relevant to the major thesis of this essay is not obvious. He had already published the material for which it might have been central. This all seems like additional evidence that we are about to deal with an inner production, at least as revealing about the writer as about the subject with which he ostensibly deals. Let us translate the actual title "Moses, His People, and Monotheist Religion" to "Freud, his interpersonal struggles, and his relationship to his most cherished object, psychoanalyses" for what it may reveal.[20]

In the opening section, "The Historical Premiss," he reviews the material he has written earlier on the origin of monotheism in the rule of Akhenaten, his death, the decline of his teachings, and the impact it had on his follower, Moses. Freud imputed to Moses "disappointment and loneliness" which moved him toward the selection of a people in whom he could instill the doctrine and thereby realize his ideals (*Standard Edition*, vol. 23, p. 60). The imagery here is strongly reminiscent of the beginning of the psychoanalytic movement, again perhaps an indication that he is reviewing his own story if we invoke the monotheism = psychoanalysis translation. Lonely and mostly isolated after the separation from Breuer, affected by the loss of status in the medical community that his early psychological work produced and by the death of his father, Freud worked essentially alone to further the basic ideas he had already detected in accounting for the origin of hysteria. His self-analysis, achieved in no small measure by his major discovery of the decoding of dreams, led to the formulation of a new psychological doctrine which he then brought to a small band of followers. Since he was the originator, it may be of interest at this point to return to the question of why Freud repeatedly emphasized that Moses was not the originator of monotheism. We have already discussed one set of reasons that could have brought this about, namely as a response to the accusation of the ethnic origin of psychoanalysis and its consequences. However, there are indications that other factors of long standing, deeply embedded, were also involved. These very likely had to do with his relationship to significant figures during the development of these ideas and his conflict about how to credit their importance. Akhenaten may very well represent the combined image of Breuer and Fliess, the two figures who shared, in different ways, in his intellectual struggle. At various times he credited Breuer with the originator's role. Clearly, though, this was a magnanimous gesture, an overstatement, which he modulated at other times by indicating that the major credit was due the person who advanced the idea and established its permanence rather than the originator.[21] On the other side of the coin, the contributions of Fliess to his thinking were later clearly minimized, quite in contrast to what one would expect in reviewing Freud's published correspondence with his one-time friend (Bonaparte, A. Freud, and Kris, 1957).

Perhaps the most important point made in this opening section, for our purposes, relates to the evaluation of the monotheistic doctrine. Freud depicts the Mosaic position stemming from Egypt as being concerned with truth and justice, simplicity and holiness, in contrast to the Yahwehistic position concerned with sacrifice and ceremony. The progression, he states, after the death of Moses went from Mosaic to Yahwehistic and back to Mosaic.[22] It is a contrast which may be described in other, familiar terms as one between calm, reasoned, intellectual forces as opposed to primitive, aggressive, affective forces. This struggle must be dominated by the "ego" rather than the "id" in order for progress to take place. This was his solution for mankind and obviously his solution for himself. The vicissitudes of this struggle, its origin, course of development, outcome, and evaluation, then become the subject of the remainder of the essay. In it he attempts to tie together a life's work, both intellectual and personal. He roams back and forth between the origins of civilization, the core of religion, the development of the neuroses, the causes of anti-Semitism, the attempts at resolution of the fundamental conflict and its control, and the success of the outcome. It is as though this piece of work had to take on the properties of a worthy exit, his final words on all that concerned him throughout life. In a symbolic sense one can see that the first relationship is ideal, true, just, simple, holy (Mosaic). It is replaced by a less desirable one highlighting opposite values (Yahwehistic), which in turn leads to the search for ways to reestablish the ideal original. The imagery is consonant with his theoretical ideas of early development, especially with regard to the role of the mother.[23] In his own life his mother was embedded in a positive context, while his father's remaining ties to his Jewishness, both in observance of tradition and in ritual customs, were held in low esteem by Freud.[24]

The underlying structure connecting all these seemingly disparate stories of origins relayed in this section of the narrative consists of an early trauma leading to a defensive struggle which then culminates in a period of latency. This is followed at a later point by inevitable inner and/or outer stress which reactivates the neurotic struggle and results in a partial return of the repressed (the original trauma). In every example given, the core of the trauma deals with the anger-aggression motif and its negative consequences. However, the trauma sources are limited for Freud. He assigns them all to the father-son relationship. The father threatens the son (castration or denial of pleasure), the son kills (or wishes to kill) the father. No matter what kind of solutions are generally reached to keep the problem under control, eventually it will resurface and lead to suffering. Anger leading to aggression (murder) is the "original sin" of mankind, a shared heritage from which there is no ultimate surcease. That it is conceptualized only within a male-male relationship should be kept in mind. Clearly there are other logical possibilities.

In the development of religion, Freud points out the cyclical nature of the progression, how after the father is killed the various stages lead back to the need for the deified father-leader who then, like Moses, demands too much and meets a similar fate. Because it is an ambivalent love-hate relationship, it is never really resolved. On the personal level, the history of the psychoanalytic movement is replete with Freud's concerns about elimination or displacement of either himself or his ideas. Certainly a review of his relationship with Jung reveals this clearly, especially in the instances when death wishes were attributed by Freud to Jung and resulted in fainting episodes by Freud (see chapter 3). Usually, when dealing with the reasons for the various defections that took place Freud would point out that the dissidents could not take the strictures imposed by the harsh but truthful reality of the psychoanalytic image of man. Thus, in Freud's mind, Jung was ready to give up the sexual theory and Adler would renounce the importance of unconscious processes (Freud, 1935, pp. 96–97; *Standard Edition*, vol. 20). But, again, in the comparison of the model for religion and the model for neurosis, Freud sees that the point at which the similarity is striking for the male child is the importance of the father in the attempt at Oedipal resolution. It is as though Freud bypasses the earlier experience, the role of the mother as the chief socializing agent, and what this could intend. If the love-hate story for father is credible, might it not also have antecedents in the relationship with the mother as well?

Yet, despite his jaundiced view of religion as a neurotic manifestation, Freud was also quick to point its value in the development of civilization, chiefly as a curb to the primitive, aggressive aspects of the species. However, such influences, like neurotic symptoms, cannot provide ultimate success. Here we can examine examples provided in the text and refer them back to their possible meaning in Freud's life, as though on one level he was really talking about himself.

Contending that religion was an outgrowth of guilt over parricide and the religion of the Jews a further instance of the general case, Freud goes on to point out the consequences of trying to repress, or of not confessing, the act. It can lead to an eventual concordance with strict superego values, imposing a greater holier-than-thou attitude, over-identifying with the image of the deity, and a sense of overinflation of the ego. This solution he attributes to the Jews and sees it as one of the root causes of anti-Semitism. Here again one can point out the similarity to Freud and further to the psychoanalytic movement. Following the model of their leader, they projected the image of an elite, anointed group. They overidentified with Freud and his teachings, and continually imposed additional strictures of orthodoxy which fostered isolation. In further explicating the aggression theme, Freud points out that the avenues of solution actually open to the Jews by the

Mosaic code did not include the open expression of a physical, aggressive side. Theirs had to be a solution of the intellect, a curbing of the aggression so as not to be reminded of the repressed sin. It is difficult to get a more direct expression of various dicta representing the psychoanalytic view: "the voice of the intellect . . . ," "where id was there ego shall be." This ideal represents Freud's conscious view of himself, which we examined earlier—a position which he finds flawed when applied to the Jews.

The other avenue possible in dealing with the effects of parricide is that of confession, a solution he assigns to Christianity. To confess leads to absolution and avoids the pitfalls of monotheistic elitism (envy by others) and in general to a less stressful existence. However, despite its advantages, he points out in a cryptic passage that the sacrificed son (Jesus) "became a god himself beside the father, and, actually in place of the father. Christianity, having arisen out of a father-religion, became a son-religion. *It has not escaped the fate of having to get rid of the father*" [emphases added] (*Standard Edition*, vol. 23, p. 136). What seems to underlie this discussion on a personal level concerns an evaluation of the available alternative to the ethnic source of his distress. Had he become a Christian, as others (Adler) had, would his path have been easier, his ideas judged on their merit? His answer seems to indicate that the problem he is confronting is more fundamental and cannot be papered over cosmetically. On another level one could say that he had confessed his own parricidal wish in his correspondence with Fliess some forty years before but the problem was not put to rest by the admission. Something more was involved.[25] No matter how many times over many years he returned to the importance of the father-son theme, or resorted to abstract biological explanations in solving the origins of aggression, he could not put the problem to rest.

### Salient Signs of Freud's Personal Involvements

In the final section of the first part of this two-part third essay, entitled "Difficulties," Freud leads us to suspect that there is an extremely high probability of a personal component contained in what he has written. Using the Judaic religion and its outgrowth Christianity as a sample of one, he has just finished trying to establish the fact that religion is a cultural neurosis by demonstrating similarities in the process between the development of an individual neurosis and the development of the religion with which he is concerned. Yet he retains some residual tension about the arguments he wishes to bring to the attention of the reader. The first of these concerns the fact that he is basing his conjecture about the analogous religion-neurosis relationship on a single case. He excuses this limitation on interesting grounds. One has to do with his limited knowledge of religion (he knows only the familiar, his own, and its derivative), the other with the conjecture that the other religions (about which he knows little) do not seem as highly developed to him and thus cannot provide the evidence he needs. He by-passes Mohammedanism as a possibility, stating that "the internal development of the new religion came to a stop, perhaps because it lacked the depth which had been caused in the Jewish case by the murder of the founder of their religion" (*Standard Edition*, vol. 23, pp. 92–93). A brief discussion of the limitations in this regard of Eastern religions follows this same cryptic explanatory course. His argument is that he can really only talk about that which he knows something about, his own experience so to speak, and the remainder of the possible data pool, the whole realm of religion, really does not meet the criteria for admission (for reasons that are not easily understood nor clearly explained). To contend that (1) he is ignorant of the general domain, (2) that he has found the unique case that makes the point, and (3) in his ignorance he attributes arrested development to that about which he knows little is an extreme position and calls further attention to the possibility of the personal element in why he was so adamant in presenting this somewhat confusing thesis to the world.

In a second and more extensive discussion of "difficulties" within the position he has taken (how to explain the generational transmission of unconscious guilt over the repressed parricide), he is forced into defending a Lamarckian view on the inheritance of archaic ideas. This he does despite his knowledge about the prevailing attitudes of biological science on this question. Indeed, this section is characterized by an attitude that he will use whatever arguments suit *him*, no matter what anyone might think. They fit his experience. This attitude pervades much of what he is writing about, but even he knows the evidence is thin. The whole thrust has the flavor of a defense. Something about it is right, but also something does not quite fit. In this instance we might conjecture that perhaps the nature of the problem is correctly identified, aggression and its control, but not the object source, nor its developmental course, especially in his own history.

One might again ask why it was so necessary over the years for Freud continually to impart the message that religion was a mass neurosis and then exemplify the argument with Judaism in this final book? In reviewing this question, Jones goes to great lengths in dealing with the various critics and criticisms of Freud's position. Ultimately Jones decides that Freud's basic intent was as always to seek the truth and that the impetus for raising the issues of origin was brought on by the figural position that his being born of Jewish parents forced on him at this point in life, as well as the mysteries surrounding his early history (Jones, 1957, pp. 362–70). It is a benign view of what turned out to be a burning issue for Freud, hardly suggesting an intellectual investigation of either the manner in which Freud pursued the question of religion or the resolution he offered. By deeming religion a mass neurosis and demonstrating by analogy the similarity in the process to individual neurosis he had by implication offered the antidote to religion, just as he had offered the antidote to neurosis—psychoanalysis. Religion in his own life, as we have seen, had never been anything more than a negative factor making it more difficult for him to accomplish a variety of goals to which he aspired and to which he felt entitled.[26] He also wished to avoid what it inevitably forced on him, the identification of him with Jewish orthodoxy, for which he had not only no affinity but rather scorn and distaste. When such a negative set toward his ethnic origin exists in a person with high personal values of courage and rationality, a conflict must result. The frustration resulting from a group of what he could only see as irrelevant circumstances threatening all he held dear was likely to force a resolution that had many of the earmarks of a dream, overdetermination and wish fulfillment. These seem to characterize the content of *Moses and Monotheism*. The book not only speaks to the condition of his inner world at the time it was written but also reveals the nature of the continuing intrapsychic problems which characterized him as a unique person. These had to do with aggression, its origin and control, a matter which not only had its particular personal referent in him but one with which he struggled in the development of psychoanalytic theory. Whereas the role of sexuality in the course of personality formation was solved early, the role of aggression had a more troubled course. It was difficult for him to establish the origin of aggression in the instincts he ascribed to man (ego and libido), and he had finally to revise his instinct theory and derive aggression from the death instinct, man's biological compulsion to return to an inanimate state (catabolism) (Freud, *Standard Edition*, vol. 18, pp. 3–44). Not even the faithful followed him in this abstract metatheoretical leap. Some even saw his solution as derived from a long-standing personal concern about death.[27]

### The Emergence of the Problem with Mother

There is yet a second part to the third essay in *Moses and Monotheism*, which is entitled "Summary and Recapitulation." In its opening sections Freud talks about the fact that this second part has very little new in it, a statement that is repeated at various points in the third essay, which leads again to the possibility that he is dealing with old unsolved problems. His claim was that he found it difficult to integrate his latest thoughts into the body of what had already been written but not yet published, and thus he decided, despite the repetition, to add this new section. What he points out as being new are "additions relating to the problem of how the special character of the Jewish people arose." Now he intends to highlight the people and their character and we should be alerted to considering his special observations with regard to how they might relate to the character of one of the Jewish people, namely Freud. At this point—the writing of this last section in England in the summer of 1938—there was, I suggest, a further shifting in Freud's identification patterns. All of the figures involved carried identification status for Freud, as in a dream. He could be Moses, or one of the people. He could be in the role of the son or in the role of the father. Perhaps even more startling is the possibility that what was assigned to the father could more easily be attached to the mother and that the figure of Moses now had the possibility of representing *both* the maternal and paternal authority figures in his life.

The exposition is divided into eight separate parts. In the first he speaks of the special characteristics of the Jews, their particularly high opinion of themselves, their chosen status, their distance from others, and the hostility and jealousy that these characteristics engendered in others. Thus far the parallel between what he is attributing to a people and what he himself clearly possessed is striking. He goes on to point out that these traits were imprinted on the people by a powerful father figure, Moses, at a time in their history when they were enslaved with little esteem or self-regard. This attribution of the source of these characteristics to the father is clearly a departure in Freud's thinking and alerts us to the possibility of a new revelation concerning the neglected importance of the mother. Self-esteem, he has told us on numerous occasions, derives from the early mother-son relationship. Furthermore, if we sort through the major biographers for character sketches of Freud's parents, it becomes apparent that his mother more closely approximated the characteristics he assigns to a powerful Moses than did his father.[28] The doctrine that Freud imputes to Moses, however, seems to be one that is devoid of the aggressive side. Moses sold the Jews a doctrine which could in its grandeur and funda-mental attraction keep them from being reminded of their original aggression (parricide). However, it also provided them with the basis for their continuing problems in life, the difficulties of living up to the demands of the law and the hostility their attitudes produced in oth-ers. A possible meaning attached to Freud's particular construction could be that the mother, through her early, exclusive love, gave him a sense of self which diverted him from the aggressive feelings that resulted from the eventual loss of her undivided attention. To have aggressed against her would have threatened the source of his self-esteem. Thus what she provided with her love was the fundamental basis of his strength and at the same time that which caused him pain with others, the inhibition of his aggression. We shall have further opportunity to return to this theme and the role of the mother in Freud's life.[29]

One of the mechanisms attributed to Moses in order to promulgate his conception of a single deity was the forbidding of the making of a graven image. This led in Freud's exposition to the triumph of the abstract, the intellectual over the sensory or real. In Moses's case, despite the gentle, regal purity of the doctrine, he as a person was supposedly aggressive and demanding. Knowing what was "the way" or "the truth" for the people did not seem to have all that much influence on his own behavior. For Freud one could make a similar argument in reverse, in that having told the world what the negative consequences of instinctual renunciation could be, he seemed to have adopted an intellectual attitude toward his fate, attempting somehow always to understand it. In some sense Freud had adopted the strategy he assigned to the Jewish people. He would not rant and rail about his fate but rather maintain his superiority and retain faith in the ultimate triumph of his views of mankind.[30]

Freud's ensuing discussion of the gradual renunciation of the instincts for the intellectual solution in the history of mankind may also be read in a personal vein. What he points to is that in the course of the development of humanity, pride replaced the power of human sensuality. If read closely, one sees that he is talking about the restrictions on sexuality and the demand for the just and virtuous conduct of life.[31] What is missing in the exposition and salient by its omission is any specific reference to the renunciation of aggression. Yet, despite his knowledge about what instinctual renunciation could produce psychologically in an individual, pride did seem to replace human sensuality for him, including the expression of his anger. He was the soul of rationality.

As the essay continues, he returns to hammer home the now oft-repeated theme that intellectuality, pride, and instinctual renunciation are limited solutions which will make easy the identification of its owner. These solutions will also become the fundamental sources of both joy and pain to their possessors. He maintains, however, that they mask the basic problem of mankind and individual *man*, namely the struggle with authority as portrayed by the core ambivalence contained in the father-son relationship. To carry his line of reasoning further, one could add that the son may eventually become the father but that does not ensure that the problem will disappear for all time. It can be revived by having to deal with coercive restrictions applied to valued objects imposed by other authoritative or competing sources.[32] More importantly perhaps, the problem of backed-up aggression would also fail to disappear if the core-ambivalence is also contained in the mother-son relationship and not in any way recognized. Could this have been Freud's fate?[33]

Throughout all of this weighty intellectual discussion dealing with the origin of culture, religion, and the characteristics of a people, Freud is trying to alert us to the following: that no matter how much power the father originally has, primal or real, the power that the father takes on in the unconscious, repressed machinations of humankind is excessively multiplied and distorted. Thus we as humans are caught in a problem which originates in a kernel of truth but ultimately results in a neurosis, individual or mass. What appears to be so striking about his revelation is that he offers it as though he is an observer, a man from Mars, for whom these far-reaching conclusions could have no personal referent. How does this insight that we create our own neuroses as people and as a people (out of distortions about the father) relate to the fabric of his own life? I should like to deal with two different but connected possibilities which will again bring to the forefront the role of the mother. For the first I would venture the guess, shared by others, that the incompleteness of Freud's own personal resolutions were largely a function of the limited investigation on his part of his relationship to his mother (see note 27). He was clearly aware of the positive side, almost blind to the negative side, which was then exacerbated, distorted, and displaced onto his view of his relationship to his father.[34]

The second possibility deals with what he is criticizing at this point, namely Judaism or religion in general, what he saw as father-dominated psychological resolutions. He presents them as inadequate because they cannot solve the fundamental problem for which they were designed. What then is the human's alternative? It seems obvious that it was psychoanalysis, in which illusions are not tolerated and both the spiritual and the earthy have their say. His doctrine was superior to those religious systems whose limitations he is exposing. It accounted for the necessity of finding a way to give vent to the instincts without threatening existence. Furthermore, his doctrine, as we shall see, may have remedied the castigated, father-dominated solutions by being a symbolic representation of the mother.

Perhaps, in a sense, these essays do accomplish a major wish-fulfilling purpose for Freud. They assert the belief that a powerful set of ideas will survive despite their momentary unpopularity and the impending death of their leader. They also attempt to demolish what he had supposed to be one important source of threat to his own psychic well-being and that of his creation—the power of the father and of religion which in his own imagery is fused into one. His anger could be assuaged through a set of civilized resources, the intellect and the pen.

In the final paragraph of this repetitive, controversial work, Freud ends in a strange manner. After having offered hair-raising possibilities to explain the perpetuation of a religious tradition, he states, "Our investigation may perhaps have thrown a little light on the question of how the Jewish people have acquired the characteristics which distinguish them. Less light has been thrown on the problem of how it is they have been able to retain their individuality till the present day." He then goes on to excuse himself by saying that this is all he is able to offer (*Standard Edition*, vol. 23, pp. 136–37). The incongruity of this weak ending after such far-reaching assertions again points to the strong possibility that it contains a personal message. Certainly one direction to follow is that he is telling us that he has only dealt with *one side* of the story, the *negative side*. Let us continue to examine the possibility that in speaking of the characteristics of the Jewish people he is also speaking about himself. In this instance, it would translate into an analysis of the origin of his guilt and what that produced in him. Although one can see that certain positive features resulted from defending against that guilt, namely ethical principles and intellectuality, he is indicating that the entire story is not told. There is more to it, to which he may not be privy. He has done the best he can.

Perhaps a lead into this question of what is left to be told will come from approaching the issue with which he concludes this essay. He wonders what allowed the Jewish people to retain their individuality, a missing aspect of his analysis of their characteristics. Indeed, it is also a missing aspect of the origin of his own individuality in anything more than a superficial sense. Freud had given us limited insight into his feeling on this matter, as we have previously mentioned. One of the clearest statements may be found in the final paragraph of his brief paper "A Childhood Recollection from *Dichtung und Wahrheit*," Goethe's autobiography. After tracing the impact of the birth of a sibling in a recounting of several patients whose stories are similar to Goethe's, Freud says, "I have, however, already declared elsewhere that he who has been the undisputed darling of his mother retains throughout life that victorious feeling, that confidence in ultimate success, which not seldom brings actual success with it. And a saying such as 'My strength has its roots in my relation to my mother' might well have been put at the head of Goethe's autobiography [and also Freud's!]" (*Standard Edition*, vol. 17, p. 156). We might now further examine the possibility that the origin of his strength was also the origin of its opposite, the core neurotic problem, which he in distortion attributes basically to the father. Let us follow this possibility for what it may reveal.

### Conclusion: A Fundamental Script in Freud's Life and Its Attempts at Revision in Moses and Monotheism

In looking back over the story told in *Moses and Monotheism* and relating it to Freud's life, we have already indicated that the origin of man's difficulties is traced by him to the struggle with the father, the Oedipal tale recast. What is behind that struggle is implied but kept from its figural significance, relegated to the background. The role of the female is downplayed and becomes salient mostly by omission or misplaced emphasis. Thus the sequence elaborated in his description of the development of civilization begins with the sovereignty or importance of the father, later switches to the importance of the sibling, and only as an interim solution turns to the centrality of the mother before the return of father dominance. This sequence seems like the very antithesis of Freud's view of the development of the individual human being, which begins with the importance of the mother and takes on sibling and father centrality largely in connection with the original tie to the female. Freud in accounting for individual neurosis, which he is comparing to the path followed by mankind in arriving at religion, gets back to the father-son relationship and its impact and stops there. It is as though he can go no further although he has pointed out at various times that there may be further to go. Certainly one step further back is the sibling rivalry, which he accents in the "Dichtung" paper and to which he referred, almost in passing, in a letter to Fliess some twenty years earlier (see note 34). This letter is central to the point in question about the origin of neurosis in Freud's life and certain portions of it demand rereading. At one point he is describing what is happening in his self-analysis and says,

> To describe it in writing is more difficult than anything else, and besides it is far too extensive. *I can only say that in my case my father played no active role* [emphasis added], though I certainly projected on to him an analogy from myself; that my "primary

originator" [of neurosis] was an ugly, elderly but clever woman who told me a great deal about God and hell, and gave me a high opinion of my own capacities; that later (between the age of two and two-and-a-half) libido towards *matrem* was aroused; the occasion must have been the journey with her from Leipzig to Vienna, during which we spent a night together and I must have had the opportunity of seeing her *nudam* (you have long since drawn the conclusions from this for your own son, as a remark of yours revealed); and that I welcomed my one-year-younger brother (who died within a few months) with ill wishes and real infantile jealousy, and that his death left the germ of guilt in me.[35]

In this letter he speaks directly to what he has discovered about the origin of his own neurotic tendencies. He discounts the actual role of his father, seeing what he ascribed to him as a projection from the negative side of an early mother figure. He only points clearly to the positive valence attached to the real mother. The negative valences are attached to a substitute mother figure, his unfortunate sibling, and the psychological consequences of his imputed aggressive wish. If one really wished to follow strictly the individual neurosis–group neuroses (religion) analogy which he uses in *Moses and Monotheism*, the problem would have had to emanate from the loss of the most valued object, the mother, and the struggle to regain it.

To make this point take on extended meaning in Freud's life it is necessary to retrace some of his history briefly. There is common agreement in the biographical sources that Freud was the life-long favorite of his mother. The relationship between them is described by Jones as a special one. He was her first child, a son, for whom greatness was forecast (Jones, 1953, chap. 1). Within a brief period of time, however, a succession of seven siblings followed, the first only eleven months later, the last when Freud was ten. What seems to be clear about the impact of the family growth upon him is that the first two siblings, Julius, who lived only eight months, and Anna, born when Freud was two and one-half, were associated with negative affect for him. The remaining five, especially Rosa, Dolfi, and Alexander, were embedded in a much more positive affective context. In Freud's own language, one can characterize this sequence as trauma, defense, and latency. The trauma was produced by the early displacements and led to a high potential for negative affect toward all of the objects, mother and siblings. The source of the defense arose from the positive aspects of the early relationship with mother. Freud's own characterization of this is found in some of his earlier writings and repeated in *"Dichtung und Wahrheit,"* which has been previously quoted. This attitude was manifested early, even in preschool days by the young Freud in his quest for knowledge. His rewards came from demonstrating his brightness, his promise for future intellectual achievement. By the age of four, when sister Rosa was born, he already was cast in and had adopted the role of the achieving child destined for greatness. The remaining children therefore presented no threat. It must be emphasized that the trauma was the loss of the exclusive attention of the mother, displaced by siblings for whom he harbored fantasized aggression.

In the previous chapter concerned with the Freud-Jung relationship, I noted the similarity between certain aspects of each man's attitude toward his mother and toward his theoretical work. In Freud's case it was represented as follows:

> If we think of "the work" as being the symbolic representation of the mother, the two men differed rather markedly in their imagery as to how to achieve and maintain relationship with the object. Freud's imagery was that of sole possession and overcoming obstacles. His early heroes were conquerors. He attacked boldly with ideas in order to achieve and then fully expected to be attacked when he had reached a position of prominence. The object had to be fought for, there were others in the way, and you were never safe when you possessed the object because someone else would try to take it from you—either directly or by modifying it or demeaning its value. The basic belief, though, was that he knew it was his but others would not let him have it.

This statement was written to account for Freud's reaction to Jung's defection as it was reflected in "The Moses of Michelangelo" and in *Totem and Taboo,* the earlier esoteric works. While I structured the relationship between the two men as that of a father to a son, and dwelt on an unexplored aspect of the displacement theme, namely the fear of father, I also called attention to the infantile roots of Freud's displacement fears. What seems to emerge from this lifelong battle to maintain primary possession of the valued object is a set of contingent, alternative means-end sequences, a script. If you are in the position of the child you must find an alternative, a substitute, perhaps a symbolic representation of the object because your relationship to the treasured object is always threatened by others. This he did by his achievements which assured the mother's adoration. Perhaps, then, the fantasy may continue, if one is an adult; in the role of the husband the return to the blissful, nonthreatening, noncompetitive state can be reexperienced. This, however, is likely to be short-lived and with the birth of children the resolution must again go to substitute or symbolic sources. In Freud's life the mother's exclusive positive influence was rapidly replaced by her necessary attention to others. The search on his part for a real-life substitute was sporadic; he seemed happy to search for knowledge instead. There seemed to be few reports of important romantic relationships with females throughout his adolescence and young adulthood until he met Martha. By this time he was already twenty-six and heavily invested in trying to establish himself in a research career. The years of courtship, as revealed in Freud's letters to his beloved, are marked by serious concern with attempts to wean her away from all other influences, to be his exclusively, and then some (Jones, 1953, chaps. 7 and 9). This exclusivity unfortunately was as brief as the one he had enjoyed in his primary family. Thirteen months after marriage their first child was born and she was followed over the next eight years by five siblings. If loss of the exclusive possession of the primary love object through having to share her with others, a form of displacement, was the core of neurotic tendencies in Freud, then, as I have conjectured in chapter 3, the early childbearing years of the marriage were very likely to redintegrate the problem.[36]

There is much evidence to support the view that the ten years following the birth of the first child were consecutively among the most difficult in Freud's life. The outside pressures were great. He had to find a way to support a growing family, and a way of establishing his mark intellectually. These pressures have been dealt with at length by both Jones (1953) and Schur (1972, chaps. 2–6). The latter, who served as personal physician for the last eleven years of Freud's life, describes in detail the physical discomforts suffered by Freud during the 1890s and their psychological concomitants, but neither Jones nor Schur seriously attempts to tie Freud's neurotic difficulties of that period to a central, nuclear problem emanating from the relationship with the mother. It is clear, however, from the correspondence with Fliess that he was trying to solve inner problems. Their appearance may have been generated in part by multiple external factors (his work and his financial situation) but more likely by the reenactment of an early life drama, the loss of the primary love object by displacement. To solve this the way he did earlier demanded an investment of a substitutive nature in an object that he really could call his own, an achievement that belonged solely to him. Perhaps one could look at the Fliess relationship through such a lens. It did have a rather commanding quality of exclusivity about it at times. Freud expressed the notions that he wrote for Fliess, that he had no one else, that Fliess provided him with relief from his misery, that their meetings were anticipated sources of joy, etc. (Bonaparte et al., 1957). But somehow the relationship came across to this reader as an overidealized fantasy for Freud, born largely out of unfulfilled needs and personal distress. Because of distance they actually had limited personal contact with one another. Fliess married early in the relationship and was wedded both to his growing family and his novel ideas. Freud's side of the correspondence can almost be read as a monologue with a fantasy friend.[37] An exclusive personal relationship was not a likely achievement.

I have already indicated that Jones acknowledged that the period following his marriage until the close of the century were filled with neurotic suffering for Freud. He dates the onset of the symptoms of Freud's neurasthenia prior to the time of the marriage and also indicates that the symptoms were exacerbated by his intense love for Martha and the pain of their long separation. Jones also importantly points out that interaction with Martha was a powerful antidote for Freud's symptoms. Yet in the same paragraph Jones remarks that, "curiously enough it seems to have reached its acme some years after the marriage" (Jones, 1953, p. 170). One could extend this bit of musing to point out that it may not have been "curious" at all. Freud's earliest theorizing about the neuroses in his letters to Fliess are filled with references to the origin of all sorts of neurotic symptoms, perhaps not unrelated to the kind that he was experiencing, in unsatisfied sexual excitation.[38] These were expanded in various ways to account for the loss of sexual desire, a condition present by 1897, when he was only forty-one, he intimated to Fliess (Bonaparte et al., 1957, p. 230). Perhaps, then, what has been generally overlooked, although not really unknown, was the central importance of his early problem with displacement, its resolution, and the "return of the repressed" brought on by the circumstances of the marriage. The progression of that struggle through the Fliess period culminated in a reinstatement of a successful reparative script. The loss again of the exclusivity of the object was replaced in time by a creation of his own, psychoanalysis, to which he devoted his life, and guarded from harm with every device at his command. It was not just a theory, a set of scientific ideas, an approximation of the nature of humans. It took on over time the properties of a revealed doctrine for him. By 1936, around the time of his eightieth birthday celebration, he wrote to Albert Einstein in response to a congratulatory letter: "I really must tell you how delighted I am to learn of the change in your judgment, or at least a move in that direction. Of course, I always knew that you admired me only out of politeness, and that you are convinced by very few of my assertions. But I have often asked myself what indeed there is to admire about them if they are not true—i.e., if they do not contain a high degree of truth. Incidentally don't you think I should have been far better treated if my doctrines had incorporated a greater percentage of error and folly? . . . And I may hope that by the time you have reached my age you will have become a disciple of mine" (E. Freud, 1960, p. 428). At the same time, in a letter of appreciation to Stefan Zweig, he deals with the truth issue by saying, "not that I doubt the content of truth in my doctrines, but I find it difficult to believe that they could exert a demonstrable influence on the development of the immediate future" (E. Freud, 1960, p. 429). The imagery is that of a man to whom truth has been revealed but who cannot make his impact felt, a veritable Moses as Freud saw him, the carrier of truth who was about to be dispensed with.

For the most part the solution involving the theory as a replacement for the loss of exclusivity, the work as a displaced symbol of the lost object, was very adaptive, as it had been earlier. His psychological difficulties were likely to return only under conditions which primarily threatened the existence of the theory. In the interval between the first appearance of Moses in Freud's writings (1913) to the last (1934–38), psychoanalysis seemed relatively secure in Freud's mind, ever increasing in recognition just as his own fame spread. The advent of National Socialism and its implications must have presented him with the return of a variety of inner conflicts which he had long since put to rest, his ethnic identity and foremost his earlier struggles with loss, displacement, anger, and guilt. If *Moses and Monotheism* was a worthy exit, it was because in it he spoke to all of these issues.

While one can by no means put aside the importance of Freud's lifelong struggle with the father-son relationship, it seems to have been overemphasized in his thinking about himself and about psychoanalytic theory, perhaps unduly limited both. He himself pointed out this overemphasis in the already mentioned October 3, 1897 letter to Fliess. In his own life the major manifestations of the father problem were reasonably clear. From his early youth to the time his father died in 1895 and beyond, Freud seemed always to be seeking a male identification figure. This was the case not because of the father's unusual power but rather of father's lack of power. In real life he appeared in no way to be limited by his father and, in fact, had demonstrably outstripped him in various ways as a young man. When Freud clearly adopted a paternal role, after taking the leadership role in the newly developing psychoanalytic movement (1902), the major fear he developed was that of displacement, and the major affect attached to it was anger which had to be mastered. Others were always possible threats who could displace you in your exclusive relationship to that which you valued most; a clear recapitulation of an early childhood conflict.

But fear of displacement and anger, easily seen in his later interactions with male figures, seem somewhat more obscured in his relationship with females. Yet we know from his own description that anger toward the female was displayed toward two females early in his life, his sister Anna (two and one-half years younger) and his niece (one year younger) (Jones, 1953, pp. 9–10; Bonaparte et al., 1954, p. 222). Although in his self-analysis he was able to turn up negative wishes toward the father, he mainly reports the uncovering of positive (sexual) wishes toward the mother. Let us further examine the possibility that the anger toward early rivals of both sexes hides the temporally prior and perhaps more fundamental problem, the anger toward the mother for abandoning the idyllic exclusive relationship in order to care for others.[39] She left him in a difficult state of ambivalence in that she continued to recognize him as her favorite but turned her attention to others. He was held by the positive impact her implicit adoration engendered in him and could not express openly his feelings about his loss. If one analyzes Freud's relationship with the most significant women in his life, one will find innumerable examples in support of this conjecture. In 1918, twelve years before his mother's death, he wrote to Abraham expressing how much he dreaded the possibility that he might die before her because of the impact this might have upon her (Schur, 1972, pp. 314–15). Yet from all that we can gather about her from biographical sources she was, especially in her later years, quite tough, vain, self-centered, demanding, and sometimes even irascible (see note 28). Perhaps his overconcern with her possible pain masked the complex web of feelings about her that had been kept from consciousness for a very long time. So far as we know his concern about the fate of his mother as survivor did not generalize to other significant people in his life, neither his wife nor his favored daughter. It was confined to his mother, who at this point in life hardly seemed as though she lived only for him. When she did die in 1930 he was not up to attending the funeral and remarked in letters to Jones and Ferenczi shortly following that, unlike his grief-stricken younger brother, he felt very little negative affect over her loss, mostly freedom. His affective response to her death is then explained in the most rational, real-life terms (Jones, 1957, pp. 152–53). In overall quality the relationship with mother had an early Edenic flavor which in later life seemed to be replaced by a distant, aloof, although properly respectful, stance. It was as though he understood least about the impact of this relationship on his affective life despite his lifelong encounter with self-analysis.

The relationship with his wife, Martha, has a similar cast, the outlines of which we have already pointed out. The beginning, as revealed in his letters to her, is filled with imagery of an idyllic, exclusive union. This is followed by a period of psychological pain on his part during the years when the children were born. With the resolution of his loss in the creation of his own "true" object, psychoanalysis, his attitude toward his wife became similar to that exhibited toward his mother—proper, distant, aloof. In both instances, however, he was seen by others as being somewhat uxorious, doting, and submissive, terms that seem somewhat strange to apply to Freud, yet understandable if the positive regard of the other remains important and the anger must be denied. In this vein I am reminded of two absolute instances of negation that were used in describing Freud. One has to do with his *never* wishing to hurt another, previously referred to in a letter from Freud to Putnam (Jones, 1955, p. 417). The other appears on the last page of Jones's second volume. Reviewing Freud's often expressed feelings in later life of being "betrayed" or "deceived" by male friends, Jones continues: "We note, moreover, that *never* in his life did Freud accuse any *woman* of betraying or deceiving him" [emphasis added] (Jones, 1957, p. 434). For Freud, who in 1932 in a chapter on the psychology of women painted the character of women in a far different way with regard to trust and conscience, this seems a paradoxical confluence explainable only if he knew about the general case but could not apply it to himself (*Standard Edition*, vol. 22, pp. 112–35). It is salient that he could not consciously perceive the loss of the female as a betrayal or deception, seeing it rather as an inevitable fate for which no lament was justifiable, the situation he described after the death of the mother. It is the same reasoning he applied to his being Jewish by birth, a fate about which he felt he could do little, and we might add, no matter the unwarranted pain it might induce. The threatened demise of psychoanalysis at this point in his life demanded a different resolution.

There were, of course, women in his life in addition to his wife who lived out part of his wishes for adoration and exclusivity on a limited basis and thus helped to keep this fundamental problem at bay.[40] Prominent in this regard was his sister-in-law Minna Bernays, who was a long-time intellectual companion. In later years he carried on extensive correspondence and personal interaction with Lou Andreas-Salomé and Marie Bonaparte, who were entirely devoted to him, as were several female professional colleagues.

Of all the women in his life, however, the one who lived out the mothering role, in the sense of the "good-mother," most faithfully was his daughter Anna. An extensive and insightful review of that relationship is presented by Roazen (1975, pp. 436–60). The recent definitive biography of Anna Freud by Elizabeth Young-Breuhl (1988) is a storehouse of additional information about the relationship of Freud and Anna. What is important for our purposes is that Freud's physical disability, the appearance of the cancer in 1923, made it possible for him to seek and accept the singular devotion of this, his youngest child. She responded to all of his most critical problems, neurotic and

real. She provided for him the comfort of an exclusive personal attendant and a potential intellectual and spiritual heir who would help to
maintain and perpetuate his ideas. Yet there is something ironic about
the imagery with which he surrounded her—indicating that her devotion alone could not provide serenity. In two separate letters written
seven years apart he refers to her as his faithful Antigone (E. Freud,
1960, pp. 382, 424). While it is simple to follow the implication of how
devoted she was and to leave it at that, one must remember that
Antigone attended an old, wandering father-brother who suffered the
guilt of a sin he neither intended nor could expiate, not even by self-
inflicted suffering. Was Freud's unsolved problem that of the relationship with the father, the theme that he kept returning to over and over
again in the so-called cultural works? These forays did not seem to
solve the problem, perhaps because the problem, as we have already
suggested, was only partially identified by him. The exaggerated, distorted form in which the problem with the father is cast masks the
unconsidered problem concerned with the loss of the mother and what
that produced.[41] By the time he reached this stage of life, cancer-ridden
and in his eighth decade, he was seriously concerned with the eventual
fate of his creation. Some of his attempts to perpetuate it during the
1920s had to do with demonstrating by implicit comparison its superiority over other forms of "truth" or "belief" to which mankind had
succumbed, and to this theme he returned in part in *Moses and Monotheism* some years later.[42] However, the major triumph in this final
book lies in the fact that in the newly developed treatment of the
origin of Moses and the fate of monotheism, Freud solves in fantasy
the problems of the value of the object, the assurance of its continuation, and the eventual perpetuation of the relationship of the object
with the one who cherishes it most. This he does despite the threatening intervening conditions of death and displacement.

# CHAPTER 5

## C. G. Jung: The Man and
## His Work, Then and Now

Some years ago I was asked to participate in a program sponsored by the American Psychological Association honoring significant contributors to twentieth-century psychology. My assignment was to review the work of C. G. Jung and assess its impact in its time and in present time. I was flattered to be asked to reflect on the work of so prominent a figure as Jung, but I also had misgivings which initiated an approach-avoidance conflict. Since I am not a "Jungian," I wondered whether I had the appropriate credentials for the task. When pondering this question, approach was strengthened by a bit of imagery which concerned my memory of a filmed interview with Jung in the closing years of his life where Jung makes the comment, with a wry smile, that he is not a Jungian.[1] Thus, clearly we did have something in common; both of us had a continuous interest in his life, his thought, and his work, and neither of us were particularly interested in the bureaucratic aspects pertaining to the dissemination of his work.

The suggested format for the presentation, to assume the identity of the central figure, also gave me pause. I could easily envisage an overwhelming image of Jung in a Jehovahlike pose thundering at me, "Nobody speaks for Jung but Jung himself." The image was reinforced by a story that Barbara Hannah, one of Jung's disciples and biographers, was fond of telling about her first seminar presentation, which met with such strong criticism from Jung that it took her ten years to venture a similar effort.[2] Indeed, Jung did speak sensitively for himself at the close of his life in *Memories, Dreams, Reflections* (1961), and following this many others have spoken for him, including Hannah (1976), Von Franz (1977), Storr (1973), and Wehr (1987) on the positive side; Glover (1950), Stern (1976), and Erich Fromm (Wehr, 1987, pp. 474–75) on the more negative side.

Perhaps a more important impediment to adopting Jung's identity might be better understood by a resort to Jung's concept of introversion as elaborated by Shapiro and myself (1975). For people living largely in the introverted mode there is a natural and automatic distance assumed between self and other never to be overcome without the impending threat of the loss of ego boundaries. Thus it is not easy for me to try to be someone else.

The final barrier to accepting the role of Jung was that I could not escape the omnipresent awareness that anything I would say would be a thinly veiled projection and somehow I felt more comfortable with owning and owning up to my own thoughts. Despite these ruminations, my decision to accept the task was based largely on curiosity about what would emerge from all I had thought about the man and his work over the past thirty years.

I followed an intertwined path between the life and the work in reflecting on Jung's contributions. His work was voluminous and, although frequently referred to as theoretically unsystematic, quite orderly in its flow from one piece to another. The journey, selectively highlighted, leads progressively from the early word association studies to his study of psychotic imagery, to his postulation of universal realms of unconscious processes, to his elaboration of a descriptive language for the study of personality, and finally to his search for the universal structure or form of mental life, its unfolding and its goal. Because of its importance, I placed major emphasis on the period between 1909 and 1922, which includes the break in the relationship with Freud, and its consequences. During this time Jung experienced great internal struggles whose resolution is important in understanding the course of his life and work. The story unfolded as follows.

Although Jung's major biographical elements are well known, especially since they are vividly portrayed in *Memories, Dreams, Reflections* (Jung, 1961) and in Hannah's *Jung* (1976), let me rapidly review the data which would bring us to 1900, where the journey begins in earnest.

Jung was born in 1875, to a Protestant minister and his wife who shortly thereafter lived in the rural environs of Basel, where Jung grew up largely left to his own imaginative devices. His lineage on both sides contains a number of prominent people (Hannah, 1976, pp. 19–22). His early life, filled with loneliness, isolation, reliance on imagination, and heroic but distant models, is not dissimilar from that of Harry Stack Sullivan, who also was led early in his psychiatric career to the study of schizophrenia (see chapter 6), and toward the quest for unusual accomplishment.

Jung's life until age nine was spent as an only child in a marriage which he identified as difficult. Father he described as dogmatic, but reliable and trustworthy. Mother he saw as having two dispositions, one somewhat unstable, mystical and clairvoyant, the other practical, mundane, and directive. He identified with mother's mystical side, which he called her number two personality, and indeed referred to himself later in a similar way.

Until age twelve, Jung described his existence as difficult and problematic. He suffered from various ailments, some of which may have had a psychosomatic base. He was little attuned to the demands of school and experienced difficulty in interpersonal relationships. At age twelve, upon recognition of the self-defeating path he was following, he initiated a change, and he later described the memory of facing up to his fears and by dint of will overcoming strong neurotic symptoms. From that time on his work continually improved until he became a superior student. He ultimately decided to follow a career in medicine, as had his paternal grandfather and great grandfather. For this purpose he entered the University of Basel in the spring of 1895—barely a year before his father died—and completed the course of study five years later.

Although I have chosen not to follow the usual path of analyzing his early experiences and memories as a guide to understanding his personality, I do wish to reflect on the incident at age twelve, which he believed opened the path to an existence free of symptoms, one more in tune with the demands of the real world. He describes being attacked unexpectedly by a schoolmate, striking his head while falling, and being dazed by the experience. His response to the attacker is handled by the statement, "I was only half unconscious, but I remained lying there a few moments longer than was strictly necessary, chiefly in order to avenge myself on my assailant" (Jung, 1961, p. 30). From then on he focuses only on the secondary gain from the unfortunate accident, namely an excuse to avoid school, and indeed describes the consequent appearance of fainting spells which kept him home-bound for several months. The revelation came when he heard his father respond to a friend's inquiry about Jung's health with great concern about the darkness of his future. Jung then reports how forcefully the reality issues struck him. After describing his successful confrontation with his symptoms, he says,

> Gradually the recollection of how it had all come about returned to me, and I saw clearly how I myself had arranged this whole disgraceful situation. That was why I had never been seriously angry with the schoolmate who pushed me over. I knew that he had been put up to it, so to speak, and that the whole affair was a diabolical plot on my part. I knew, too, that this was never going to happen to me again. I had a feeling of rage against myself, and at the same time was ashamed of myself. (Jung, 1961, p. 32)

From this description the following threads emerge, which I think are important ones in Jung's life. The first is that the external stimulus for the distress, the unwarranted aggression of the other, is essentially by-passed and the focus goes to the resolution of an internal problem instead. Secondly, the distressing affects identified, although not quite in appropriate context, are anger, rage, shame, and humiliation, which are constantly referred to in his descriptions of childhood and student years. These are affects which might easily result from the aggressive action of another but in this case do not. They are admitted to awareness when they result from an intrapersonal conflict instead. Thirdly, the displaced external problem is then fought out in a confrontation with self which leads to the antidote to all ills, work. These threads we shall see revealed again.

When in December 1900 Jung took up his first post as "Assistent" at the Burghölzli, he was twenty-five, largely without research experience, with only recently professed interest in psychiatry. Although he identifies the source as Krafft-Ebing's text read earlier that year in preparations for the state medical exams, we do know that his interest was already demonstrated in 1898 when, following a series of unexplained occult-like events at home, he began a two-year observation of seances held by a young relative of his who exhibited attributes of dual personality. This work, submitted as a doctoral thesis in 1900, became his first publication in 1902 (Jung, 1970, vol. 1). For Jung, the reading of

Krafft-Ebing's text made clear that psychiatry would allow him to pursue the mysteries of mind, a calling to which he had been devoted for many years without formal recognition of its appropriate designation.

He feverishly devoted 1901 to learning the basic tools of his trade in typical medical-school, frenzied fashion. It took him six months to devour the contents of fifty years of the *Allgemeines Zeitschrift für Psychiatrie*. The lessons were well learned, because by 1902 he already published a complete case history of a hysterical attack in an accused, incarcerated person, which appeared in the *Journal for Psychology and Neurology* (Jung, 1961, chapters 3 and 4).

This tremendous capacity for work, along with unusual perceptive and observational abilities and the talent to rapidly translate his thoughts into written communications, were features that clearly identified Jung's scholarly career. Within ten years of his first publication more than ninety bibliographical entries followed, including several books and monographs, countless clinical papers, a major series of empirical research reports, and numerous reviews of the significant publications in his field.

But let us return to the beginning psychiatrist and review the early work, its impetus, its content, the messages intended, what impact it had in its time, and what lasting value it may have carried.

The association studies stimulated by Eugen Bleuler, his chief at the Burghölzli, had as their real source the desire for understanding dementia praecox. No matter its origin, all that emerged in the ensuing ten years bore the particular stamp of Jung's thinking even though influenced by his relationship with more senior mentor-figures like Freud and Bleuler. In Bleuler's case, we can quickly sense his influence by reading his introduction (chapter 1) to *Studies in Word-Association*, a collection of many of the papers that emanated directly from work that Jung or his students did in the Burghölzli laboratory, set up by Jung in 1904 (Jung, 1918/1969). Bleuler was centrally concerned with the ever-present problem of psychiatric diagnosis and more specifically with the etiology, prognosis, and possible therapy of dementia praecox. Having adopted the association methodology as a tool, he desperately sought an agent to gather the necessary data to hone that tool for use in answering his questions. Such a person he found in Jung. The background details of Jung's participation is given in the opening paragraph of Jung's first important paper in this series, entitled *The Association of Normal Subjects* (Jung, 1918/1969, p. 8). It states specifically Bleuler's influence, including the task he set for Jung and Riklin, his collaborator. What is obvious is that Jung embarked upon this journey to do the necessary scientific work so that his chief could continue with greater precision the investigation of his central concerns. That this turned out to be only part of the story, a clear reflection of Jung's life-long need to pursue his own path no matter what his momentary allegiances demanded, is suggested by a statement of Bleuler's in the introduction. After indicating that Jung's studies have opened the possibilities of answering many of the diagnostic questions, he says (p. 6), "But this does not exhaust the results. By ingenious interpretations, which can be readily proved correct, Jung and Riklin have shown that the unconscious mechanisms are accessible to this method far more extensively than we dared hope." This aspect of the work did not stem from Bleuler; it was a continuation of the work started with Jung's dissertation subject. He was still searching for the key to the "world behind the world" which he had observed in his young relative. He thought he found it in the analysis of controlled associations—as a unified core of ideas in the unconscious, accompanied by excessive or inappropriate affect—a complex. That this would attract him to Freud's position expressed earlier in *Studies in Hysteria* (Freud, *Standard Edition*, vol. 2) and *The Interpretation of Dreams* (vols. 4 and 5) goes without saying. What is important to see is that Jung was already embarked on a path of his own. He did not discover this path through the assignment by Bleuler nor by his reading of Freud's work.

Why then, if Jung was an internally directed person destined to follow his singular path, did he embark intensively on Bleuler's journey and then Freud's? One clue stems from aspects of Jung's personality clearly recognized by others but probably hidden from his self-awareness until later in life. At various times and by various people he was described as arrogant, vain, unusually ambitious, status seeking, highly competitive, and even untrustworthy. These designations, alongside others such as humble, caring, undefensive, even saintly, will give some flavor of Jung's complexity, which he describes as an old man in terms of his #1 and #2 personalities. He was clearly the possessor of both sets of attributes, but it was the power of his ambition and competitiveness, part of his #1, that made those mentor alliances so attractive. Frequently in the narrative of *Memories, Dreams, Reflections* he refers to his attitudes toward ambition and competition. The following excerpts provide rich material for analysis in this regard. During gymnasium days, he indicates that although he enjoyed success, it came at too heavy an internal price. He says that he even succeeded in reaching the top of the class but his pleasure was spoiled by the envy of his classmates. "I hated all competition," he writes, "and if someone played a game too competitively, I turned my back on the game" (Jung, 1961, p. 43). Here he gives evidence of his ambition but cannot deal with the interpersonal aspects involved in its achievement, aggression toward others and hostility from them. At another point he is recalling his medical student days, circa age twenty-five, his choice of psychiatry as a specialty, and the consequent disappointment of his teacher and his friends. He tells us that he came out at the top of his final examinations, tripped up only by an unexpected error in a subject in which he excelled. He then says, "Had it not been for this I would have had the highest mark in the examination." His thoughts take him then to the following:

As it was, another candidate received the same number of points as I did. He was a lone wolf, with a personality quite opaque to me and suspiciously banal. It was impossible to talk to him about anything except "shop." He reacted to everything with an enigmatic smile, which reminded me of the Greek statues at Aegina. He had an air of superiority, and yet underneath it he seemed embarrassed and never quite fitted into any situation. Or was it a *kind of stupidity?* I could never make him out. The only definite thing about him was the impression he gave of almost *monomaniacal ambition* which precluded interest in anything but sheer facts. A few years afterward he became schizophrenic. I mention this as a characteristic example of *parallelism of events.* My first book was on the psychology of dementia praecox (schizophrenia), and in it my personality with its bias or "personal equation" responded to this "disease of the personality." I maintained that psychiatry, in the broadest sense, is a dialogue between the sick psyche and the psyche of the doctor, which is presumed to be "normal." It is a coming to terms between the sick personality and

that of the therapist, both in principle equally subjective. My aim
was to show that delusions and hallucinations were not just specific symptoms of mental disease but also had a human meaning.
(1961, p. 110)

This is a fascinating aside written almost sixty years later about
what seems like a dreamlike episode, filled with gaps and nonse-
quiturs. No matter its reality quality, we can see that the thing he
abhors in the other is his ambition, monomaniacal persistence to
achieve, and arrogant disregard of others, things of which others later
accused him and to which he seemed to be oblivious in himself. This
memory was perhaps a screen for what he feared if he allowed himself
to be solely directed from either of his two sides. If he pursued his place
in the world as his #1, he would be haunted by internal pressures
produced by envy from others and aggression toward others. These
pressures would be reflected in dreams and fantasies. This actually
came to pass. If, on the other hand, he withdrew into self, he feared
being overwhelmed or lost in unconscious material. We shall see later
evidence for this. A conflict of this sort could easily lead to the balancing of opposites as an ideal solution.

The three major products of this first decade of work were *The
Psychology of Dementia Praecox* (1906/1972, vol. 3), *Studies in Word-
Association* (published as separates from 1904 on and collected into a
volume in 1909) (1918/1969), and *Symbols of Transformation*, sometimes translated as *The Psychology of the Unconscious* (1916/1949).
Although these works deal with disparate subject matters, the underlying theme in each of them relates to the orderliness and meaning of
the products that emanate from *undirected* thought, as opposed to
directed thought; these are revealed through controlled associations,
the fantasies of psychotic people, and the creative fantasies of an
ordinary person. In this respect he was very much in the tradition
established by Freud in the study of hysteria and in the examination of
the meaning of dreams. He did, however, immediately go further in
extending the importance of the power of unconscious (undirected)
processes to the development of dementia praecox, emphasizing its
psychological origin, a position not shared in psychiatry then and of
limited popularity in psychiatry now. Additionally, Jung's work enlarged the scope of imagery to be studied as a key to the understanding

of personality and of psychopathology. The path went from dreams to any form of undirected thought, and the mode of interpretation broadened from the uniquely personal or idiosyncratic to that which could be learned from common thinking as reflected in symbols and myths.

If we ask the question as to how well these early contributions have stood the test of time, the response would have to be strongly affirmative. The methodology for examining unconscious processes not only still exists but flourishes in a variety of ways, from personality assessment measures, to police detection aids, to literary criticism, and even to the understanding of history. Certainly the importance of psychogenic factors in the development of the psychoses led, after a long period of time, to the psychological treatment of psychotic states, a development that was initially impeded by Freud's dictum on the lack of amenability of the psychoses to respond to psychological intervention and later slowed by the development of electrical, surgical, and pharmacological therapeutic aids.

If one asks what impact the work had in its time, the answer must also be resoundingly positive. The recognition that accrued to Jung in a relatively brief period of time is astounding. In less than five years after his medical degree was granted, he was a senior staff member and director of a research laboratory in one of the most prestigious psychiatric facilities on the European continent and also held an academic appointment in the university. Within the next five years he was awarded an honorary degree from a foreign university (Clark) in light of the impact of his empirical research on association, and he was elected to serve as the first president of the International Psychoanalytic Association, a clear recognition of his role as heir apparent to Freud. Certainly for a person not yet thirty-five he seemed destined to fulfill whatever worldly ambitions he harbored. What then conspired to interrupt this triumphant march?

As is most often true in life, there were multiple forces, some objective, some subjective, some realistic, some neurotic, some highly personal, some seemingly transpersonal. In general, though, this confluence of forces was represented in the *Psychology of the Unconscious* (Jung, 1916/1949), a book whose production and consequences forced him into a path much more suited to the ultimate expression of his unique intellectual and personal discoveries, without the encumbrance of allegiance to others. The content of this work deals with an expansion of the concept of libido beyond sexuality to general interest, and considers incest to carry a meaning beyond the sexual to more general concerns with the issues of union and separation. But as well as it indicated his dissatisfaction with the restricted arena of psychoanalytic conceptualizations, it also reflected the return of a neurotic problem which was fostered by his interaction with Freud. Jung knew that the publication of these ideas would bring to an end their relationship. From his own reports of his childhood, one can deduce the conflict. Reliability and safety were afforded by the father, and separation from the father figure implied the loss of these features. On the other hand, maintenance of the status quo, protection under the father's aegis, meant an ultimate cessation of growth, a reliance on dogma. It perhaps was no accident, as others have intimated, that Jung became so fascinated with the analysis of Miss Miller's fantasies, the essential data of the book, since Miss Miller's problem he analyzed as related to separation from the like-sexed parent in order to fulfill her gender destiny. One could easily attribute this same struggle to Jung at the time. Freud was clearly cast by him in a parental role, a parent who demanded loyalty to his particular ideas. Jung enjoyed the gratification afforded his #1 personality through his allegiance to Freud. Jung was clearly the second in command, the heir apparent. It was, however, at a cost to the perusal of his own bent, his #2 side. The conflict was of such intensity and had such profound manifestations that he knew at some level that it had to come to resolution. He later recalled those days after the return of the trip to America with Freud as ones in which his dreams increased in symbolic and archaic material. His attempts to understand the unconscious processes through reading in mythology and mysticism led to increased feelings of confusion.

The *Psychology of the Unconscious* speaks to separation issues and their consequences. After quoting a poem by Hölderlin, he interprets,

> This recognition, that man must sacrifice the retrogressive longing (the incestuous libido) before the "heavenly ones" tear away the sacrifice, and at the same time the entire libido, came too late to the poet. Therefore, I take it to be a wise counsel which the unconscious gives our author to sacrifice the infantile hero. This sacrifice is best accomplished, as is shown by the most obvious meaning, through a complete devotion to life, in which all the

libido unconsciously bound up in familial bonds, must be brought outside into human contact. For it is necessary for the well-being of the adult individual, who in his childhood was merely an atom revolving in a rotary system, to become himself the centre of a new system. (1916/1949, pp. 453–54)

What Jung is doing here in his discussion of the more general meaning of both libido and incest is expanding the attraction and separation problem from son to mother to include also son to father and child to family. This is clearly seen in the ensuing imagery which concerns male-male and male-family relationships as represented by Christ trying to wean Nicodemus from the retrogressive longing for the family and its customs to a new and more personal relationship to a heavenly figure. The text then becomes a bit more opaque and perhaps more indicative of the personal struggle with Freud.

> Both tendencies serve the same goal—the liberation of man; the Jew from his extraordinary fixation to the family, which does not imply higher development, but greater weakness and more uncontrolled incestuous feeling, producing the compensation of the compulsory ceremonial of the cult and the religious fear of the incomprehensible Jehovah. When man, terrified by no laws and no furious fanatics or prophets, allows his incestuous libido full play, and does not liberate it for higher purposes, then he is under the influence of unconscious compulsion. For compulsion is the unconscious wish (Freud).

He winds up this discourse with a remedy for the threat of this retrogressive longing. "The best liberation is through *regular work*" (Jung, 1916/1949, pp. 453–55) (a solution already recognized at age twelve). What I am intimating here is that the need for separation was powerful; this included separation from the father figure and separation from the path directed by his #1 extraversive side, ambition, status, and position. The neglect of these needs threatened his mental well-being. Why he could not act easily on these needs we shall shortly see. The publication of this work in 1912 did in fact hasten the ending of the relationship with Freud and entered Jung on a solitary path which he followed assiduously for almost a half-century.

Jung's work up to this point centers upon the importance of unconscious processes, decoding their meaning, and understanding their dynamics. The direction indicated in the *Psychology of the Unconscious*, using mythology, theology, literature, and mysticism as interpretive sources, was a new one. No longer was the mystery simply to discover what consciousness repressed, but how to bring to awareness the vast store of experience already contained in the unconscious and reflected in undirected imagery. Jung became aware of the possibility that the structural properties and dynamic operations of mind were already known and told in the more esoteric imaginal productions of societies, their symbols, rituals, mythology, folk and fairy tales, and mystical speculations. Explicating the statics and dynamics of mind as he conceived it eventually became the central task.

For the next decade (1912–1922), Jung was in a position analogous to that of Freud between 1890 and 1900 (the period that Jones [1953] describes as one of "splendid isolation"). From these years a number of important works emerged, including the first part of the *Two Essays on Analytical Psychology* (1916/1953, vol. 7) and *Psychological Types* (1921/1971, vol. 6). The break with Freud cut him off from a great many of his "in-the-world duties," editing of journals and the presidency of the International Psychoanalytic Association. It is reported that his psychiatric practice declined. He had already resigned from the Burghölzli and the university and retained contact with only a limited number of his Swiss psychiatric colleagues. He himself comments on how difficult a time this was for him, how his dream material and fantasies increased in complexity, threatening to overwhelm him. He describes this period as a "confrontation with the unconscious" (Jung, 1961, chapter 6). Of all the personal material he reveals about this period in his life, I should like to recall to you a dream he reports for what I feel it reveals about him, the struggle of that time, and its resolution in the work. It is also strangely reminiscent in several ways of his intrapersonal encounter at age twelve which we have already discussed. The time is December 1913, just two months after the final letter from Jung to Freud in the continuous correspondence that began in 1906. In that letter Jung resigned his editorship of the "Jahrbuch" because he had heard that Freud doubted his "bona fides" (McGuire, 1974, p. 550). After recounting visions dealing with the devastation of European soil and with death and rebirth themes, he had the following dream.

I was with an unknown brown-skinned man, a savage, in a lonely, rocky mountain landscape. It was before dawn; the eastern sky was already bright, and the stars fading. Then I heard Siegfried's horn sounding over the mountains and I knew that we had to kill him. We were armed with rifles and lay in wait for him on a narrow path over the rocks.

Then Siegfried appeared high upon the crest of the mountain, in the first ray of the rising sun. On a chariot made of the bones of the dead he drove at furious speed down the precipitous slope. When he turned a corner, we shot at him, and he plunged down, struck dead.

Filled with disgust and remorse for having destroyed something so good and beautiful, I turned to flee, impelled by the fear that the murder might be discovered. But a tremendous downfall of rain began and I knew that it would wipe out all traces of the dead. I had escaped the danger of discovery; life could go on, but an unbearable feeling of guilt remained. (Jung, 1961, p. 180)

When he awoke from the dream he could not understand its meaning and was plagued with the thought that if he could not decipher its message he must shoot himself. Relief came from his recognition of the symbolic meaning of the content. Siegfried represented the German nation and its people, their ambition, their need to impose their will on others, and he saw the personal meaning this had for him in that it characterized his worldly, ambitious, power side. He decided that he had to kill this side of him in order to continue to grow and develop. As you may recall, this theme already emerged in his reminiscences about the year 1900, some thirteen years earlier, in both his loathing for ambitious people and the calling to attention of the inevitable consequences of ambition, interpersonal alienation and schizophrenia.

The necessity of following his own path was an important lesson which certainly can be gleaned from the content of the dream, and what he took away from it. The solution served to relieve his great distress. However, one cannot help but wonder why the break with Freud produced such inner upheaval in him at all. On the surface he felt as though he did nothing improper, since Freud was the intolerant one who could not stand anyone else's independence of thought.[3] Jung was a man of means by this time who could not have been concerned about loss of income. His accomplishments in the world were also considerable. What then might have produced this internal unrest? One possibility is that, although he was aware on some level of the need to separate from Freud, he was quite unaware of the hostility he bore toward Freud for the loss of the favored position, including the status that went with it. It is one thing to separate—still another to be cast out. The latter implies humiliation, an affect I think he found intolerable. Jung became cognizant through the analysis of the Siegfried dream of the importance of abandoning the ambitious status-seeking path, an internal, almost abstract solution. What he perhaps missed in the dream were the immediate interpersonal referents, his repressed anger toward Freud and his role in the dissolution of the relationship. Even in his own terms of dreams as compensations the conscious attitude was one of the victim, having been aggressed against by an intolerant, power-exercising colleague (recall the incident with similar features at age twelve). However, the dream content reveals the slaying of Siegfried, or with little distortion "Sig Freud," already recognized in an aside by Samuel Rosenberg, the literary detective, in his book entitled *Why Freud Fainted* (1978). Corroborating evidence for the conjoint anger and Jung's wish not to give up his position may also be gleaned from an examination of the correspondence between Freud and Jung from December 1912 to its effective end in October 1913, two months before the dream appeared (McGuire, 1974, pp. 534–50). Jung, after the angry diatribe in the letter of December 18, 1912 (see note 3), comes back in succeeding letters to a softer and more reconciliatory position even after Freud indicates his wish to discontinue any personal aspect to their relationship. In that last year of active correspondence, Jung wrote, from the time of the return from the Munich conference in late November, some twenty-two missives, while Freud wrote nine. The last two are dated February 1913 by McGuire, a surmise from Jung's letters since their content is missing. Jung continued to write for almost eight months without reply. A perusal of the frequency of correspondence for the previous years will indicate that Freud was clearly the more frequent and persistent correspondent.

The ultimate consequences of the psychological resolutions indicated in the dream material are evident in the *Two Essays* (1953, vol. 7) and *Psychological Types* (1971, vol. 6). In the first, one can see what became Jung's major attitude toward Freud and psychoanalysis from then on. He did not oppose it, he subsumed it. It was not wrong, just limited; a one-sided view, whose opposite was provided by the Adlerian position, both parts of a larger framework already envisioned by Jung but not yet worked out in detail. On the personal level, it could be translated into the thought that one did not really have to slay the authority in order to survive. One need only to see authority in perspective, as one element in a duality not to be feared but understood. The whole idea of benefiting from that which you fear, that which is largely unknown to you but to which you are intimately attached, that which has the power to overwhelm you, is given at the close of the first edition of the *Two Essays,* in a small section entitled *General Remarks on the Therapeutic Approach to the Unconscious* (chapter 8). This section seemed particularly autobiographical and perhaps indicative of what Jung was experiencing in the years surrounding the separation, the fear that the individual path could lead to being lost in the unconscious, an underlying theme in the analysis of the Miller fantasies.

After pointing out the dangers inherent in exploring the unconscious, especially when neurotic symptoms are present, he goes on to say what appears to be applicable to himself:

> But the neurotic cases are not by a long way the most dangerous. There are cases of people apparently quite normal, showing no especial neurotic symptoms—*they may themselves be doctors and educators* [emphasis added]—priding themselves on their normality, models of good upbringing, with exceptionally normal views and habits of life, yet whose normality is an artificial compensation *for a latent psychosis* [emphasis added]. They themselves suspect nothing of this condition. Their suspicions may perhaps find only an indirect expression in the fact that they are particularly interested in psychology and psychiatry, and are attracted to these things as a moth to the light. [This is a theme of one of the Miller fantasies.] But since the analytical technique activates the unconscious and brings it to the fore, in these cases the healthful compensation is destroyed, the unconscious breaks forth in the form of uncontrollable fantasies and overwrought states which may, in certain circumstances, lead to mental disorder and possibly even to suicide.

After further explication of hidden negative possibilities in the unconscious, he goes on to say,

> It would be wrong, however, to dwell only on the unfavorable side of the unconscious. In all ordinary cases the unconscious is unfavorable or dangerous only because we are not at one with it and therefore in opposition to it. A negative attitude to the unconscious, or its splitting off, is detrimental insofar as the dynamics of the unconscious are identical with instinctual energy. Disalliance with the unconscious is synonymous with loss of instinct and rootlessness.
>
> If we can successfully develop the function which I have called transcendent, the disharmony ceases and we can then enjoy the favorable side of the unconscious. The unconscious then gives us all the encouragement and help that a bountiful nature can shower upon man. It holds possibilities which are locked away from the conscious mind, for it has at its disposal all subliminal psychic contents, all these things which have been forgotten or overlooked, as well as the wisdom and experience of uncounted centuries which are laid down in its archetypal origins. (Jung, 1916/1953, pp. 112–14)

These rich paragraphs, in their condensed wisdom typical of the "two essays," contain much of what emerged as Jungian psychology after forty additional years of intense, scholarly elaboration. However, from the personal point of view, what we can clearly see is a resolution to rely most on an intrapsychic path, where human relationships will assume an importance secondary to that of internal psychological experience, an attitude explicitly expressed much later, in *Memories, Dreams, Reflections* (1961).

What I am trying to draw together from these bits and pieces of historical data is that Jung in 1913 lived through the deep difficulty of separation from the internalized father image, first slaying him, and later incorporating him as a positive but lesser figure. It was evident by 1916, when the early sections of the "two essays" were finished, that Jung had moved from the angry, fearful position of the Oedipal son, to the more independent and benign role of the leader and father. I hesitate to say Oedipal father because he certainly gave no evidence from then on of the classic fear postulated by Freud and demonstrated in his life, namely that of displacement.[4] In fact, for a long time afterward Jung worked alone, much as a father without a family or a leader without a tribe.

The "two essays" clearly marked both the freedom of Jung from his allegiance to psychoanalysis and the freedom to explore the essence of those things that had originally attracted him to psychoanalysis, his fascination with the concept of the dual nature of things and the dynamic products resulting from the interplay of opposites. The two kinds of thinking formally introduced in the *Psychology of the Unconscious* (1916/1949), although earlier intimated in his study of dual personality and the association process, resulted in a variety of expressions of duality in the two essays—perhaps the most direct and important of which is the initial delineation of the attitudinal types introversion and extraversion. From this point the step to the elaboration of a theory of types follows. Jung tells us it is in part an attempt at a descriptive psychology of consciousness, an effort to provide a view of his own unlike those of Freud and Adler. The book, *Psychological Types* (Jung, 1971), begins with a more than three-hundred-page foray into type structures in the history of ideas, as seen in the work of philosophers, poets, and writers. It is an impressive product of an inquisitive intellect. There follows a clear delineation of Jung's two-by-four-by-two typology, probably his greatest point of articulation with American psychology both then and now. By the time this work was published, Jung had lived through a ten-to-twelve-year period, roughly the second decade of his scientific career, in which the three works which contained in seed or in essence the elements of Jungian theory were produced. The principles, the structures, and some of the dynamics of a theory of mental life were already set out. In the next twenty years, through the study of gnostic and alchemical tests, Jung felt that he uncovered the direction, the process, and the goal to which mental life was attuned, the path of individuation. The major works of that period, a most prolific one which included numerous papers on psychopathology, dream theory, psychotherapy, the problems of culture and mind, were the concluding section of the two essays (1935/1953), *Psychology and Religion* (1938/1964, vol. 11), and *Psychology and Alchemy* (1944/1968, vol. 12). It was as though the basic ideas set free in the earlier works were orchestrated into the fabric of life, ancient, modern, and future.

The year 1944 marked a turning point in Jung's life. At age sixty-nine he suffered a massive heart attack and hovered between life and death for weeks. What he experienced during that time he describes vividly in *Memories, Dreams, Reflections* (1961, chap. 10). The outcome of this was to follow even more stringently his own inner directions. Important manuscripts were produced. The major ones were *Mysterium Conjunctionis* (begun long before the attack and finished in 1955) (1970, vol. 14), *Aion* (1951/1968, vol. 9, pt. 2), and *Answer to Job* (1952/1969, vol. 11). In these, he returns to earlier themes and their resolution, duality, separation and union, good and evil as contained in the concept of God, the individuation process and its outcome, selfhood. Unlike the previous periods of work where fundamental issues of mental life were liberally interspersed with real-world problems of psychopathology, psychotherapy, and cultural change, problems more connected with the outer world, we see instead a man almost totally directed by his inner life.

Jung died in 1961 at a time when his ideas were beginning to receive a hearing, both in psychology and in the larger world, that they had never previously enjoyed. Until the end of the Second World War, I feel reasonably certain that Jung's major impact was on a very limited group of followers, mainly psychotherapists and a restricted segment of the European intellectual community mostly interested in esoteric, symbolic, cultural forms or products. In more general circles he was referred to as a dissenting student of Freud's and the originator of some ideas about introversion and extraversion. What then served to bring Jung's name and his work to the fore? In some ironical way, I would contend, the conditions for recognition were somewhat fortuitous and not at all in keeping with what I think he would have wished. There are several avenues that led to a renewed and increased interest in the man and his theory.

The first had to do with the continued controversy over Jung's relationship with National Socialism after Hitler's rise to power in 1933. This issue, focal during the period when Jung edited the *Zentralblatt für Psychotherapie*, the official organ of the German-controlled General Medical Society for Psychotherapy, seemed to fade away with the demise of Hitlerism, only to be revived immediately following World War II by accusations concerning Jung's sympathies with the racial attitudes promulgated by Nazi doctrine. The matter lingered even after Jung's death, and as late as 1966 Aniela Jaffé was commissioned to write a historical review of the issues involved, which she did in admirable fashion (Jaffé, 1968/1971). Without entering into this controversy or assessing the extent of Jung's culpability, let it suffice for our purposes only to point out how this served to bring Jung's name to the public eye. Despite the fact that the context was potentially negative, it brought to attention the man and his work.

A second factor concerns the tremendous growth in mental health interests in the wake of the devastation produced by World War II. In our country this led to the rapid development of mental health specialties, including clinical psychology, which in turn called attention to training needs. The study of personality theory and especially its application to the psychotherapeutic process became a fundamental aspect of training programs. There was no question, then, that Jungian ideas would receive a much more extended hearing. Adjunctive to this was the limited opportunities for advanced training in psychotherapy available to psychologists, given the restrictions placed on nonmedical personnel by psychoanalytic training institutes in America. Thus, after the opening of the Jung Institute in Zurich in 1948, a sizable contingent of foreign professionals, including many Americans, were attracted over the years to the opportunity to study Jungian theory. The results of this effort may be seen in the increased number of Jungian training centers now evident in the United States with the resulting increase in the dissemination of Jungian ideas.

A third and I believe an extremely important factor resulted from cultural changes that took place in this country and throughout the world starting in the late 1950s and continuing until today. I am referring here to the increased interest in inner imaginal processes experienced through the use of consciousness-expanding or hallucinogenic drugs. The step to an interest in Jungian ideas is an obvious one. These ideas now contained the fascination for a larger and more diverse population, whereas earlier they were likely to attract only those with strong introversive propensities.

A fourth factor, not completely independent of the third, relates to Jung's continuous concern with the problem of religion as it is represented in the psychology of the individual. There were clearly points of articulation between various aspects of modern Protestant theology and Jungian notions of individuation. Thus, people struggling with the relationship of God to man, in the individual rather than in the dogmatic sense, were likely to find their way to an interest in Jung's ideas.

Having traced some aspects of its development and recent history, it is not unreasonable to reflect on the future of Jungian psychology. For my own part I see this as a complex question whose answer bears only partly on what may turn out to be the ultimate explanatory power of the ideas. What one tends to get from global, seminal thinkers like Jung is a direction, a path, a fundamental set of concepts through which one might order experience and some evidence pertaining to realms in which the fit between the world and these ideas seems compelling. Whether the ideas increase in attractiveness is usually a function of the incremental power that occurs as their limits are extended to include new realms not yet considered. These avenues are not usually traversed by the innovators, for man lives but a limited lifetime. They are usually left for others to explore. Thus, not only must the ideas contain intrinsic merit, but they must also attract people who will continually attempt to assess their ultimate value, and not simply those who will accept them uncritically. The history of the Jungian movement has not yet produced these kinds of people in number. Consequently, I see this moment in time as a transitional one for Jung's ideas. Whether they will turn out to have power similar to those of the great figures in human thought or recede into the company of interesting esoteric thoughts I do not know, for too many degrees of freedom still exist in the matrix which leads to success.

Some things do seem clear to me, however. Jung was an unusual man with a most fertile intellect who contributed much to various aspects of the study of personality, no matter the ultimate resolution of the value of his general theory of mind. His connection to modern efforts are legion—the importance of imagery and its revelation of scriptlike aspects, his emphasis on the study of the entire span of life with its attention to the problems of the second half of life; his attention to various aspects of the psychotherapeutic relationship which do not stem solely from transference sources; his awareness of the countertransferential aspects of the therapeutic process and their impact on the work; his broadened perspective on the nature of dream material—these are but a few of the ways in which his more general influence may be detected.

Lest one come away from this discussion feeling that I have glorified

Jung's achievements or not paid sufficient attention to his shortcomings, let me close by reminding you of one of his life-long insights—one that began in childhood with his forbidden image of God dropping a turd on the church and demolishing it (Jung, 1961, p. 39)—and ended some seventy years later with the publication of his book *Answer to Job*. He was convinced of the dual nature of God, good and evil—the dual nature of man—and I am convinced of the dual nature of Jung. He was led to emphasize his relationship to his introverted, abstract, imaginal side, not infrequently at the expense of his touch with the real world, the world of people and relationships. Even at the end of his life, he expressed a density about the meaning of his encounters with others, in comparison to the clarity he felt about the meaning of inner, imaginal events (Jung, 1961, p. 95). It was a price that he had to pay.

# CHAPTER 6

## On the Life and Work of Harry Stack Sullivan: An Inquiry into Unanswered Questions

### Introduction: The Biographers

The appearance in 1982 of Helen Swick Perry's biography of Harry Stack Sullivan (1892–1949), *Psychiatrist of America,* was a long-awaited event in mental health circles. Little more than the bare outline of his history was known, and so much mythology had grown up around the person of this very private, somewhat eccentric, and perhaps unconventional individual that a retelling of his life in the context of his time seemed almost imperative. Certainly no single person, on general balance, could claim better credentials for the task. While clearly there were others whose personal knowledge of Sullivan through shared intimacy far exceeded that of Perry, she had been involved for at least twelve years after his death in reading his notes and listening to his recorded professional utterances in order to edit his work for posthumous publication. Prior to that time, for the last three years of his life, she served him well as the managing editor for the journal he co-founded and edited, *Psychiatry.*

Perry, as she tells us, began her research into Sullivan's life in 1961 after a disagreement with the members of the editorial board supervising the publication of his lectures and scattered writings (1982, p. 3). She had indicated in the introduction to a newly emerging volume that Sullivan had told her that he had been hospitalized with a schizophrenic break during his earlier, perhaps adolescent, years. This she felt was common knowledge, and she was much surprised when she was told, by the psychiatrists who constituted the board, that no tangible evidence of that hospitalization was known to exist and thus its validity was suspect. She set out to establish that evidence only to realize over time, as is commonly experienced, that the initial question led to far more interesting and important ones in the life of her subject. After long years of searching Perry was not able to point to any record of Sullivan's hospitalization, although she indicates that she is the possessor of information that verifies that he was indeed hospitalized (1982, p. 4). However, what she did do was to present us with a complete biography, a fleshed-out version of a fascinating human story replete with honest attempts to fill in missing connections and unobvious sequences.

In all such endeavors, however, the work must, of necessity, be incomplete. The uncovering of heretofore unknown data raises new and perhaps unresolved issues. The relationship of the author to the subject undoubtedly influences interpretation of the material and thus invites response and further exploration. No better example of this process need be mentioned than Ernest Jones's biography of Sigmund Freud (1953, 1955, 1957). In the more than thirty years since its publication it has stimulated a honeycomb of scholarship and speculation about Freud's life, his personality, and the relationship of these elements to his theoretical and psychotherapeutic work.

In many respects Jones's task was much easier than Perry's. So many people "knew" Freud. He was so intimately connected in various ways to a multitude of others. Besides, his unquestioned international standing had stimulated a number of others early on to write biographical material about him. He himself had written a lengthy autobiographical sketch in his later years, which at least was a reasonable chronology of the evolution of his ideas up to that time (Freud, 1926/1935). Sullivan was much more veiled about most of his human relationships. Not all that many people knew him well, and those who did seemed especially to honor his lifelong need for privacy. His work, relatively sparse in publication during his lifetime, has made its way slowly into the literature mainly between the period 1953–1973 largely due to Perry's efforts. Thus the whole story, so to speak, has not been available for study for any appreciable length of time.

Until Perry's volume the most extensive source of material on Sullivan's life was the opening chapter in A. H. Chapman's *Harry Stack Sullivan: His Life and His Work* (1976). This condensed, fast-moving biographical account agrees in all essential elements with the factual aspects of Sullivan's existence previously published by Perry in brief biographical sketches (1962, 1974). It differs, however, in significant ways from Perry's full-length biography in interpreting the meaning of the events of his life. To these differences we shall consequently return.

Immediately prior to the publication of Perry's book, another volume on Sullivan appeared, written by Kenneth Chatelaine (1981). This book, an outgrowth of a Ph.D. dissertation, was little publicized, and in fact did not come to the attention of this writer until 1983. Chatelaine's work, which concentrates on Sullivan's life and work until 1930, what he titles "the formative years," draws heavily on both Chapman and Perry's earlier work as sources. This material is then supplemented by interviews with a number of figures in Sullivan's life, mainly around controversial issues highlighted in Chapman's work and considered in detail by Perry. It should be noted in fairness, however, to forestall invidious comparison, that Perry's major focus was biographical, while Chapman, a psychiatrist, was primarily involved with the explication of Sullivan's work to a more general audience. Chatelaine, a psychologist, was more concerned with establishing the relationship of Sullivan's contributions to a larger body of scholarly knowledge.

Although Perry's book will undoubtedly take its place as the definitive work on Sullivan's life, and both Chapman and Chatelaine have important questions and information to add to our pool of knowledge, there remain unsolved issues in the relationship of the life to the work and in the unfolding of the life itself. There are large gaps in the story pertaining to the development of his personality, his sexual development, and his career development. It is to these general issues, as they are affected by the details of the life history, that our attention will turn. Sullivan himself recognized the difficulty of the biographer in relating the individual's personal life and professional development in a review of Ruth Benedict's *The Chrysanthemum and the Sword* which Perry quotes in the opening of her book (Perry, 1982). It begins before the chapter entitled "Prologue" with, "Biography usually fails to integrate the subject person with the significant others who facilitated and handicapped his durable achievements as a contributor to culture history and rarely indicates whence came his skills and limitations in the interpersonal relations which made his contribution effective." In the following pages we shall examine various aspects of Sullivan's life, always with his reservation concerning biographical analysis in mind and always with the intent of overcoming this limitation.

## An Overview of Sullivan's History

To launch our inquiry into the mysteries of Sullivan's life story, let us begin with a brief sketch distilled from the various aforementioned biographical sources. Sullivan was born in 1892 and lived almost all of the first sixteen years of his life on a farm in the vicinity of a rural village in south-central New York State. He was the only living child of Catholic parents of Irish immigrant background who dwelt in an overwhelmingly Protestant, "Yankee" area. His preschool years were largely devoid of continual, daily contact with age-mates. In the following years, while school in the village was for him a successful experience intellectually, it was largely a failure interpersonally. Throughout his school years in Smyrna he was known to have only one close associate, who was five years his senior. This relationship lasted roughly from 1900 to 1906, when his friend graduated high school and left to study medicine. Much has been written by the biographers about this friendship and its impact on Sullivan and we shall return to a consideration of it at a later point.

The period from Sullivan's high school graduation in 1908 to his entry into the U.S. Army in a medical capacity ten years later is beclouded by the unavailability of certain facts and the lack of clarity surrounding others. We do know that his graduation from high school in 1908 was highlighted by the award of a state scholarship to attend Cornell University to study physics. At the end of the first year in Ithaca, under cloudy circumstances, having failed all his courses the second semester, he was put on academic probation and asked to leave school for one semester. There followed a two-year disappearance during which his whereabouts are not definitely known. The life continuity was resumed in 1911 when Sullivan entered the Chicago College of Medicine and Surgery. The following years, while roughly traceable in terms of whereabouts and activity, are almost entirely blank with regard to knowledge about human relationships. His academic record was spotty, and in 1915 he left medical school without a degree in hand. He then took up employment for only six months before disappearing a second time, for four months. We next pick up the trace of his movements in 1916 when he joined the National Guard; as with college, his tenure was ended abruptly and under cloudy circumstances. This sparse personal narrative takes on more definite human contours after the rather mysterious granting of his medical degree in 1917 and his entrance into the U.S. Army during World War I in 1918. The path becomes clear and traceable from the time of his move to Washington, D.C., in 1919, as a medical administrator in government service, and considerably more detailed from his beginnings in the psychiatric world at the end of 1921 until his death in 1949.

By the end of his life he had achieved much professionally. His fame among psychiatrists grew from his early success in the treatment of schizophrenics to his later recognition as an outstanding teacher and lecturer, a brilliant but unsystematic theoretician. Privately it was rumored that he was schizophrenic and/or alcoholic, and/or homosexual.[1] Much of the analysis of the biographical data involves these issues and their place in Sullivan's history. Let us begin this work by tracing the origins and development of his career path, which is by no means clear.

### The Puzzling Road to Psychiatry, 1909–1923

In reconstructing Sullivan's personal and professional development, two major questions arise. One essential unresolved mystery rests in his somewhat meteoric career rise: how is it that a person with no formal psychiatric training or openly expressed interest in psychiatry prior to 1921, one year later entered into the treatment of schizophrenics with a clear set of ideas as to how to proceed which bore no obvious relationship to ideas or treatments then or previously in vogue? Certainly his medical school record, as described by Perry, indicates no interest in this specialty and almost no aptitude for the one course on the transcript that could be identified as having either psychological or psychiatric content. Perry, who recognizes no mystery, seeks to explain his transformation largely by the acceptance he received from the staff in the benign setting of St. Elizabeth's Hospital in Washington, D.C., a large mental institution where he was assigned by the Veteran's Bureau as a liaison officer in 1921. This, coupled with his own life struggles, including perhaps one or more schizophrenic or schizophrenic-like panic episodes, and his perceptive brightness while treating his first psychiatric patients, were for her the necessary ingredients (Perry, 1982, chapters 22 and 23).

A second puzzle involves how a person with as many adolescent psychological difficulties as he is purported to have had, a shy, schizoid, sensitive, sexually naive person, evolved into a brash, assured, innovative professional over a twelve-year period—from the time he left Cornell in 1909 to the time he came into contact with psychiatry at St. Elizabeth's in 1921. Perry points out in her opening paragraphs of the chapter titled "The Impact of St. Elizabeth's Hospital" that until he joined that company "one can safely assume that he had had few meaningful relationships either socially or intellectually" (Perry, 1982, p. 179). Thus she is forced to rely on that source for his transformation. The picture of the social misfit is then further fostered by a quote she attributes to Clara Thompson, a long-time colleague and friend whom Sullivan met in the 1920s, to the effect that his poverty and social ineptitude even after entering medical school "kept him still isolated from his contemporaries" (Perry, 1982, p. 179). Was he really "remade" either psychologically or professionally by less than a year at St. Elizabeth's? It hardly seems likely.

The key to what transformed him from a shy, isolated, socially backward person to one described quite differently by William Alanson White, the eminent chief psychiatrist at St. Elizabeth's, in November 1922, must be sought in a more careful psychological analysis of those years of struggle, 1909 to 1921. In this regard, a reproduction of White's letter of recommendation for Sullivan to two prospective employers in the fall of 1922 may be informative, not only as to how Sullivan was seen by others at this time but as to how extensive and lengthy his psychiatric role at St. Elizabeth's had been. This may be important in solving our mystery since so much of what he later did was attributed to all that he got at St. Elizabeth's during that brief time. It is neither the picture of a shy, retiring person nor the transformation of such a person to a more outgoing one during that year:

> I have your letter . . . inquiring about Dr. H. S. Sullivan. I could not consider Dr. Sullivan's application for this staff because the administrative positions were all filled with no prospects of a vacancy in the immediate future. Dr. Sullivan functioned here for

sometime as a liaison officer between the Veteran's Bureau and the hospital. During that period our relations were eminently cordial and we got along nicely. As regards my opinions as to his availability for a staff appointment, I should say as I told him once, that I do not feel that I know Dr. Sullivan very well. He is a keen, alert, somewhat witty Irishman, who has a facade of facetiousness which is a bit difficult to penetrate. One or two occurrences have made me think that back of that facade was a considerable discontent that might perhaps express itself in alliances with other discontented spirits. However, this is perhaps an unfair presentation of his character. He probably is better equipped than the average State Hospital assistant, has had a considerable experience, is a genial and pleasant individual, and I should have very seriously considered appointing him in some capacity if I had really been in need of assistants. (Perry, 1982, p. 187)

At best the letter might be seen as a lukewarm recommendation filled with ambivalence. Clearly, Sullivan was not seen as a protégé by White. In fact it appears as though White did not know him very well and what he did know did not make an unequivocally positive impression upon him. The letter hardly argues for a person with unusual professional capabilities or promise at that time. Perhaps the attribution of White's influence arose from the close relationship that he and Sullivan later enjoyed, when Sullivan's work at Sheppard and Enoch Pratt became known.

Chapman, in dealing with this period, feels that Sullivan was most likely not interested in psychiatry until he reached St. Elizabeth's, but that he learned a great deal there under White's tutelage. This seems doubtful in light of White's letter. Chapman also believes that he did a great deal of work with patients during that time because his administrative work was not demanding, thus preparing him for a psychiatric career. This also seems dubious after reading White's letter. Most of all, Chapman (1976, p. 32) sees him as learning from the patients. Given his relative lack of expertise, one would have to surmise that he would likely learn what he was set to learn, what he had experienced before, a point to which we shall return.

Chatelaine is more trusting about the matter of professional preparation on Sullivan's part. He refers to Sullivan's various applications for government service, which list courses and training opportunities in which he participated. This may be the reason White thought that he had considerable experience (Chatelaine, 1981, chap. 5). Unfortunately, neither his registration for, nor his attendance at, any of these has ever been verified. Thus again we are pointed toward a more careful analysis of the years between 1909 and 1921, where the data is sketchy, to determine the origins of his psychiatric interest, his novel therapeutic efforts, and their relationship to his personality development.

If one paints with large brush strokes or sketches in broad outline the "known" periods in Sullivan's life which surround our era of particular interest, 1892–1909 and 1921–1949, the similarity is not difficult to see. As a child he was largely isolated from experience with other children until he was sent to school. He was intellectually precocious, demonstrating this fairly early, and basically derived a fair amount of self-esteem from the recognition by others of his cognitive gifts. As a farm child in a "town" school, in the beginning the single Catholic child among Protestant peers, he lived for the most part the life of a "social" outsider whose status derived from his intellectual superiority. The fitting climax of this role designation took place at the time of his graduation from high school in 1908, when he was chosen valedictorian and was awarded a scholarship to Cornell, a unique event in Smyrna history. What is critical to extract from this brief sketch is that his self-esteem depended almost solely on his intellectual achievement.

The professional period of his life, 1921 to 1949, has a similar flavor. He was seen as "special," highly innovative, and intellectually gifted at Sheppard and Enoch Pratt Hospital, his first psychiatric post, in Towson, Maryland. He was given freedom far beyond others of similar experience in psychiatric work. Despite his idiosyncrasies, his association socially with ward attendants, his "adoption" of a young schizophrenic boy, his overspending of personal and public funds, and his remoteness from others, he was highly valued as a person who had new ideas and one who was planning new paths for psychiatry that had intellectual roots in the social sciences. He made liaisons with people in the academic community and was concerned with the social, economic, and cultural aspects of the illness he studied and treated, schizophrenia. One prominent difference between the end of the first and the beginning of the third periods was his exquisite awareness of the importance of, as he called it, "interpersonal relations," especially with respect to mental health and its development. As in the earliest period, his life could be described as that of a social outsider whose self-esteem derived from his demonstrated intellectual superiority. In both periods, because of the return for his accomplishments, his self-esteem was largely intact.

### The "Missing Years," 1909–1911

It would be pleasant and simple if we could fill out this story by reporting that the period 1909–1921 was continuous with the time preceding in that he went on to college to excel in his studies. It would be even better if we could say that, unlike earlier, he found kindred souls with whom he shared a variety of adolescent experiences. Or further, that several of these friends remained close to him during his medical training and were supplemented by a new complement of like-minded cohorts from whom he learned the value of friendship and interpersonal intimacy. Or that from his variety of contacts there emerged lasting relationships which served as models for how to avoid reliance on a single source of income for self-esteem (intellectual achievement), ones that led him to experience multiple sources of gratification, including love of others.

Unfortunately the story of Sullivan's life did not unfold this way. The difficult period in question was ushered in by the disastrous year at Cornell, which ended in academic failure and suspension, and was further complicated, in Perry's account (1982, chaps. 17 and 18), by a suggested brush with the law occasioned ostensibly by the action of a group of students who apparently used him as a scapegoat. To emphasize how much of an outsider he might have been, Chapman (1976, p. 25) reports on an inquiry he made to the 239 survivors of Sullivan's entering class at Cornell, 1908, as to whether any of them knew Sullivan or could tell Chapman anything about the circumstances of his suspension. No information was forthcoming; no one knew or remembered him.

The next two years, 1909 to 1911, were even more cryptic. None of the biographers could gather any clear evidence of what happened to

this bright, somewhat socially isolated, seventeen-year-old in the ensuing period after his major and continuing source of self-esteem had
been removed by suspension for academic failure, although each
thought a different path likely. Perry conjectures that he was probably
hospitalized for some period of time, most probably at Bellevue Hospital in New York, either helped by A. A. Brill, the pioneer American
psychoanalyst, then a consultant at Bellevue with whom Sullivan
was later friends, or by Sarkis Gregory, a medical staffer at Bellevue
from 1904 to 1936. Gregory was a close friend and colleague of the
neurologist-psychiatrist son of the Sullivans' family physician in
Smyrna, thus a possible tie could be established (Perry, 1982, chap.
19). Chapman, on the other hand, believes he was likely working,
probably somewhere in the Midwest, to earn enough money for medical school. Chapman attributes Sullivan's admission to friends that
he had been hospitalized to his well-known tendency to dissemble
about the events of his life—in this instance, in order to justify some
special claim to sensitivity or knowledge about schizophrenia. In
pursuing this question about possible hospitalization at this time,
Chapman makes an interesting distinction—almost a hedge—which
may be critical in eventually understanding this issue. He says that
"it is conceivable that Sullivan was briefly hospitalized for a lesser
kind of adolescent emotional turmoil" and goes further to point out
that Sullivan's use of the term *schizophrenic* was synonymous with a
"panic state accompanied by some degree of interpersonal incapacity." He also indicates that this usage of the term was somewhat
eccentric and idiosyncratic (Chapman, 1976, p. 26). Was Chapman
referring here implicitly to homosexual panic, a term which Sullivan
did use with reference to the onset of schizophrenia? This connection
will become more obvious subsequently. Chatelaine, pursuing this
same problem, investigated the possibility that Sullivan was hospitalized in the Binghamton State Hospital where Ross McClure Chapman, his later boss at Sheppard and Enoch Pratt, was serving. The
inquiry came to no avail. No record of Sullivan's admission came to
light in the entries covering the years 1909–1911 (Chatelaine, 1981,
pp. 43–44). It should be pointed out that Perry investigated a wide
number of possible institutions in the effort to establish Sullivan's
hospitalization, also without success, although she indicates as I have
already mentioned that she is in possession of "other information

that establishes the fact itself that he was hospitalized at least once" (Perry, 1982, p. 4).

It seems entirely reasonable that the biographers have touched upon some important features in the development of Sullivan's ideas about schizophrenia while speculating about the two missing years. Sullivan's belief later on in his work at Sheppard and Enoch Pratt that schizophrenic panic in male adolescent patients could be reduced or alleviated by reassurance about homosexual imagery or behavior suggests that this was essentially the process he went through at that time. The panic was acute, related to homosexual "cravings," and "resolved" in a relatively brief period of time. Whether he was hospitalized at this time is problematic, and my guess is that he was not. In support of this guess, I would offer the following bits of data extracted from Perry (1982, chaps. 17, 18, and 19).

There was no report from anyone from whom Perry could gather actual evidence in his home community that Sullivan appeared out of his mind at that time. In fact, some felt that he may have feigned mental illness for legal purposes to escape whatever punishment would have derived from an apparent brush with the law. Furthermore, if in fact he was floridly psychotic toward the end of the academic year (spring 1909), it is highly unlikely that Cornell would have suspended him for six months, and for academic reasons. It is much more likely that they would have put him on leave indefinitely for medical reasons. If we take literally the newspaper items cited by Perry as reported in the Norwich *Sun*, they indicate that Sullivan was in his home territory, either Smyrna or Norwich, in November 1909 and April and August 1911. Although Perry doubts that he was actually there in these two instances, I would tend to think he was, for in small towns too many people would be likely to know if such announcements were false. If his incarceration took place between leaving Cornell (probably May or June 1909) and Thanksgiving of that year, then it was of a few months' duration and not generally known since the newspaper item described his being home from Cornell for the holidays. If he was schizophrenic during that period and had been released from a hospital, it does not seem likely that he would have been allowed consequently to wander on his own. Some suggested that he was sent to live with his Aunt Margaret in Brooklyn during that period. Since she was a full-time school teacher, it again seems unlikely that she would have been able to take on a psychotic late teenager. Where then was he and what psychological condition was he in?

Perry's suggestion that he was in Bellevue attended by Brill or Gregory, or Chatelaine's speculation that he was in Binghamton State Hospital treated by Ross McClure Chapman, although not substantiated, at least raises the possibility that he was influenced by a model during this period. This would make sense in understanding why he elected to study medicine, for which he had not shown any clear prior interest. Perry's highlighting of the fact that Sarkis Gregory remained unmarried may be of value in unraveling other aspects of this puzzle.[2] However, her attempts to explain Sullivan's belated interest in medicine and also in psychiatry by the events in the Norwich press during 1908, a succession of lurid news items including murder trials which stressed the mental illness aspect, are very unconvincing.

We know that when Sullivan was at Sheppard and Enoch Pratt he demonstrated two models for reducing the panic of young male schizophrenics, a state in which he found a large measure of confusion and fear over homosexual impulses. Both really involved lessening the guilt about the homosexual struggle, only the source person instrumental in reducing the guilt differed. In one model the work was to be carried out by assistants who were age-mates or near age-mates, homosexuals or people tolerant of homosexuality who could offer friendship and reassurance about homosexual fears. The other model was exemplified by his taking in to his home a fifteen-year-old boy who was allegedly suffering schizophrenic panic (read homosexual impulses which were disorganizing him through guilt). Since it is not likely that if Sullivan had been hospitalized between 1909 and 1911 congenial and reassuring age-mate attendants would have been available, no matter what hospital, would it be too improvident to imagine a circumstance in which he was taken in by an older man, a physician, who was understanding, reduced his guilt and fear about homosexual gratification, and even stimulated the interest in him to study medicine with perhaps a small financial stake to get him started? In a section of the chapter on male adolescence in Sullivan's *Personal Psychopathology*, written in the early 1930s but not released for publication until 1965, he speaks of the male mid-adolescent with little prior sexual experience with others who is introduced to sexuality by an older male (1972, p. 198). He sees this essentially as leading to positive outcomes if not encountered in unfortunate circumstances, e.g., on the streets in urban low-income areas, in groups isolated from women (jails, hospitals), or initiated by predatory men (cacocunes). How positive the outcome will be is distinguished by the degree of personality warp prior to adolescence. He tells us that if there is a continuing primitive attachment to the mother, then the encounter with sexuality will remain at a homosexual level. If no such warp exists, then an introduction to sexuality by an older male will lead eventually to a seeking of heterosexual gratification because of the negative valence of societal pressures toward homosexual gratification. The autobiographical ring of this analysis is striking; in his case a warp with the mother existed.

The point to be made from all of this is that if Sullivan had experienced a prolonged schizophrenic episode at this particular juncture in his life, 1909, it would be very difficult to understand how he would have arrived at a medical school (after a traumatic school failure), a long distance from home or from anyone he knew, alone and without adequate financial resources, and without any desire to study medicine. Beginning a new life in Chicago at nineteen years of age, in light of what we know about his personality as a child and his Cornell experiences of 1908–1909, doesn't support a serious or extended bout with schizophrenia in the period referred to by Perry as "the disappearance of Harry." It does, however, suggest a period in which a male model helped him over his sexual panic and modeled his occupational path. The acceptance of James Inscoe—a fifteen-year-old boy in a schizophrenic-like panic—into his home years later, in 1927, may have been the recasting of a scene he had already enacted. The origin of the treatment by the use of sympathetic age-mates we shall return to consequently.

### A Sketch of Sullivan's Personality Circa 1911

Although we can be reasonably secure in the belief that the two years 1909 to 1911 were filled with difficulty for Sullivan, certainly, whatever happened, he reconstituted himself enough then to begin again a period of education, this time leading to a professional goal. While we have no reports from others of what he was like as a person at that time, we may be able to construct an image from two sources of data.

One is Perry's extended description of what he was like as a child. The other is Sullivan's own theoretical writings on self-esteem and sexuality and his description of the warps in the preschool years and their later consequences, in *Personal Psychopathology* (1972), the first book and the most obviously autobiographical piece in all of his work. The data fit acceptably together and seem to stand up well, although incompletely, when compared to descriptions of him in later life. If anything, Perry's view may be on the benign side. At the other end, deriving characteristics of his personality solely from his explications of pathology is a narrow and limiting procedure erring on the harsh side. These are, however, the available data from which we must work, and they probably provide us with reasonable approximations of the limits of the spectrum.

Perry's extended description of Sullivan as a child pictures him as isolated, not terribly at home with age-mates, lonely, imaginative, bright, and not clearly aware of his impact on others. She tells of his being invited on geological walks at school with the older children because of his precocity and his subsequent alienation of them by the constant demonstration of his own knowledge. At home he seemed to be protected by his mother, indulged by his aunt, and ignored by his father. His intellectual potential was recognized by all and his undesirable behavior somewhat tolerated or excused accordingly. She portrays him as a child with reasonable self-esteem stemming from the regard he received from others for his knowledge, not timid, able to defend himself, but eager to be and make a friend without the apparent wherewithal to do just that (1982, pp. 73–74).

That Sullivan's discussion of the warps of the preschool years is a portrayal applicable to himself without great distortion is apparent after reading the biographers. In this regard it is interesting that obsessive and psychopathic characteristics are those seen by him as the "major difficulties" of that period, given all the known possibilities for psychological deviation that exist. Certainly later characterizations of him by others include these designations.[3]

He describes the obsessional and the psychopathic personality, "the grave disorders of growth in childhood," at length in his chapter on "the chronology of difficulty" (1972, especially pp. 118–25). I shall not quote all that he says about each but rather extract elements that seem to be particularly relevant to what we know about him.

A. Developmental and behavioral aspects of the psychopathic personality
1. "If now, in the learning of adjustment to parental authority . . . the emphasis is placed on the acquisition of chiefly verbal techniques which prevail over other aspects of interpersonal reality, then the growth of self is severely affected. The acquisition of stereotypes does not proceed to anything like the usual extent, and, instead, there are incorporated fantastic patterns of people as foci for verbal and other expressive gestures useful in 'having one's own way.' "
2. ". . . the failure of the *psychopathic child* applies only to factors of interpersonal events" (not like mental defectives); "and thus shows increasingly *an incapacity to be personally real in interpersonal situations.*"
3. "Fantasy processes thus continue to predominate in interpersonal situations" (no learning of consensual validation).
4. "In later life the psychopath often comes to be considered a great liar, although this judgment can scarcely survive a close study of his statements. There is little or no clearly conscious determination to deceive. . . . the statements of the psychopath are for the most part remarkably well adapted to the immediate interpersonal situation in which he happens to be."
5. "Even in the case of the psychopath . . . so-called *pathological liar,* the intention to deceive is not as conspicuous as is his inability to believe the facts that he has experienced."
6. "Whenever his motivation of an interpersonal situation miscarries, the 'set' is usually dissipated by grief or anger, and the impression of the inexplicable unpleasantness is replaced by a fantasied success. If, subsequently, one insists on hearing about the event, the recall takes the form of a retrograde falsification. If pressure is applied with a view to securing greater accuracy of recall, anger is generally elicited, but it is not so much anger at being disbelieved, as it is anger at aggression; the inquisitor is treated as if he were hostile and attempting to injure the psychopathic individual."
7. In the juvenile era psychopaths "begin to sense a difference from others, emphasized . . . by the long recurring series of failures in their social efforts."

8. "Because, however, of the singular deficiency of their self-formulation, they are incapable of correcting erroneous actions which apply to other people" and they don't learn from experience.
9. "No psychopathic personality is capable of a sound sexual adjustment, and in this field their efforts are an unfailing source of troubles to themselves and their very temporary mates."
10. "In situations requiring their submission to authority—excepting only in regimented groups such as the armed forces—the psychopathic individuals are generally inadaptable."

B. Developmental and behavioral aspects of the obsessive personality
   1. "The *obsessional personality* is characterized superficially by an excess of personal uncertainty and scrupulosity. These children tend to express doubts and uncertainties about everything. This is not to be mistaken for timorous uncertainty or insecurity; for example, these folks are usually tenacious and stubborn to a degree—especially in doubting."
   2. "The obsessional child shows neither signs of fear nor tendencies to resort to tantrums. His peculiar device is *thought*."
   3. The obsessional youngster is "apt to be of superior intelligence . . . learns easily, shows excellent ability to profit from all experience *except* that pertaining to other people significant in his total situations."
   4. The obsessional child becomes preoccupied with his thoughts, especially with doing and thinking the right thing.
   5. "Loveless marriages complicated by hypocrisy and imposture are the prime sources of this deviation."
   6. "The child of parents of this sort undergoes a thorough disintegration of the primitive mother sentiment very early."
   7. ". . . and the obsessional child comes chiefly to be distinguished by a specious thoughtfulness that turns all the virtues into instrumentalities of aggression and aggrandizement of his self."
   8. "The obsessional child is one in whom rage and anger tendencies have been sidetracked."
   9. In obsessional children, "their self never sheds its original omnipotence *anlage*."

This material, clearly supported by later incidents from his life, can provide the basis for a thumbnail sketch of Sullivan as he arrived in

Chicago in 1911. On some level he was quite knowledgeable and secure in what he thought he knew or could learn, which allowed him to attempt medical school. On another level he was doubtful after the Cornell experience that he was capable of learning anything. He was expecting somehow to get what he needed, to be indulged. He thought he had the verbal capacity to bring this about, and yet he was not convinced that he could accomplish his goals. He was no longer in panic about his sexual role but uncertain about what the ultimate patterning would be. This aspect of his growth struggle was superimposed on *the continuing struggle with self-esteem*, the major battle of his late adolescent and young adult years. With regard then to the question of personality development, it may be a mistake to view the period between 1909 and 1923 as involving some sort of transformation. It is more likely that the major patterns were set and vacillated as a function of self-esteem. Thus in his better moments he was witty, self-assured, knowledge spouting, oblivious to his impact on others, expecting to be indulged, etc. In his trying moments, when self-esteem was threatened or impaired, he was more patently obsessive, schizoid, and/or psychopathic.

With regard to self-esteem it is interesting that although early in his professional writing he saw the problems of sexual development in adolescence as the immediate source of serious mental disorder, there is evidence that eventually he understood the difficulties as being chiefly those of self-esteem. In discussing early adolescence in *The Interpersonal Theory of Psychiatry* he states,

> Since lust has a peculiarly strong biological basis, and, in some people, may be an ever recurrent and driving force in early adolescence, this preoccupation with lust can lead to serious destruction of self-respect because of the unpleasant situations one is driven into, because of the disapproval one encounters, and because this type of preoccupation literally interferes with almost any commonplace way of protecting one's self-esteem. A great many people whose self-esteem has been somewhat uncertain, depending on scholarship only, find their standing as students rapidly declining as they become preoccupied with the pursuit of lust objects. Thus they become the prey of severe anxiety, since their only distinction is now being knocked in half. (1953, p. 273)

This, we must remember, was conceived in 1944–45 and delivered in lectures some two years later, in the twilight of his life. Perry, in her introduction to *Personal Psychopathology,* while pointing out Sullivan's somewhat overlooked indebtedness to the published work of Edward Kempf, refers to their separate but similar discussions of homosexuality. She says, "Sullivan later suggested that homosexual problems were often only symptoms of deeper disturbances in the realm of self-esteem," a derivation perhaps from the above quotation from Sullivan (1972, p. xviii). If we take his insight at face value we might hypothesize that the major problem facing Sullivan in his "years of isolation," roughly the period between his departure from Cornell in 1909 and his appointment in 1918 as a first lieutenant in the Army Medical Corps during World War I, was the recovery of his self-esteem. This was accomplished through status gained by the reflected recognition by others of his knowledge, his prime source of self-esteem in childhood. His bout with sexuality in some ways could be seen as an appendage of that struggle, although in his mind's eye, until he was close to forty, he was not clearly aware of the relationship between self-esteem and sexuality. In fact, his position earlier was somewhat antithetical to the one he later adopted, the one we have already considered. For example, in the chapter discussing dynamisms of difficulty in *Personal Psychopathology,* written in the early 1930s, he wrote,

> If one has no difficulty in securing his sleep and food, and if he makes some fairly successful resolution of his sexual needs, there is no great difficulty in securing the rest of his personality needs by compensatory substitution. It is true that his self-esteem *may* be uncertain, so that he is somewhat tense and inclined to defensive operations, but whether by tennis championship, big-game hunting, world travelling, by the less glorious methods of talespinning, movie patronage, or even the ignoble course of keeping himself an object of sympathy—in any or all of these cases, he struggles through, rather to the envy of his fellows. If, however, he includes the sexual drives in those to be solved by compensatory processes, then he is the envy of very few, he is a much harassed man. (1972, p. 57)

In this discourse he does not even consider a resort to his former source of self-esteem, intellectual recognition as a compensation for flagging self-esteem, nor does he consider it possible that sexual frustration could be compensated for at all, a dubious omission. The major point to derive from this quote is that self-esteem is essentially a function of the reflected feelings of others and has little to do with one's own evaluation. This point will become central in tracing his struggle with self-esteem during these critical years. It seems important to consider that the primacy of intellectual achievement over sexual achievement or vice versa may ultimately be subsidiary to the problem of reestablishing self-esteem through acceptance by others. The path to acceptance by others in his imagery is accomplished by the achievement of status in their eyes, intellectually when he was young, sexually while adolescent, and a return to intellect in adulthood. The quoted statement may also be an indication that sexual gratification was not a continuing problem for him in that period of his life.

### The Chicago Years and the Struggle with Self-Esteem, 1911–1917

The years in medical school, 1911–1915 (Perry, 1982, chap. 20), are in many ways as mysterious interpersonally as the two "missing" years, 1909–1911. In all of Perry's exhaustive twenty years of searching into Sullivan's life, she found only one indication of a meaningful relationship that may have taken place during that time. James Inscoe Sullivan (Sullivan's long-time companion and designated foster son and heir) reported to her of Sullivan's alleged despair in early 1917 over the death of a friend from medical school. The only identifying feature of the friend was a French-sounding name which Perry had difficulty in tracing. The medical school records show only one such person in Sullivan's class, and there is no record of him in the school from 1912 on. What may be important here is to identify only that in early 1917 Sullivan was distressed over *loss*, a situation to which we shall return in time (Perry, 1982, p. 168).

About the period 1911–1915 we do know from his grade record in medical school that his performance was entirely undistinguished and that by the end of four years of study he had not completed the requirements necessary to obtain a degree. This is especially important information in that the school itself did not enjoy a very strong image academically. From information that Perry supplies we are aware of the fact that Sullivan's failure in embryology resulted from non-attendance in laboratory sessions. Perry's major explanation for his performance was his having to work to help support himself and his dislike of rote, regimented learning (1982, pp. 156–62). While undoubtedly these factors were influential, one could wonder what impact his struggle with adolescent sexuality had on his academic progress during those years. Sullivan, from his own thinly veiled autobiographical descriptions of sexual difficulties in adolescence, pictured himself as having a prolonged stage of preadolescence, probably culminating at age sixteen when he entered Cornell. Adolescence he described as the period starting with the frank eruption of genital lust to the stable patterning of sexual expression. The eruption of genital lust and the inability to satisfy it in his case led to the multiple difficulties in his year at Cornell. The two missing years following Cornell we can see as being reparative in some way, in that although the medical school years are seen as trying and difficult financially and perhaps academically, he manages without serious interruption; that is to say, he maintains himself in school each semester, works enough to keep body and soul together (with some financial help from his Aunt Margaret and sporadic aid from his financially stressed parents), and generally holds together. From whence then came the sources of self-esteem? From the writings of the Sheppard and Enoch Pratt years, we know that he came to the conclusion that there is no compensation for the discharge of genital lust. Certainly his medical school performance could not have supplied him with the self-esteem he formerly derived from intellectual accomplishment. What he likely sought was an avenue for his sexual expression within the context of approving peers. I would submit that these conditions could probably be met without too much trouble in the surround in which he lived, the "streets of Chicago" (Sullivan, 1972, p. 198) and that the extended discussion of the various avenues to homosexuality and the fine distinctions made about sources of gratification in sexuality (auto, homo, hetero, erotic and sexual) found in *Personal Psychopathology* are largely autobiographical, personally known to him through his own experience or others with whom he interacted (Sullivan, 1972, chaps. 6 and 7). My conjecture is that he found an accepting peer group in working-class Chicago who accorded him status for his place as a medical student and were accepting of and perhaps participants in his working out his sexual patterning. This set of experiences, during the years 1911 to 1915, were the ones that led him immediately to the use of peer-level attendants to befriend and reduce the homosexual panic he expected would exist in adolescent male schizophrenics in his now famous work at Sheppard and Enoch Pratt. Thus the mystery of where his treatment ideas came from can be answered by resort to personal experience during the period of his own distress and immediately following. I have, however, indicated that the major struggle of this period was with self-esteem; let us follow its vicissitudes in the period after medical school.

The events of 1915 precipitated another period of crisis in Sullivan's life which lasted for more than two years, with some intermittent period of relief. The crisis was initiated by his failure to graduate from medical school, which could have acted to redintegrate the loss of status and self-esteem that followed the dismissal from Cornell. In later life he attributed his not receiving the degree with his class to financial difficulties, in that he owed the school tuition monies. Perry, however, uncovered his academic ineligibility to graduate on schedule. He had simply not completed all the requirements and nothing about his record indicated that he showed such high promise of future performance as a physician to convince anyone to waive the requirements still outstanding. As far as it is known, he proceeded from this point as though the medical school episode was over. He never returned to complete the missing requirements, nor is there any evidence that during the period that he was employed in a medical-type capacity (from August 1915 to February 1916 in the Illinois Steel Company) he used any of that money to reduce his debt to the school (1982, pp. 156–78).

That he was in psychological distress during this time is indicated by the fact that he held the job for only six months, and without any other visible sources of income disappeared for a period of four months. Neither his whereabouts nor his source of income during that time has ever been identified, and he followed this period by enlisting in the Illinois National Guard in late June 1916 (Perry, 1982, chap. 21). Now I do not wish to call into question any patriotic motives that he may have had in joining a military organization. Certainly there is enough evidence from his later life that he gave willingly of his time and expertise to help his country in time of need. However, we are dealing with a time when military need was not that great—the major preoccupation was a border skirmish with Mexico. It seems much more likely that the military presented a haven at that time for a harassed individual who had not solved the problem of finishing his medical studies and thus was limited in embarking on a career. Without doubt, a stint in the military could have helped him solve the financial side of his problem, if he could have saved enough to pay off his debt, but it could do nothing to help him complete his academic work. In this sense, the problem was only put on "hold."

From Perry's report (1982, p. 166) it seems as though his sojourn in the military on a post outside San Antonio was a relatively happy one. He worked in a medical unit with the rank of sergeant, which was likely to produce status, and he had opportunity to ride horses, which he loved. He later recounted in his lectures a light and playful story about the military which included a clear reference to a friendship (Sullivan, 1956, p. 40). Although he used this tale to illustrate the phenomenon of selective inattention and Perry cites its levity to support her contention that he was relatively untroubled during that period, I would like to call attention to why this may have been so. The contents of the tale supply the lead. Preparing his audience for the concept of selective inattention by describing how much concentration is needed to hit a target at one thousand feet on a rifle range, he says, "And people who are very deeply interested in that sort of thing and who are, at least part of the time, very good at it, cannot be reached when they are getting ready to fire." He goes on, "I have literally been so much of a scientist as to stick a pin into a *very, very dear friend* of mine [emphasis mine] on one such occasion. And sure enough, as I had expected, it was only after having fired that he reached around to the injured area and gave me the devil. Literally, on the rifle range, things are suspended from any disturbance of one's consciousness until it is time to notice them" (Sullivan, 1956, p. 40).

What I find important about the content of this story are the things that become salient when you disregard the apparent point that he is trying to illustrate and focus upon the elements that serve to make it up. In the first place, it seems ludicrous to think of him out on the rifle range contemplating the nature of selective inattention and acting the scientist in order to demonstrate to himself the power of the concept.

It also seems ludicrous to think of sticking someone in the rear (which I believe is intended in what he says) when that person was concentrating on firing a rifle unless you knew him extremely well and could count on a positive response from him. It is an intimate gesture under trying conditions. When coupled with the unusual phrasing "a very, very dear friend" it has the flavor of greater intimacy. When further placed in the context of a person with an isophilic sexual adjustment, it suggests the possibility that some of his happiness associated with this period could have come from a satisfying homosexual affair. When one further considers that the entire length of his stay in the National Guard barely exceeded five months, there didn't seem to be all that much time to build a deep friendship, especially for someone who suffered from interpersonal difficulties.

I am raising this issue because of the next bit of data with which we must deal. We know that he was discharged from the National Guard after a brief period of duty for reasons of physical disability. Perry, in recounting this time, indicates that, aside from a broken jaw which he incurred riding horses and which didn't seem a likely physical disqualification, she could find no physical reason for dismissal and thinks perhaps he suffered psychological stress which led to the discharge (1982, pp. 167–68).[4] My own conjecture would be that his homosexuality was revealed and the military handled this knowledge discreetly by discharging him for physical reasons. Since the period was pictured as a happy one for him and it seems to have ended precipitously, apparently without justifiable cause, I would be led to the possibility that he violated some moral standard which led to a rapid dismissal, a procedure probably not unknown in the military at that time—a physical disability discharge to hide a violation of military sexual mores. It was this failure to survive in the military, coupled with the loss of a valued friendship, that led to an acute crisis for him in the winter of 1916–17.[5]

What we know about the ensuing period indicates that the stress was psychological, and there is a reasonable likelihood that he received some professional help. He at later times reported receiving seventy-five hours of psychoanalysis during that winter. Perry and Chapman both feel that this was probably not quite the case for a variety of reasons, including his lack of money, his limited interest in psychoanalysis, and the fact that there were no known analysts in

Chicago at that time (Perry, 1982, pp. 167–68; Chapman, 1976, pp. 35–36). Chatelaine concurs with this interpretation (Chatelaine, 1981, p. 154). Perry reveals that on later applications Sullivan listed receiving psychiatric training at three different hospitals in Chicago in 1916–17, a claim that has not been supported. She speculated that "he himself was hospitalized at one of these hospitals for some brief period after he got out of the National Guard" (1982, p. 169). The evidence she cites to support this speculation is persuasive. It stems from later statements he made about his interest in, and contact with, schizophrenic patients beginning in the winter of 1916–17 (Perry, 1982, p. 169). At any rate, if he was hospitalized at that time, and I am inclined to believe that he was, it was not for a schizophrenic-like acute homosexual panic but more likely to have been for a severe anxious depression that resulted from the experience in the National Guard and was probably more amenable to a "talking cure" if he was in an institution. That he may have had the opportunity to observe cases of male adolescent schizophrenic panic on a ward to which he was admitted was highly likely. Having had the medical training that he did and the earlier experience with panic after Cornell may even have given him some opportunity to help with others on the ward and may even have been a source of recovering self-esteem as well as the source of the fantasy that he had formal training. The fact that James I. Sullivan reported to Perry that Sullivan told him he was depressed during this time adds credence to this conjecture and ties together his later statements about his interest and training with schizophrenics (Perry, 1982, p. 168). Perry reports that after the crisis of the winter Sullivan was in some form of private practice. If so, it was very likely, according to Chapman, to have been industrial medicine and less likely to have been in the employ of insurance companies doing medical examinations (1976, pp. 31–32). From these descriptions of his activities it seems highly unlikely that he suffered a schizophrenic episode and could reconstitute so quickly. Recovery from a depression would make more sense.

Whatever actually happened in his life after that winter is not firmly established until the beginning of 1918, when in January he appeared in Smyrna to visit his parents, whereupon he was referred to in the local newspaper as Dr. Harry Sullivan (Perry, 1982, p. 170).[6] The only other bit of information of relevance is that his medical degree, which, as Perry writes, "was found in Sullivan's effects" (and not prominently displayed as is usually the case), was dated September 1917, thus indicating that he had to do something prior to that time to convince the appropriate authorities that he was now eligible for certification as a physician (Perry, 1982, pp. 164–65). Certainly he had to present himself as a person whose psychological condition was not in question, something possible in the recovery from depression, less likely after a schizophrenic episode.

The issues surrounding the granting of this degree have not escaped the attention of either Perry or Chapman, and each resolves them differently. We shall return to this matter subsequently. For the purposes of the thesis I am attempting to explicate, the most important fact was that Sullivan was in possession by early 1918 of a certificate entitling him to the rights and privileges of a doctor of medicine. This was the critical element in the return of status and attendant self-esteem. From that time on we see nothing other than a continuous growth in responsibility as measured by the positions that he held. Never again are we able to detect a period in his life when the stress he was under seemed able to disrupt seriously his psychological functioning. In fact, no matter how difficult the circumstances, whether as a novice heading a research effort with schizophrenics at Sheppard and Enoch Pratt, or a man seeking to establish a point of view in psychiatry against the odds of the psychoanalytic establishment, or a person physically disabled before his time by heart trouble, he seemed to draw on a reserve of strength forged from the memory of ancient suffering overcome, as long as self-esteem was intact.

The year 1918 marked the end of ten years of suffering, parallel to similar decades in the lives of Freud and Jung from which several insights and experiences came that laid the groundwork for their productive years. Freud's decade was 1890–1900, Jung's 1910–1920; both were entering their middle years when this isolation occurred. Sullivan was much younger, only sixteen at the onset, but he lived considerably less time than the other two. For Sullivan the onset is marked with loss of status and self-esteem, the end with the return of these elements, in some sense a path guided by external direction. The others, older, more settled, with more status derived from professional regard, turned inward.

With regard to Sullivan I do not feel that the return of self-esteem led to an obvious professional path and that he knew what he wanted to accomplish after that. It is more likely that in his case he had re-established a constant spring for positive feelings about self, similar to that which he experienced in the days before he left home. Along with that were the necessary interpersonal experiences, already referred to, which when later utilized led to his professional success. With shame and anxiety reduced he was then able to perform well at the succession of medical administrative posts that he held until he finally entered full-time, uninterrupted psychiatric practice at Sheppard and Enoch Pratt at the end of 1922.

The story could easily end at this point, in that I feel that I have satisfied my curiosity with regard to the two initial questions raised: (1) how was it possible for someone with no apparent psychiatric training or professed interest to enter the profession as a novice with a clear set of ideas as to what schizophrenia was all about and how to deal with it therapeutically, and (2) how did a shy, schizoid, sexually naive adolescent emerge twelve years later as an assured and innovative professional? In essence, I have contended that his idea of the relationship between schizophrenia and homosexual panic came from his experiences in the year at Cornell and in the period immediately following, which is clearly spelled out in his various writings on both adolescence and schizophrenia. I have also reviewed the vicissitudes of self-esteem in Sullivan's life during this critical period. Furthermore, I have ventured to reflect on the possible manner of his struggle with adolescent sexuality, the path it likely took, and the impact of his resolutions on his later work. Again, it is no revelation that he was known to have an isophilic sexual preference. Certainly Chapman states it openly (1976, pp. 12, 23, 38, 50), Chatelaine presents affirmative opinions of others to this effect although his own position is not clear (1981, pp. 445–58), and Perry also concurs with this idea of his sexual resolve, although in a subdued and more extended contextual framework (1982, p. 334). To know how he got from Cornell to Sheppard and Enoch Pratt, one had to reflect in detail on the known facts of his life as they related to sexuality and self-esteem.

Perhaps the better part of wisdom would dictate leaving the story at this point, but a few nagging residuals remain, stimulated essentially by the biographers. They relate principally to the issues pertaining to homosexuality in his life and force a further examination of his relationship with two of the most important male figures in his life, Clarence Bellinger from his childhood and James Inscoe Sullivan from his mature years. Prior to that, however, I would like to address two issues. I will first explore the mystery surrounding the granting of his medical degree in 1917, a matter which was previously introduced, and then turn to the analysis of an internal conflict about treatment when he began his full-time career in psychiatry and its resolution.

### The Mystery Surrounding the Awarding of the Medical Degree, 1917

Both Perry (1982, p. 165) and Chapman (1976, p. 32) point out the strange fact that Sullivan's degree was not recorded in the appropriate files of either Valparaiso University, to which the Chicago College of Medicine and Surgery was originally attached, or Loyola University, which eventually bought it out. They further stress that the original degree was not found among his effects until after Sullivan's death. Each also points out the difference in the name on his diploma, Harry Stack Sullivan, with the one carried in the school records, Harry F. Sullivan (Perry, 1982, p. 85; Chapman, 1976, p. 32). Chapman, who believes that the only reason his degree was not granted in 1915 was because he had not settled his tuition debt, resolves the problem readily by indicating that when Sullivan cleared up his debt in 1917, the degree was granted and that the negligence involved in the recording of the degree was a clear indication of the carelessness with which the school was administered.

Perry deals with this issue of the degree more extensively, and it may be well to quote this section of her narrative in preparation for what is to follow. On page 162, in the last paragraph of her very brief, six-page chapter on "the Chicago College of Medicine and Surgery," she states: "However spotty his education, Sullivan had finished *in some fashion* [emphasis mine] the required courses at the end of the term in 1915, but his education in medicine had just begun." Just two pages later, in a new chapter, she returns to this matter with the following two paragraphs.

When he stopped going to classes at the Chicago College in 1915, he was not eligible for a degree, as indicated by the final report sheet on his grades. Moreover, the rules of the school required that he pay all back fees and complete a year of internship before the formal degree could be granted. Neither the records of Valparaiso University in Indiana nor those at Loyola University show that Sullivan ever received a medical degree. But the diploma, *properly signed and executed* in September 1917 [emphasis mine], was found in Sullivan's effects, and a copy of it has now been placed in the files of Loyola University.

This story is as puzzling and as complex as many stories in Sullivan's life. In the same month that the buildings and equipment of Chicago College were purchased by Loyola University, Sullivan received his degree from Valparaiso, signed by many of the same professors who had been his teachers in medical school. In that transition period from one university to another, Sullivan *apparently straightened out his credentials* [emphasis mine] and paid his back fees, or as many as he could. Undoubtedly the tradition of Valparaiso University, as set up long ago by its founders, held sway over the decision of the faculty to waive some requirements, probably both financial and academic. Also it seems quite likely that Sullivan himself was persuasive and determined to overcome the irregularities of his record. The decision was obviously wise, whoever made it, and at twenty-five years of age, Harry Stack Sullivan's name was inscribed on the duly certified diploma. It was his first use of the name Stack at medical school. And it seems to have been the last medical diploma issued by Valparaiso University; no other degrees are listed for September of that year, although a list of graduates from Chicago College is given for May 1917. (1982, pp. 164–65)

What Perry conveys to this reader in her description of events is that it was a "puzzling" and "complex" sequence which really has never been adequately explained. Her own sense of residual tension or lack of closure is indicated by such things as stating in the first quotation that he had "in some fashion" completed the required courses by the end of 1915, and following that with the opening of the second quotation in which she states, "He was not eligible for a degree, as indicated by the final report on his grades." Later she says, "But the diploma, *properly signed and executed* [emphasis mine] . . . was found in Sullivan's effects." After indicating something about the confusion of the transition of administrations, she is quick to point out something that almost has the quality of a non sequitur: "Sullivan received his degree from Valparaiso, *signed by many of the same professors who had been his teachers in medical school*" [emphasis mine]. Why did she feel it necessary to indicate that the document was "properly signed and executed"? Similarly, what was so unusual about faculty members signing a degree? She goes on to say, "In that transition period from one university to another, Sullivan *apparently* [emphasis mine] straightened out his credentials and paid his back fees, *or as many as he could*" [emphasis mine].

She then goes on to resolve the puzzle by appealing to the power of the tradition of the school, which she explicated earlier: "Everyone is to be given 'an equal opportunity to obtain a medical education in a high grade medical school . . . regardless of financial circumstances.' The instruction 'shall not be inferior' to that of any other school in the country, even though their fees may be higher. And the school shall continue to grow and prosper from the excellence of its work rather than denouncing the work done by other schools." One is led by her to believe that somehow Sullivan was persuasive in his appeal and that this fortunately won the day.

While it is an entirely conceivable story, it is not terribly compelling to this reader. In the first instance, the importance of the money issue appears to be somewhat inflated and obscures what was more likely the major concern—his lack of fulfillment of the requirements. Let us examine in greater detail the debt. Since the school was devoted to the ideal of providing equal opportunity for a medical education to people of limited financial means, how likely is it that they would have held up the degree on those grounds alone? Given the fact that the degree was a necessary card of admission to an increased earning capacity makes it even more dubious that the degree would have been withheld on financial grounds alone. Certainly if the world of 1915 was remotely similar to the world of today, a person who only needed a limited sum of money to ensure a considerably greater earning capacity in a reasonably high-status occupation would have been an excellent credit risk.[7]

We must then turn our attention to the lack of completion of the academic requirements and how that could have been overcome.

Since there is no record that he ever returned to school within the period 1915–1917 and Perry (1982, pp. 159–60) listed his academic deficiencies as multiple (histology in the first year, embryology in the second—at least the laboratory work—an E for two years of embryology, probably a conditional grade in an A–F grading system, and no final grade for a course listed as "psych" in his third year), what could have convinced an appropriate administrator or faculty panel that he was now worthy of a degree? There is no evidence that leads us to believe that if there were academic deficiencies he did anything in the ensuing period to make them up. Since Perry also indicated that a formal year of internship was an additional requirement for the degree, Sullivan had a formidable set of barriers to overcome—money, course requirements, and practical requirements.

With regard to money, the situation is not clear. There is no reference anywhere to any outside person helping him financially. The biographers, following Sullivan's lead in the 1942 sketch in *Current Biography*, indicate that he worked for two years to acquire the money to pay off the debt. In following the sequence of events of those two years described by Perry, it is not easy to see how he could have amassed any reasonable sum. Let us briefly review what is known. For six and one-half months, from August 1915 to sometime in February 1916, he worked without his medical degree as an assistant surgeon for the Illinois Steel Company. While he could have accumulated some savings from this continuous employment, his whereabouts and means of income for the next four months are unknown. That they were not likely to have been terribly secure or remunerative is probably indicated by the fact that immediately following this period, in late June 1916, he enlisted in the Illinois National Guard, where he remained for most of five months with the rank of sergeant. He may well have been able to save some money during this period, but this was then followed by a period of distress after his discharge in November. The next several months, covering the winter of 1917, seem very unlikely to have produced income. He talks of seventy-five hours of psychoanalysis; Perry thinks he may have been hospitalized. Neither situation is likely to add to one's income. Thus the burden would rest on the spring and summer of 1917, a time when he indicated that he was doing work for a variety of insurance companies. This is certainly possible but would likely have demanded a person who could work vigorously and not one who was in any obvious psychological distress, another argument for the likelihood that the distress of the winter of 1917 related to depression rather than to a schizophrenic episode.

As far as the practical requirements are concerned, it is conceivable that he could have offered his combined employment at the Illinois Steel Company (six and a half months) and his stint in the National Guard (five-plus months) in lieu of an internship, since both positions involved medical duties and were undoubtedly under the supervision of trained medical personnel. The one unexplained barrier that remains is the unfulfilled course requirements. How was this overcome?

In trying to make sense out of the bits of data we have, I attempted to construct a set of logical possibilities over and above the ones provided by Perry and Chapman. The first that came to mind centered on the historical fact that the United States entered World War I on April 6, 1917, coincident with the conclusion of the "winter of 1917" when he was supposedly hospitalized and/or analyzed.[8] It is quite conceivable that Sullivan could have appealed for the degree to be granted in order to enlist in the military, where he could utilize most effectively his nearly completed medical training. In the hysteria surrounding military mobilization and especially in the search for appropriate medical support personnel, it would not be too surprising that the unfulfilled requirements would not have loomed quite so large.

There is some evidence to suggest that this speculation is not an idle one. Within a few months after the date of the degree, September 1917, Sullivan applied, in February of 1918, for a commission in the Army Medical Corps. Not a great deal of time had actually elapsed since in January he had made a visit to his family in Smyrna. The conjecture about appealing for a waiver of requirements in order to join the military might be more convincing had he applied for a commission immediately upon receiving the degree, but there might have been sufficient reasons for the apparent delay. In the first instance there was the curious situation that when the application was finally made he falsified his age, claiming that he was born in 1886 rather than 1892. Perry is quick to point out the risk that was involved in such behavior, in that if anyone had looked closely they would have noticed that he presumably graduated from high school at age twenty-two, as well as other puzzling things relative to age and developmental progress. Perry also points out that this false date of birth existed on a variety of applications and records and was not really brought into line until 1930, some twelve years later and, I might add, when he already had established for himself a clear and impressive professional identity (Perry, 1982, pp. 170–71). Why then did he feel the need to falsify his birth date? The possibility exists that he did not want to have to own up to his previous service in the National Guard, especially if the reason for his discharge was related to homosexuality. Even though the discharge stated that he was released for a physical disability, this in itself would have reduced his chances for commission in the regular forces. One wonders if this dilemma about the possibility that his prior record might be discovered did not lead to some procrastination in enlistment until he decided on the drastic step of falsifying his age and modifying his name, from Harry F. to Harry Stack. It seems almost obvious that the deception was in the interest of hiding some important information, and once having made the decision to deceive, he had to maintain it for quite a long time. To return, however, to the origin of this inquiry—namely, to explain the grounds on which he may have made the appeal to waive the unfulfilled requirements for a medical degree—one could then understand why he had to risk the possibility of exposure if it was part of the bargain that he volunteer for medical military service.

Another possible scenario leads in an entirely unappealing direction but nevertheless deserves an airing. It is that there was no waiver of requirements by the school and that the degree was in some manner fraudulently acquired. This certainly would bring unity to a set of small, nagging bits of information that remain part of Sullivan's history. These include (1) the lack of original registry of the degree in appropriate annals; (2) the difference in the name to which the degree was issued and the name on the school records; (3) the apparent burying of the degree in his personal effects only to come to light after his death; (4) his forgoing the use of the title M.D., especially in the latter part of his career;[9] (5) his involvement (after the acquisition of the degree and the eight to nine months in the army) in governmental jobs for most of three years, which were essentially in medical administration and not in medical therapeutics; (6) his not joining the American Medical Association until 1930, although he had indicated that such application had been made in 1918 when trying to qualify for a commission. That this part of Sullivan's life involved considerable dissimulation is amply pointed out from the records Perry examined. In this regard it is interesting to recall material cited earlier from what Sullivan wrote about childhood psychopathology in *Personal Psychopathology*:

> In later life the psychopath often comes to be considered a great liar, although this judgment can scarcely survive a close study of his statements. There is little or no clearly conscious determination to deceive to be found behind his apparently fraudulent utterances; if past performances and probably future circumstances can be ignored, the statements of the psychopath are for the most part remarkably well adapted to the immediate interpersonal situation in which he happens to be. Even in the case of the psychopath who cannot be brought to give an authentic account of any of his doings—the so-called *pathological liar*—the intention to deceive is not as conspicuous as is his inability to believe the facts that he has experienced. (Sullivan, 1972, p. 121)

This description may be very revealing of how he was functioning during this period. Detailed knowledge of this sort, without long-term study of this particular process in others, and lack of conscious awareness of its relevance to self, is very likely to be the result of a projection. But one does not have to defend the notion that Sullivan in his adult life displayed psychopathic behaviors. Perry's book contains convincing examples involving his lack of responsibility concerning money and its impact on his relationship to others. An especially poignant instance of this, which would illustrate clearly what he was talking about in describing the relationship between psychopathy and lying, is contained in the incident surrounding his father's funeral when he, by then a prominent psychiatrist, ran up a sizable bill of expenditures and left Smyrna unannounced (Perry, 1982, pp. 306–7). The behavior becomes somewhat more understandable after reading the previous quotation. Pointing out the possibility of a fraudulent acquisition of the medical degree is not intended as a blasphemous act, but rather as an indication of how desperate his life situation may have seemed at the time and how critical the return of self-esteem was to his consequent development.

The possibility of establishing any evidence to support such a conjecture is remote and this adds severe reservations to bringing it to open consideration. Two obvious avenues exist as to how such an event could have occurred. The first would have involved collaboration by an authorized official of the school to have the degree issued without appropriate recourse to official regulations. The second would involve outright forgery. The first of these possibilities would be impossible to investigate more than seventy years later. The second seems somewhat less remote to assess, since a copy of the original document has been deposited, according to Perry, in the files of Loyola University.[10]

### Prelude to the Work at Sheppard and Enoch Pratt

From this review of certain aspects of Sullivan's history which could have led to his development of a set of novel ideas in the treatment of schizophrenia, it would seem as though he was not entirely free of conflict with regard to the direction he would take. While there is nothing in Sullivan's writings that would lead directly to that conclusion, a consideration of several factors would make that seem likely. The conflict I would suggest may have been between what he had learned from the experiences of living, which we have just reviewed, and the promise of what he could learn, contained primarily in the tenets of psychoanalysis. More simply stated, the conflict could be characterized as being between teaching people to deal with life or plumbing the secret recesses of mind. That Sullivan had a continuing interest in psychoanalysis is attested to by the biographers. Sullivan claims to have undergone seventy-five hours of psychoanalysis largely in the winter months of 1917 (Perry, 1982, pp. 167–68), which Chapman seriously doubts (1976, pp. 35–36). Chapman also tells us that during the 1920s Sullivan's published and delivered papers identified him superficially as sympathetic to Freud's position (1976, p. 44). Both biographers tell of his urging his colleague Clara Thompson to pursue her analysis with Ferenczi in Budapest so she could teach him of Ferenczi's new and more compatible approach to psychoanalysis. This Thompson did and returned in the early 1930s to work analytically with Sullivan (Chapman, 1976, p. 53; Perry, 1982, p. 214). Clearly, then, he retained an interest in the products of the unconscious.

The resolution of conflict with regard to his impending work at Sheppard and Enoch Pratt is indicated in one of the rare personal dreams reported in any of Sullivan's work (already briefly introduced in chapter 1). The dream appears in the chapter on sleep, dreams, and myths in *The Interpersonal Theory of Psychiatry* (1953) and is reproduced by Perry in discussing Sullivan's trepidation about the new assignment (1982, pp. 190–91). The dream content, although brief, has the quality of being rather profound and important. When introducing the dream, Sullivan is trying to illustrate the intrusion of dreamlike material into waking life, its relationship to schizophrenia, and the balance in that state between reality and fantasy. A few pages prior he has conveyed a thought which leads directly into the dream. He says, "Quite a number of people who are tense and extremely uncomfortable while awake, have a frightful nightmare one night, which they cannot awake from, even though they objectively 'wake up'; and not very long after that such people become unquestionably schizophrenic throughout their apparent waking life" (Sullivan, 1953, pp. 334–38). Then, a bit later he reports his dream, which I shall reproduce in its fullest context. Perry attributes this dream to the period just prior to his leaving for Pratt, since he refers to Washington in his discussion of his reactions immediately following the dream. The content surrounding the dream, however, seems more indicative of the time when he was already at Pratt and beginning his research. It would be my guess that the recall some twenty years later combined similar feelings that he experienced both before and during the time at Pratt. He writes,

> Some of you will recall having had occasionally an extremely unpleasant dream which awakened you, but did not awaken you completely; in other words, it moved you from deep sleep to very light sleep. The evidence of your still being in light sleep is that while you have every feeling of being awake, and certainly have every freedom of voluntary motion—which is rather strikingly curtailed in anything like deep sleep—you cannot get what you know to be reality to behave. In this connection, I will mention fragments of two or three dreams which come to my mind. One was a dream which I had to undergo very early in my study of schizophrenia, in order to realize that I had some grave barriers to the task which the gods had brought me. To give some background on this dream, I should say that in my very early childhood it was

discovered that I was so repelled by spiders that the body of a dead spider put at the top of the stairs would discourage my ambulatory efforts, which had previously often resulted in my falling downstairs. Now, of course, if one considers that the spider is a mother symbol, and that this occurred around the age of two-and-a-half to four, one can picture what profound problems I had in repressing my hostility to the mother, or something of the sort. But I prefer to say, simply, that I didn't like spiders, and I disliked them so much that I wouldn't pass one. As the years rolled by, I never got fond of spiders. I haven't very much objection to most living things, but I have never appreciated spiders and other predatory creatures of that kind, and I fear I never shall. I had the following dream at the time when it became possible, finally, for me to start on an intensive study of schizophrenia, partly by my own efforts and largely by accident; and I had decided on this study and all the arrangements were satisfactory. You all recall the gometric designs that spiders weave on grass, and that show up in the country when the dew's on the ground. My dream started with a great series of these beautiful geometric patterns, each strand being very nicely midway between the one in front of it and the one behind it, and so on—quite a remarkable textile, and incidentally I am noticeably interested in textiles. Then the textile pattern became a tunnel reaching backward after the fashion of the tunnel-web spiders, and then the spider began to approach. And as the spider approached, it grew into truly stupendous and utterly horrendous proportions. And I awakened extremely shaken and was unable to obliterate the spider, which continued to be a dark spot on the sheet which I knew perfectly well would re-expand into the spider if I tried to go to sleep. So instead, I got up and smoked a cigarette, and looked out the window at one thing and another, and came back and inspected the sheet, and the spot was gone. So I concluded that it was safe to go back to bed. Now, I'm not going to tell you all about what that meant, because only God knows what I dreamed; I've just told you what I recalled. I'm trying to stress the hang-over, the utter intrusion into sensory perception, which required the shaking off of the last vestige of sleep process, the definite reassertion of me and mine, Washington, and what not, in order to prevent the thing from going on. Fortunately, with some assistance, I guessed what might be the case, and thus escaped certain handicaps for the study of schizophrenia. I might add that spiders thereupon disappeared forever from my sleep—so far as I know. (Sullivan, 1953, pp. 334–38)

Perry uses this material very well to illustrate Sullivan's concern about the kind of impact he feared the work might have on his own state of being and the kind of motivation and courage it took to sustain his effort to understand schizophrenic patients. There is, however, much more that is compelling about both the dream material and the associations in which he embedded the retelling, and this requires further examination for what it may reveal about Sullivan and the work at this time in his life.

Let us begin by pointing out what the dream was all about. In this regard, let us stay close to the actual material produced in the dream and the associations and eschew the kind of symbolic interpretation which aroused antipathy in Sullivan. In his explanatory introduction to the dream Sullivan provides us with the following equations: spider = fear, and patterns (textiles) = interest. Furthermore both affects derive from a single object. The first, fear, from the object itself, the second, interest, from that which the object produces. The pursuit of interest, in this instance schizophrenia, leads inevitably to a confrontation with what is feared, one's own propensities in this direction. But where in the dream did it actually lead? To a tunnel reaching backward—perhaps a dark, uncharted course embedded in past time. The pursuit of that interest to its origins or core, and to its relationship to past time, is barred by an overwhelming immediate threat whose fear-generating properties forces one away from that particular avenue of inquiry. If one persists, the fear may pervade consciousness—the spider image on the bed sheet—and precipitate a condition in which reality and fantasy cannot be reliably distinguished, as in schizophrenia. The only antidote presented in the description is one that reestablishes the "real things," smoking a cigarette, looking out the window, so that one again is firmly anchored. At the end of the description Sullivan tells us that although he did not really know what the dream meant somehow he recognized enough about the dangers of the situation to allow him to avoid the dreaded pitfalls. Whatever this secret was, which he with some assistance guessed, he chose not to share it—partly because his ostensible intent in presenting this material was only to illustrate the possible pervasiveness of dream imagery. But perhaps he himself was not fully cognizant of the solutional aspects embedded in the dream and its content, even though his consequent actions would indicate that on some level he had integrated the implied solution admirably. That it was a resolving dream is given by his final bit of communication that spiders then disappeared permanently from his dream repertoire. The resolution was his implicit recognition that his fears would effectively bar him from going where he should not go and thus in order to pursue his interest he need not necessarily delve deeper into the past. He rather needed a firm anchor in the present, in reality, in order to understand and to treat schizophrenia. This then resulted in the wish to study the verbal productions of patients. It also led to the emphasis on dealing with the problems of the here and now. No matter what the origin, he saw two of the major problems of young male schizophrenics as being related to loss of self-esteem generated by poor personal relationships and anxiety arising from homosexual fears. Certainly various aspects of his treatment program were geared to dealing with these reality issues. The role and importance of the real, as opposed to the implied, remained critical for him in his work. It certainly was reflected in his search for the missing "facts" in interviewing, the stress on the larger environmental antecedents of human psychological difficulty, and on the assignment of role of expert to the therapist, who could then feel free to manipulate the environment for the benefit of the patient.

While this analysis highlights some dynamic aspects involved in the evolution of Sullivan's views on schizophrenia and its treatment, it does not intend, either implicitly or explicitly, a value statement regarding whether the true path to the understanding of an individual is to be found in his "unconscious utterings" or in his "interpersonal relations." What is being said is that the path that was set by psychoanalysis proved unappealing for both intellectual and personal reasons to Sullivan, which then led him to focus on relevant matters which he could handle in himself and others without the fear of being overwhelmed. The whole sequence which I have reproduced seems to be indicative of the process. The dream and its associational context is really not considered as primary material from which self-understanding might emerge. In fact, to the contrary, it is seen as being unknowable to man, perhaps known only to God and furthermore full of symbolic nonsense. While it could provide one with hints of things to be aware of, its real value was as an illustration of the intrusiveness of the "unreal" into the "real" world and its possible damaging consequences. The latter is by no means unimportant, but in its exclusivity it leads one away from important data contained in the content of the dream material itself. A further instance of what I am trying to portray, namely Sullivan's avoidance of obvious but dangerous paths, is contained in still another example of his explication of the concept of "selective inattention." The circumstances are somewhat complex and need to be spelled out.

In the lecture material that later became *Clinical Studies in Psychiatry* (Sullivan, 1956), one chapter is devoted to selective inattention, of which concentration without awareness or overconcentration to the exclusion of other input may be typical examples from everyday life. He goes on in this material to trace the process in various more pathological circumstances. In the original lecture, according to the editors of that volume, he included an example of the process of "normal awareness" which concerned an incident of Sullivan's with his father, and which they edited out of the script. They included it, however, as a footnote in a later chapter on dissociative processes because he referred back to the story told earlier. Perry, who was one of the editors of *Clinical Studies in Psychiatry,* included this story in that section of her biography on Sullivan, just after indicating that Sullivan had fully achieved an understanding with his father after his mother's death, in contrast to the distance that had existed between them up until that time. The story unfolds thusly:

> During my father's period of being a widower, I visited him. On this occasion we sat and talked in the room which I had always liked best in the house. In the process, I noticed that the old gentleman was getting a bit distracted. In my usual fashion, I went over the context of our conversation and found nothing at all offensive to him. And so, in the margin of my mind, I grew more and more puzzled over what was clear to me as some unsatisfactory mental state in my father. Finally he said, "Well, what do you think of the wallpaper?" On hearing this question I was able vividly to recall that in an hour and a half's conversation, I had

studied every damned line at which the wallpaper came together. I had not only observed that it was new wallpaper applied since my last visit, but I had made a minute study for any poor workmanship or regrettable defects in its application. But that had in no sense disturbed my consciousness. It required this intervention by my father to attach any awareness in my mind either of the new wallpaper or of the great care with which I had been studying it. (Perry, 1982, pp. 305–6)

This seems like another instance in which the fascination with some process of mind acts to divert attention from some painful aspect of being. He focuses on the unawareness of his studying the wallpaper as being an instance of selective inattention. It is to be wondered if what was being selectively inattended to was the difficulty of the relationship with his father that caused his eye contact to be directed to the wallpaper. Or was the selective inattention really about the impact he had upon the father by staring at the wallpaper during a ninety-minute interaction. The frustration of the experience of the father, given by the apparent non sequitur, "Well what do you think of the wallpaper?" seems evident. The question carries with it the kind of implication of "if you aren't interested in what I'm saying, at least share with me what you think about wherever your interest seems to be directed toward." In some way, ironically enough, Sullivan seems oblivious to the interpersonal implications of the example. In this sense it is very reminiscent of Jung's description, in *Memories, Dreams, Reflections*, of his attendance at the bedside of his dying father, with whom he had not enjoyed a close relationship. He wrote, "A little later I went in to see him again. He was alone, my mother was doing something in the adjoining room. There was a rattling in his throat, and I could see that he was in the death agony. I stood by his bed fascinated. I had never seen anyone die before. Suddenly he stopped breathing" (Jung, 1961, p. 96). Here also was an instance in which the intellectual focus on the process of dying masks the possible affective impact that the meaning of the event could induce.

### Homosexuality and Its Role in Sullivan's Life

A remaining incomplete chapter in trying to understand this man, whose impact on twentieth-century psychological thought was considerable, involves his homosexuality and its relationship to both his ideas and his path through life. Thus far we have traced the relationship between his sexual development and his ideas through the events of his life between 1909 and 1923, from the onset of schizophrenic-like panic with its conflictful homosexual component at Cornell to his ideas for treatment of adolescent male schizophrenics at Sheppard and Enoch Pratt. Within that time period a coherent story has been created from limited bits of evidence. The major features regarding homosexuality are (1) that between 1909 and 1911, when he disappeared, his homosexual panic was resolved through a safe outlet for the satisfaction of genital expression probably under the aegis of an older male, perhaps a physician; (2) that in the ensuing period in medical school, 1911–1915, he lived a homosexual existence with varied experiences, among the working class population where he was accepted and perhaps even admired; (3) that in the period 1915–1917, after he left medical school, he had a meaningful sexual relationship with a comrade in the National Guard, which was eventually exposed and led to his dismissal from that service; (4) that his first opportunity to relate his own experience with homosexual panic to the experience of others occurred in the winter of 1917 when he might have been hospitalized for severe depression in a Chicago mental institution; (5) that by this time, 1917, he was twenty-five years of age and more or less reconciled to live out a homosexual existence, although he saw this as a partial but understandable failure in his own psychological development; and (6) that with the status and self-esteem that accrued from his position as a physician he became more circumspect about his homosexuality and channeled his knowledge about this subject into his theoretical views about personality development and the nature of schizophrenia and its treatment.

Although it is now commonplace information, since the recent biographical publications, that Sullivan's life experience included a dominant homosexual pattern, this was known only to a few of his close friends both during and after his life. While it is thought that his sexual preference was suspected by many, there was a great reluctance to accept this idea, certainly by those who were influenced by his work. How pervasive this reluctance was may be illustrated by some material appearing in 1976 under the title *A Harry Stack Sullivan Case Seminar* (Kvarnes and Parloff, 1976). In this book five sessions of a case seminar supervised by Sullivan in 1946–47 are reproduced from edited recordings and are then commented on by a group of trained professionals some twenty-five years later. The editor, Robert G. Kvarnes, was a participant in both phases of the work. During the final seminar session in the original series a group of more general questions were put to Sullivan to reap the benefit of his expertise. In one, the central point involved what Sullivan thought about his relationship to the patient as part of the therapeutic process. His answer to this question, and both the flavor and content of the discussion many years later, will prove instructive to the point I am making. Sullivan's answer was:

> This question is practically answered in the psychiatric interview course. I have come to define my role as that of expert with client. Nothing more and nothing less, but to be expert in psychiatry. I have to handle the patient in a fashion that works. It is nothing that I will fight about but I insist that this is my role. Because I set up this role for myself, I have been able to avoid two of the great evils that complicate psychotherapy. I learned to avoid the first by a ghastly disaster, and that is, do not permit anybody to develop transcendental expectations of you. Another patient is in a state hospital because I permitted that boy to develop transcendental dependency. All I have to offer is skill, and as the years roll over me I find it is best to offer just that. That does not necessitate rebuffs or anything. The relationship of psychiatrist to patient is that of expert to client. The expert has continuously to act like an expert. I can't take time out and act like a damn fool. *I can't be lover and friend and whatnot, unless I expect to devote the rest of my life to that patient, and even that does not work out well* [emphasis mine].
>
> Because of increasing firmness in holding to that type of relationship, the solution of the transference, resolution of the transference, which is so important in certain psychotherapeutic problems, has, I think, in my case, usually preceded the appearance of the transference. *Just as when the gay and wealthy woman patient gallops in and announces, after two or three interviews, that she is madly in love with me, she hears me muttering in my corner, "You may find it a little difficult in my case, baby"* [em-

phasis mine]. We have obsessional enough processes and if you do try to be the good father or mother or some damn thing, it is welcome, and I have no doubt when you get bored with it, or can't get the patient to pay for it, then it needs some attention, but if you go to a lawyer to have some business handled, Christ, he doesn't have to resolve the transference at the end of the transaction. If you go to have your watch repaired, you don't have to fall in love with the watchmaker. People come to me to have difficulties in living untangled—that is what I do. Sure they are interested. Who the hell is not, and I think well of them, but no—no, not that! I am glad to have a question about my role. It is, insofar as I know, a person who keeps track of what he is supposed to be doing, and it is not getting involved in anything except transient disorders which require being dealt with, *and I toss out another hint which might be relevant to homosexual panic. Not uncommonly with schizophrenics, with extreme chagrin they announce some desire for genital intimacy with my person, to which it is traditional that I say, "I know I would enjoy it, but it would gum up the work terribly and the work is more important." They sometimes try to pursue it under pressure, but my pose is unalterable. "Sure, I think zonal pleasures are all right, but I am selling expert service and not having a good time." It works if you get used to it. I may add that I go to considerable trouble to let them know that I would have no objection at all except that it would interfere with the work, and I mean it, what the hell!* [emphasis mine] (Kvarnes and Parloff, 1976, pp. 215–16)

It would not be too difficult to extract a hypothesis about a homosexual resolve on the part of the narrator if one compared Sullivan's response concerning interest in sexual liaison with male and female patients, especially not difficult for people who are trained to comb material for implied but not clearly expressed meanings. Let us then look at how this material struck the members of the group reviewing it some twenty-five years later.

In explicating the way that Sullivan structured the therapeutic relationship as one of an expert to a client, one participant quotes only the opening portion of the material I have just cited, ending at the point at which Sullivan introduces the transference material from the female client. There follows a brief discussion of a technical point about transference, which then leads to the quoting of the material about the female patient ending with Sullivan's comment "You may find it a little difficult in my case baby!" The interaction proceeds from there as follows:[11]

> Participant A: Don't know what the hell that says.
>
> Participant B: I don't know what the hell that says either.
>
> Participant A: He knows he's not lovable among other things.
>
> Participant B: What he's referring to is the earlier spot that links up with that, "Due to certain idiosyncracies of personality, I feel at no particular disadvantage in dealing with homosexuals. I have in fact due to those circumstances, discovered that homosexuals have one of thirty-two different types of problems!" Now what the hell is he saying there? What are the idiosyncracies of personality he is talking about?
>
> Participant C: The mythology about Sullivan has something to do with being a homosexual, functioning as one, or something like that. The data are awfully sparse. I don't know of any instances of acknowledged homosexual relationships.
>
> Participant A: I think that no one knows, but it does seem more like a myth, since you would assume that there would be some evidence. I think that what he is alluding to there is the fact that he found himself one of the few people who was genuinely at home in this area—that is, he was not put off by homosexuality. He could stay with it, and share the experience of what homosexual experience was like, I think to a greater extent than many other people at that time. Or even now, for that matter—it's not easy to stay with that kind of thing. I think he was sort of bragging about that.
>
> Participant B: Bragging about it in that kind of way would tend to develop the myth.
>
> Participant A: *One of the phenomena about Sullivan is that, despite this vague myth, no one really wants to know, and no one pushes the point.* [emphasis mine]
>
> Participant C: But I think that in the revival of interest in Sullivan which I certainly experience—the William White group is busy with it and something is going on here in Washington—there has

been a time interval and a lot of this has sort of settled down and become sort of "so what" data.

Participant A: I agree with you, that kind of stuff is not going to be important about Sullivan.

Participant C: But that is the kind of question that gets asked, "Was Sullivan a homosexual?"

Participant B: And was he schizophrenic?

Participant C: And was he an alcoholic? I'm afraid what a lot of people do with that process of applying a disparaging label is that they then unfortunately discount the person and his work—a lot of this type of discounting of Freud occurred when the evidence of his own psychoneurosis came into the picture in various biographies.

Participant A: But that's why that kind of question is asked; it's easy to discount the person's ideas when you say somebody is homosexual, schizophrenic, alcoholic.

Participant B: There is the other side of that, though, which is trying to understand what it takes to be able to understand other people—you have to be one to know one.

Participant A: That's another myth about Sullivan. That he could understand the sick ones because of his proximity to schizophrenia.

Participant C: Let me take a shot at these "labels." That Sullivan had strong schizoid and obsessional features in his personality I don't think anyone would dispute. As far as I can determine, there was no schizophrenic break requiring hospitalization or treatment in his adolescence. His history from medical school on is well documented. That's all I can say about the myth of Sullivan's schizophrenia. *Concerning the homosexual label, it is true that Sullivan never married nor apparently could he tolerate being around the hysterical type of woman. As I said, I know of no evidence of homosexuality as practiced by Sullivan. I can't help wondering whether his formulation of how the male arrives at adolescence emotionally unprepared to assume the male role in an intimate relationship with a woman didn't pertain to Sullivan himself* [emphasis mine]. As far as the disparagement about "alcoholic" goes, as I understood and remember it, Sullivan had had a couple of coronary accidents, which probably accounted for his taking small drinks of brandy throughout the day in his later years. In all the gossip I never heard one account of Sullivan's being drunk. So I think this unconventional pattern of nipping on brandy got incorporated in some people's need to cut him down. Goodness knows, he was irascible and cutting enough to have hurt a number of his colleagues' feelings.

Participant B: Let me try a different kind of thought. . . . (Kvarnes and Parloff, 1976, pp. 224–26)

I have reproduced this lengthy episode to try to highlight how important the homosexuality issue remained in Sullivan's later life. Furthermore, I wish to conjecture about its relationship to what I have already suggested as one of the most important dynamics in Sullivan's life, the maintenance of self-esteem through the recognition by others of what he "knew"—and its corollary, the fear of loss of status and its derivative, self-esteem, through failure. The former is a thumbnail description of a major script of his early life, the latter a similar summary of some of the salient experiences of the adolescent years, the Cornell and the National Guard "incidents." A later life analogue was the fear that his professional status would be discredited by an exposure of his homosexuality, what he openly considered a "failure of development."

The major thing I would like to extract from the material cited is that there remained always around Sullivan a kind of tension concerning his homosexuality, a tension that existed in him and in those with whom he interacted. He both wanted others to know, in order for him to be free, and feared the consequences to his freedom if they were in fact to know. This resulted in hints, veiled references, the citing of experiences which were his own but attributed to others.[12] What I mean by this is that some of his closest friends knew and this made no difference in their assessment of his professional contributions. This is the kind of freedom he may have wished for from the world in general and led to the plethora of veiled references in his remarks. Yet he was not unaware of the harshness of moral authority. He was angered by it and at the same time fearful of its possible consequences and thus felt that he could not afford to reveal himself openly.[13] On the other hand, the people with whom he communicated were puzzled by these somewhat cryptic references. In one sense the references were too obvious and thus not above suspicion. In another sense they were threatening, for all of the reasons cited as pertaining to what others would think. Sullivan probably knew and feared that no matter what conscious attitudes others displayed toward homosexuality, he would lose regard in their eyes and the value of his contributions would be reduced. The reluctance on the part of the discussants to face the obvious is clear. Perhaps it is because the destruction of the hero by people who identify with him is a serious and distasteful task to be avoided at all costs, including denial, rationalization, and other typical defensive operations. On Sullivan's part the conflict between the wish for freedom and the fear of the consequences of exposure may also have been contributing factors in his limited public output of theoretical work during his lifetime. He had no problem in "testing exposure" to relatively safe groups through the spoken but somewhat "embedded" word, as material reproduced from his supervision session demonstrates. Recording was the perfect compromise between telling and not fearing the consequences. It would remain ready to be heard by sympathetic listeners.

## Two Important and Enigmatic Male Relationships in Sullivan's Life

### A. Clarence Bellinger

No discussion of the importance of the issues surrounding homosexuality in Sullivan's life can by-pass an examination of Sullivan's relationship to his boyhood chum, Clarence Bellinger, about which Perry and Chapman have much to say and Chatelaine less (Perry, 1982, chapters 10, 11, 15, 34; Chapman, 1976, pp. 22–23; Chatelaine, 1981, pp. 34–37). These biographers clearly differ in how they structure the early relationship, which has in turn some bearing on how they see the origin and patterning of Sullivan's sexual preferences in later life. Bellinger and Sullivan were closely related as children but completely alienated from one another as adults. Why this was so is not fully understood.

The basic elements of the relationship which seem incontrovertible are that Sullivan's and Bellinger's lives intersected in the fall of 1900 when Sullivan was eight and a half and Bellinger five years older. By the following fall, when Bellinger began to attend the local school regularly, he and Sullivan traveled together in Bellinger's horse and buggy to and from school each day. There is some evidence that they shared common interests in books and were especially allied despite the differences in their age. They were the only Catholic children in a village school attended exclusively by Protestants. From what we know this arrangement continued until 1906 when Bellinger graduated from the local school and entered Syracuse University Medical School. Various avenues of data point to the now accepted view that they were both "outsiders" among their school peers and that both were intellectually superior to the others, a superiority which they took no pains to hide. As far as we can ascertain they remained friends in the two years between Bellinger's graduation and that of Sullivan, and no one has pointed to any clear breach in their interaction with one another during this or any other time. The prevailing image of the relationship is one of a dominating older boy to a bright, shy, and somewhat subservient younger boy. Chapman, in his description of this period in Sullivan's life, depicts the relationship as actively homosexual (pp. 22–23). His supporting evidence (not documented) comes from the expressed views of people in their home community, as well as Sullivan's writings on preadolescence and adolescence, especially as they emerged in his earlier, long unpublished, and thinly disguised autobiographical book *Personal Psychopathology*. Chatelaine, who disagrees with Chapman, cites counter evidence that there were those in the community who did not even consider Bellinger and Sullivan good friends (1981, p. 36). In his view the relationship was probably nonsexual.

Perry also argues quite differently from Chapman. She is much more persuaded, because of the inhibitions fostered by the mothers of the two boys about sexuality, their particular personality constellations, and certain salient and repeated pieces of evidence from Sullivan's writings, that the relationship was asexual (1982, chapters 13 and 34). She feels that, as a function of the lack of previous sexual experience, Sullivan arrived at Cornell in 1908 totally naive about sex, a late bloomer whose genital desires blossomed in this new atmosphere. Further, she conjectures that his attempts at sexual gratification with others led to rebuff, which increased his solitary fantasy attempts at gratification and eventually led to his panic state.

The differences in these views are not unimportant in trying to understand Sullivan's struggle in his adolescent years. Chapman's view would more likely lead to a script based on fixation. That is to say that if the relationship with Bellinger was an enduring one which had led to sexual gratification, this would lead to an attempt to reproduce it in kind in the outside world. It would suggest the image of a somewhat sophisticated homosexual sixteen-year-old boy rejected by agemates who had moved beyond him to heterosexual interests. The consequent rejection could then have led to his panic. The implication of a fixation hypothesis, however, is that he would have been led in the future to reproduce that idealized first relationship.

Thus we have two different images projected by the biographers. My reading of Chapman would present Sullivan in 1909 as a person with an extensive homosexual history with Bellinger, acutely anxious about school failure but capable of rapid recovery, which allowed him to work productively for the better part of two years to earn money for medical school.

My reading of Perry would lead me to a sexually naive, disorganized seventeen-year-old in homosexual panic whose difficulties were severe and extended in origin; one who was probably hospitalized consequently and perhaps even treated by a sympathetic psychiatrist. Can a review of the known data help us ascertain whether the relationship was sexual and why it had such an alienated outcome?

We have already established that Bellinger left Smyrna in 1906 for medical school, returned each summer at least until Sullivan left for Cornell in the fall of 1908, and that there was no known breach in the relationship. What then could have occurred to produce a rift between them which seems to have lasted from sometime after Sullivan left home throughout the remainder of their lives, despite the fact that they both pursued life careers in psychiatry and both remained connected to Smyrna through family long into their adult years? Perry is not unmindful of this problem and in one way or another treats it at great length. Her intention is to show that the basis of Bellinger's constant and unrelenting disparagement of Sullivan all through their adult lives was Bellinger's jealousy over Sullivan's success. She begins this journey with Bellinger's upset in 1908 after returning from the completion of his second year of medical training to be faced with Sullivan's publicized successes, namely his being the valedictorian (in a class of three) at graduation and his successful competition for a state scholarship to Cornell. The jealousy path then winds through Sullivan's special relationship in the 1920s to William Alanson White and Ross McClure Chapman, prominent psychiatrists to whom Bellinger had been exposed earlier without creating any undue positive impression, to Bellinger's jealousy over Sullivan's receiving greater recognition for his research, as evidenced by the absence of a clearly relevant Sullivan paper in a Bellinger bibliography. Without stating it overtly, Perry buttresses her argument by embedding this fanatical jealousy in the envelope of an unenviable character structure (Perry, 1982, chap. 34). This message is driven home relentlessly in the descriptions attending Bellinger wherever he appears in the book. No other character's personality is either so carefully and repetitively scrutinized; in fact there is not even a serious rival in this regard. No other character is painted in such consistently negative terms and no other character's possible positive attributes are consistently diminished by comparison either with Sullivan or some implied standard. This was especially striking to this reader in that it seemed such a departure from the tone of the rest of the book. The work is, overall, such a testament to the devotion to scholarship that it tends to illuminate any material that seems to be seriously overinterpreted.

If we try to characterize Bellinger's attitude toward Sullivan in their adult lives, it is given in a quotation cited by Perry. It is attributed to Bellinger in speaking to others about Sullivan and says he was "a homosexual and a son-of-a-bitch" (Perry, 1982, p. 313). That simple declarative statement contains a great deal of possible meaning which may help us to reflect on what that relationship was like in light of the various things that were attributed to it. What does it tell us about whether the relationship was sexual or not? On the one hand, it reduces the possibility that this was the case, at least in the sense of an open, acknowledged, sexual relationship between consenting parties. Since Bellinger was not known to be openly homosexual in his later life,[14] and in fact is painted in many ways as being defensively straight (Perry describes his unusual attention to administrative order, and his underdeveloped, eunuchlike physical appearance), it seems highly unlikely that he would be continually calling attention to anyone's homosexual status if he were a closet homosexual. In another sense it may relate back to the suspicion about the relationship held by the townspeople as referred to by Chapman. The statement then has the flavor of "you see, it was him and not me." This in fact may be a more defensible image of what actually transpired between them as delayed inhibited adolescents, namely that the sexual experiences were sporadic, furtive, almost fuguelike in quality, and largely initiated by a small, curious boy attempting to show his love for a chum in the way that he as an adult defined love. If this was the situation between them it would fit with the attribution of homosexuality made by others, Bellinger's alleged character structure, and the manner in which he later referred to Sullivan.

Bellinger's statement about Sullivan may also be analyzed with regard to Perry's attribution of extreme jealousy. It should be expected that somewhere in the characterization of Sullivan by Bellinger themes of jealousy would emerge if that motive was paramount. One would expect the imagery to contain expressions in which Sullivan displaced others by unfair means or was given things by others which he did not deserve. This does not seem to be the case. The imagery appears to be angry, derogatory, and strongly suggestive of an unclosed wound, as though the evil person had done something to the declarer which violated his values and was never rectified. Since we don't know of any such instance that took place during the period before Sullivan left for Cornell, let us speculate that it could have happened in the so-called "two missing years," 1909–1911, when Bellinger was in his last year of medical training at Syracuse or later in his first job at St. Lawrence State Hospital. If in fact there was no clear breach in the relationship before Sullivan left for Cornell, it doesn't seem too unlikely that he might have sought refuge after leaving Cornell in disgrace, with the one long-term friend that he had while growing up. It also appears possible that Bellinger might have been prepared to help a friend in need. Despite the generally negative picture of Bellinger that emerges from Perry's data, she also describes him as a person who devoted his life to the service of others, who felt some sense of alliance with attendants and patients as a hospital administrator, and who left his accumulated assets to those who were deserving and less fortunate than he was. There is a piece of incidental data which suggests the possibility that Bellinger might have had additional contact with Sullivan during that time. Perry refers to a statement by Kempf (a psychiatrist whose writing influenced Sullivan), which she conjectures came originally from Bellinger, ascribing the writing of bad checks to Sullivan at an earlier age (Perry, 1982, p. 313). If the reporter was indeed Bellinger it follows that he would have been the recipient of such knowledge if he was a victim. It would also account for the appellation "son-of-a-bitch," one who would take advantage of the kindness of a friend. Thus a possible sequence emerges. Sullivan could have visited Bellinger during the period in question, shared with him some aspects of his homosexual struggle, and taken money from him which he covered with a worthless check. That Sullivan was capable of such behavior is well documented in Perry's honest journey through his life. Only two instances need be cited at this juncture to make the point, although others are interspersed in Perry's narrative. One concerns the already discussed incident of the unpaid bill that he ran up in connection with his father's funeral. The other refers to his borrowing of money from a relative to pay for an expensive dinner to which he had invited her in New York in the 1920s, only to renege on the payment which he had promised to be immediately forthcoming (Perry, 1982, pp. 211–12). For anyone to do this sort of thing to Bellinger, whose need for order, sense of righteousness, and propensity for anger were great, it could easily have led to a continued feeling of outrage which was refueled by sporadic events in Sullivan's life which were known publicly and thus inevitably known by Bellinger. Two such events may have been the recognition that Sullivan was receiving for the work at Pratt, especially as it related to the treatment of incipient psychotics through attempting to relieve homosexual panic, and the news of his declared bankruptcy in New York City in the early 1930s.[15] Since Sullivan's reputation in Smyrna remained suspect from 1909 throughout most of his life, jealousy alone seems hardly enough to explain the strength of Bellinger's unrelieved negative expression. Some personal insult appears a much more tenable source to account for Bellinger's continued outrage.

Before leaving the Sullivan-Bellinger relationship, one other point that appears frequently and prominently in Perry's analysis of their interaction deserves comment. It concerns the fact that Bellinger seems to have taken every opportunity to tell people that he knew Sullivan in their formative years and followed this by impugning his character, while Sullivan on the other hand never let on to anyone that he ever knew Bellinger, even when a seemingly appropriate occasion

arose (Perry, 1982, p. 313). Perry offers an implicit logic for this difference which in its simplicity is somewhat suspect. She attributes it
mostly to Bellinger's negative character structure on the one side and
to Sullivan's benign, almost innocent need to preserve in his imagery
the idealized figure of his first and perhaps only chum. The behavioral
differences that she points out are very striking and seem like over-
statements for both participants. Bellinger's response I have already
attempted to explain in previous passages. Sullivan's response of silence bears further scrutiny for what it may indicate about important
aspects of his personality.

In trying to understand the use of silence about things for which
silence is not expected, and how it may have operated in Sullivan's life,
I combed through the various biographical sources hoping to find a
clue. One appeared in something that Perry wrote which may, when
added to her image of Sullivan's sensitive side, make the picture more
complete. In discussing his bankruptcy episode in 1932 she wrote, ". . .
and he was declared bankrupt. But the problem was not over; it embarrassed him for the rest of his life, although *he maintained a rather
stoic front on the subject*" [emphasis mine] (Perry, 1982, p. 320). While
Perry may have intended my underlined portion to mean brave and
unemotional, it also has the implied meaning of bearing pain silently.
Since she ties his behavior to embarrassment it does not seem unlikely that in general his response to embarrassment was silence. If he
had in fact done anything earlier to justify Bellinger's rage, it would not
be too surprising that he was silent about that relationship. It would
also make sense of the fact that almost no data about specific people
seemed to flow from Sullivan's imagery regarding the period from
1908 until his appearance in Washington more than a decade later. It,
too, may have been, as I have already suggested, a period of embarrassment for him. Perhaps the most persuasive bit of evidence in this line
of reasoning comes from such an obvious source that it is very likely to
be overlooked. We know that a profound and traumatic source of
embarrassment for him was the combined set of events surrounding
his year at Cornell. School failure, accusation of criminal action, and
severe psychological distress, each in itself a possible effective source
of shame, when combined might have had devastating impact. These
events were followed by a symbolic "silence" of two years, in that he
never really disclosed what had occurred during this period. We have

then uncovered two forms of silence, lack of disclosure (verbal silence) and disappearance (physical silence).

### B. James Inscoe Sullivan

Perhaps the most important and unanalyzed aspect of the story of Sullivan's homosexuality and its role in his mature years requires an understanding of his life with James Inscoe Sullivan, the most constant source of human concern and human interaction in the final twenty-two years of his life. This we may never have unless the only living participant chooses to share his memories with the world. That he may be reluctant to do this is implied by the fact that Perry certainly knew and had access to James Sullivan and also knew how considerably he shared in Sullivan's life, yet in her acknowledgments he is cited for allowing permission to use certain documents and for preparing useful memoranda on different establishments in which they lived. As a source of information about Sullivan's life and personality he undoubtedly could be invaluable, yet very little that is terribly personal about their life together was revealed by him to Perry.[16] Chatelaine, who also used him as a source, fared no better.

It is of some fascination that although all three biographers were fairly certain that Sullivan had had homosexual encounters, and that he had not achieved a heterosexual resolution in his interpersonal life, none of them opens the question of Sullivan's relationship to James Inscoe as it influenced his later life. Perry has characterized the relationship as basically a helping one in which the dominant helping role was somewhat reversed over time. It was known that James Inscoe had begun his association with Sullivan in 1927, when Harry was thirty-five and James fifteen. It was furthermore established that James at the time was in severe psychological distress, perhaps suffering a schizophrenic episode, and that Harry was treating young male schizophrenics at Sheppard and Enoch Pratt Hospital. It was at that time that James became a permanent member of Sullivan's household. Since we are in possession of much information about Sullivan's views of male adolescent schizophrenic and homosexual panic, and we are also informed about Sullivan's own sexual progression by examining his writings on adolescence, it seems reasonable to believe that the issue of homosexuality had to be an important one between them, no matter how it was resolved, either at the beginning or over time. In Chatelaine's account of the latter years of Sullivan's tenure at Sheppard Pratt, he presents testimony from former employees that they believed Sullivan to be homosexual and in fact involved at the time with a male secretary of his, someone other than James Inscoe (1981, p. 450).

There are two bits of esoteric and apparently unrelated information that may be helpful in pursuing the issue of Sullivan's relationship to "Jimmie," as he was most often called. One is contained in a long book review that Sullivan published in the *American Journal of Psychiatry* in 1927 on the social adjustment of the male homosexual. Perry does an excellent analysis of this review and its information about Sullivan's life at that time. She points out that he was rather convinced that a person with a homosexual resolve that produced reasonable satisfaction would not be likely to change after age thirty (he was thirty-five when this was written). Of more critical importance is the sentence from the book that so impressed him that he quoted it in his review: "In the whole series of parallels between the invert and the normal man there is none more striking nor more pitiful, than the invert's attempt to find peace and satisfaction in the achievement of a permanent union with some similarly conditioned man" (Perry, 1982, p. 339). This was written around the time when James Inscoe came to live with him and may very well reflect the difficulties he was experiencing in establishing what was to become a permanent union.

The second bit of data that may be of value was uttered by Sullivan twenty years later, less than two years before he died. He is responding to a question on the therapist-patient relationship, the entire response to which I have reproduced earlier in another regard. Here I wish to recall but one sentence: "I can't be lover and friend and whatnot, *unless I expect to devote the rest of my life to that patient, and even that does not work out well*" (Kvarnes and Parloff, 1976, p. 216) [emphasis mine]. We must remember that this is a spontaneous response to an unanticipated question. The answer is quite relevant and general until the point where I have indicated emphasis. From then on it takes on a different flavor, as though after having made a general statement, there is recalled to mind the limiting case and its consequences from personal experience.

Why then did the biographers, and his colleagues, despite the multitude of possible cues, offer a benign interpretation of the relationship? There are of course countless reasons that one could generate which relate to matters of privacy, discretion, evidence, and impact, and any of them could easily act as a deterrent. However, on a more subtle level, there may have been more powerful influences operating which were, by design or otherwise, generated by Sullivan. The first of these is indicated by the almost immediate familial designation, variously described as "son," "foster son," or "adopted son" assigned to Jimmie by Sullivan. Chapman, in his three limited references to Jimmie, calls him Sullivan's son once and his adopted son twice, and his work was published in the mid-seventies. Chatelaine follows a similar pattern. Yet Perry, after years of devotion to the search for verified biographical material, informed us that no legal adoption ever took place although it was assumed by all (1982, p. 209). She does not speculate about why not. The second bit of evidence was the insistent designation of Jimmie by Sullivan as a former patient long after that label was of any real identifying use. How important it was for him to identify Jimmie this way is portrayed very well by the events surrounding his entry in *Current Biography, 1942*. This entry, attributed to Sullivan, is a rose-colored and somewhat distorted history, not too uncommon, perhaps, which ends with a sentence that introduces Jimmie for the first time. The sentence is embedded in a present description of Sullivan, his home, and his interests, and reads as follows: "There his avocation is breeding day lilies, and there *his adopted son, Jimmie, a former patient* [emphasis mine] helps him to look after his two Cocker Spaniels and his other pet, a handsome mutt of none-too-clear ancestry" (Sullivan, 1942, p. 814). Perry indicates that Jimmie was not too happy in typing this description of himself and registered some protest, but to no avail (Perry, 1982, p. 209). It is rather difficult to understand what could have prompted one to maintain such accuracy within a self-description that in itself contained false embellishments and distortions. This is especially true when one considers Sullivan's definition of love and the importance he attached to interpersonal relationships.[17] One hypothesis that would at least make sense is that the communication was intended to avoid any sort of suspicion about behavior that could lead to a loss of self-esteem. In that one sentence the name Jimmie is bracketed by two descriptions, one a mild distortion (adopted son), the other an unnecessary and possibly painful identifier (former patient). Think now of the probability that anyone would suggest the possibility of an intimate liaison between the writer and his son who was also his former patient. The multiplicative inhibitory potential of incest, violation of professional ethics, and homosexuality, especially between father and son, is staggering. This was probably the first time that Sullivan was exposing this relationship for all the world to know.

I have gone into this incident and its possible implication at some length for one specific purpose, to indicate the continuing struggle that Sullivan endured with regard to the specter of homosexuality and its possible effects on his life and career. It is not even important to know whether the relationship with Jimmie was sexual. If it was, he would fear detection, and if it wasn't, sexuality might be falsely suspected. In either case it would loom as an important element in his existence. If we use the content of the material from the book review and from the earlier discussion of countertransference as the anchoring points in this relationship, we might be led to believe that it may have changed over time with regard to its possible sexual component. The first, written in 1927, is filled with awareness of difficulty, but hope for positive outcome. The second, spoken twenty years later, indicates resignation over negative outcome.

### The Intellect-Self-Esteem Script: Review and Summary

Although we have considered various aspects of Sullivan's life (and commented on what seemed to be residual questions unresolved by the biographers), it has been a circuitous journey. Thus I wish now to return to what I believe is central in the understanding of his life—his struggle to maintain self-esteem. At this point it is necessary to recall the importance that Sullivan ascribed to the role of self-esteem in the development of personality. It is also essential to remember that Sullivan saw this attribute as the product of the reflected appraisal of others. As Perry clearly intimates, and Chatelaine as well, his major source of self-esteem as a child stemmed from his intellectual ability, which was recognized both by intimate family members and teachers. This recognition from others sustained him in the face of interpersonal difficulties with rejecting age-mates. In some sense the culmination of his intellectual efforts was embodied in his winning of a state scholarship to Cornell in 1908. It was a rare and celebrated event in the town of Smyrna, New York.

The first major crisis of his life followed within a year of this great success when he was dismissed from Cornell for academic failure. No matter what led to the failure—and there has been considerable speculation by the biographers, from too much sex to too little sex to a brush with the law—the result had to be a loss of self-esteem. Failure erased the possibility that the significant others would continue to reward him for intellectual achievement, and in his history there were no clear alternative gratifiers for its maintenance. This was an enactment of a nuclear scene. The ensuing struggle to regain self-esteem was chronicled in the events of the next eight years, complicated by a concomitant bout with emerging sexuality which also had secondary implications for his feelings about self. Nevertheless, I would strongly argue that without intellectual failure his difficulty in sexual adjustment would not have led to crisis, as indeed the events of his later life indicated. In his own thinking, stated in various places, the inability to achieve heterosexual gratification was a *failure in ultimate development.* Yet despite continuing difficulties in this regard, he avoided the crises that were apparent in the critical years 1909–1918. Crisis, in his case, refers to a scriptlike pattern that contains the following ingredients. In the first instance, there is failure connected with intellectual achievement, or, analogously, failure to live up to an expected role that was conferred by such achievement. This failure is then followed by disquieting negative affect (of different descriptions at different times) which culminates in silence and/or disappearance. The sequence is continued by a new attempt to reestablish self-esteem. During the nine-year period in question, we have three instances in which the same script was lived out. In the first two the attempt at reestablishing self-esteem failed, beginning the sequence anew. In the third, the outcome was successful and the pattern was not lived out in major proportions again. Let us retrace these various steps in somewhat more detail.

The dismissal from Cornell, from a variety of accounts reported by Perry, led to psychological distress (perhaps extreme anxiety or depression or both), which was then followed by a two-year disappearance, the end of which was marked by an attempt to regain self-esteem by his entry into medical school. The sequence might have been successful had he graduated in 1915, but this was not the case. Obviously his lack of completion of tuition payments was not the only reason for failing to graduate with his class. It is clear that he did not meet all the academic requirements, another failure in his scheme of things. The events following this, a six-months work period in industrial medicine which is later reported as a period of unhappiness (disquieting affect) leads to another disappearance of four months, which is followed by an attempt to regain self-esteem by enlisting in the National Guard as a sergeant in a medical unit. This five-month interval is pictured as one filled with positive affect, a not too frequent occurrence in Sullivan's story. It also unfortunately ended in failure, initiating the third example in this repetitive script, one whose content is a bit more speculative, as I have already indicated earlier, and one worthy of retelling.

The first part of the sequence involves failure, in that he was discharged from the Guard for medical reasons of unknown origin, which I have considered to be related to the discovery of his homosexuality. That the following period, early 1917, was one of affective distress seems to have good support. It was the period in which he claimed to have had seventy-five hours of psychoanalysis. I have also considered the possibility earlier that the distress of failure might have been complicated by the loss of an intimate other and resulted in severe depression. The period from November 1916 through the winter of 1917 is largely unaccounted for. It is another of the disappearances, leading to the conjecture of many that he may have been hospitalized. The new movement toward the return of self-esteem involves his successful effort to obtain his medical degree, which was granted in September 1917, under mysterious circumstances. From then on, with the status conferred by the medical degree, even though he drifted from the military in World War I to some attempts at independent consultative work, to a succession of government medical administrative positions before arriving at Sheppard and Enoch Pratt in December 1922, he showed no signs of the pattern that dominated his life from 1909 to 1917. In fact, by the time he was at St. Elizabeth's in 1921–22 he is characterized by William Alanson White, the head psychiatrist, as keen, alert, and witty, with a facade of facetiousness, and perhaps an underlying discontent. This is hardly the picture of a panic-stricken, depressed, or schizoid person, the condition more likely seen after his failures.

What is important to see here is that failure of any kind was not sufficient to initiate the script, since we can point to failure connected with his leaving Sheppard and Enoch Pratt in 1930. He was denied the directorship of the new research wing which he had helped plan, a position which he had been led to expect. Furthermore, he was taken to task over his irresponsibility in the handling of institutional funds. This was not, however, failure in intellectual achievement, the necessary condition for the emergence of the script. His reputation by that time was established in psychiatric circles both for his research reports on his therapeutic work and for his work on national administrative committees. The list of important people writing in support of his being licensed for practice in New York (despite his lack of qualification) attests to the high esteem in which he was held, and in turn the high esteem in which he held himself (Chatelaine, 1981, pp. 509–18). That the script did not entirely disappear, however, or at least could be recognized in microcosmic form, can be attested to by a later incident described by Chatelaine. He writes, "The difficulty and complexity of Sullivan's thinking and writing is well known. Dr. David McK. Rioch, a close friend and colleague of Sullivan's who worked with him at Chestnut Lodge, a psychiatric hospital in Rockville, Maryland, tells the following anecdote. Rioch said to Sullivan: 'Harry, why the blazes can't you write so people can understand you?' Sullivan's response was to abruptly leave the party" (Chatelaine, 1981, p. 3). The sequence of loss of self-esteem through intellectual failure followed by embarrassment followed by disappearance is obvious. The fear of the depreciation of his work by the detection of his homosexual life pattern would then have posed a great problem, especially if silence and/or disappearance were its typical solutions.

Harry Stack Sullivan's life was lived with a fair amount of mystery, which until recently has hardly been probed. Various people, the biographers, colleagues, friends, all in good faith, have attempted to fill in the missing pieces or at least speculate on the basis of certain bits of evidence as to what might have been the case. There are, unfortunately, at this point not too many people who can still provide data which might prove clarifying. Perry has indicated that she is in possession of some such unreported material, as has Chapman. The most important link, however, is James Inscoe Sullivan, who, although he at times has intimated an intent to share his knowledge, has thus far chosen not to speak.

To review hidden aspects of another person's existence and speculate on their meaning is not a task to be taken lightly. This is especially so when the material from which inferences are drawn is sparse. In dealing with people who have made intellectual contributions to knowledge there is also the feared consequence, often expressed, that the evaluation of the work may be confounded by moral or ethical judgments about the lived life. The major intention of this review of some aspects of Sullivan's life was to increase our understanding of the relationship between his life and his work. Aware of the extent to which difficult problems have been aired, I am reminded of the closing statement in Aldo Carotenuto's recent book, to which I heartily ascribe. After reviewing the intimate relationship between Jung and Sabina Spielrein, a former patient and later colleague, from letters recently brought to public attention, he said, "As for us, who have flung open secret doors, nothing remains but to live with greater humility" (1982, p. 214).

### Epilogue

In expressing my views on the study of an individual, I have emphasized the extraction of the dynamic sequences (mainly unconscious) which can direct, regulate, or govern existence. Most frequently these scripts contain nodal or nuclear problems which a person engages all too often in the life history and with varying degrees of success. In one sense, they are the core units of the psychotherapeutic search. Despite the attraction of this analogy, the study of personality, especially in the personological mode, cannot be left as a byproduct of psychotherapy. In such an instance the emphasis, if history serves us well, is likely to remain on psychopathology. We are more likely to focus on what is problematic in the individual and how to fix it rather than on what is productive and how it got to be that way. Obviously both aspects and more are needed to understand how any individual personality functions. I raise these issues to point out the danger inherent in focusing on the understanding of some cryptic aspect of a life already lived or a life in progress. The outcome of that investigation may be unwittingly magnified by the writer or reader to represent the totality of that personality. To see Freud as nothing more than the outcome of an unresolved struggle over the loss of the mother would be a gross oversimplification, a tragic impediment to understanding the complexity of his personality development. The same would obviously be true of the scriptlike aspects we have discussed in reviewing the lives of Jung and Sullivan. What I wish to recall, however, is a point I made earlier in introducing the methodology which I employ. The method by no means restricts the user to the extraction of important negative dynamic sequences. Positive scripts are likely to be found as well in the personality. In still another vein, we must remember that either positive or negative outcome may be the result of either positive or negative antecedents. From the data of lived experience, one can study any aspect of personality to which one is directed in accord with any predilection one has about personality theory.

# NOTES

### 1 A Personological Approach to Personality Assessment and Psychobiography

1 The term is used here to indicate nonsequitorial aspects of communication rather than in the psychoanalytic sense of the separation of affect from cognition in imagery. The process would be largely covered by "omission" in this schema.

2 The story is as follows: The woman's husband was getting ready to leave the house when she asked where he was going. He told her that he had a few things to finish up in the office and thought he would go back. She turned to him saying that she was lonely and thought he should stay. He responded by turning away from her and telling her that he was tired of hearing about what she wanted. There was something about his action that produced a gnawing reaction in her stomach. Was he growing tired of her? She quickly smiled and reassured him that his work was important to her as well. She asked him to regard her request as giving in to a childish whim. He left seemingly mollified. She cried.

3 This may have resulted from a study done on selection data at that institution. I have not been able to locate such evidence. For a clear discussion of this issue, see Landy and Trumbo (1976), chap. 6.

### 2 A Format for Teaching Personological Inquiry

1 This work was exemplified in chapter 7 (The Case of Earnst) of Murray et al. (1937), *Explorations in Personality.*

2 Princeton undergraduates in those years were exclusively male.

3 On occasion a set of rating scales for characterological assessment (Schafer, Zimet, Levin, and Prelinger, 1958) has also been used.

### 3 The Freud-Jung Relationship: The Other Side of Oedipus and Countertransference

1 The list of contributors to this literature is extremely long and attests to the importance of the two men and their ideas. The most thorough and comprehensive efforts on Freud's life are those by Jones (1953, 1955, 1957), Schur (1972), Roazen (1975) and Gay (1988). Jung, who died in 1961, twenty-two years after Freud, has not

yet had "the definitive biographer," partly because he dictated an autobiographical volume before his death. Among the recent attempts, Barbara Hannah and Marie Louise Von Franz, long-time Jungian disciples and friends, have added considerably to our knowledge of Jung's life (Hannah, 1976; Von Franz, 1977). Wehr (1985, 1987) has joined the growing list of biographers.

2   Jung was actually preceded by another child who died in childbirth. Thus he was the first surviving child.

3   From an analysis of early memories reported in his autobiography of interactions with male authority figures (father, teacher), we may derive the abstraction that authority is associated with dogma and truth with self (Jung, 1961).

4   The attitude is symbolized in the oft told story of Freud's disappointment with father's unheroic response to a gentile who knocked his cap from his head and uttered anti-Semitic remarks (Freud, 1958, p. 197).

5   Jung's suffering from childhood eczema may be one indication of this anger. Certainly his numinous image of an all-powerful figure dropping a turd on the church (father was a minister) could be construed as a sign of this negative affect (Jung, 1961, pp. 8, 39).

6   Freud's early heroes as reported by Jones were Hannibal and Alexander the Great (Jones, 1953, vol. 1).

7   This statement is based on the deference shown Fliess in their correspondence. Fliess, who was younger, was treated as the one with real originality and creativity while Freud's own efforts were frequently depreciated. This attitude was not a general feature of Freud's personality, as revealed by his voluminous correspondence with a host of accomplished people. Freud's inferior role in the Fliess relationship, or Fliess's transference properties were already recognized by Buxbaum and by Van Der Heide some thirty years ago (Buxbaum, 1951; Van Der Heide, 1952).

8   Jones in volume 2 indicates that there was every reason to believe that Moses was of tremendous significance to Freud. He then asks, "Did he represent the formidable Father-Image or did Freud identify himself with him? Apparently both at *different periods*" (Jones, 1955, p. 365 [italics mine]). Wallace (1977) analyzes the psychodynamic determinants of *Moses and Monotheism* and relates them to the unresolved aspects of Freud's Oedipal problem.

9   As Roazen points out, Freud himself later alludes to the "religious movement" aspect of psychoanalysis as reported by Ludwig Binswanger in discussing the defections of Jung and Adler from Freud (Roazen, 1975, p. 244).

10  Shades of father and orthodoxy!

11  I am here using the language of Tomkins as expressed in his "script theory" of personality (Tomkins, 1979) and explicated by Carlson (1981).

12  The difference between the two men's attitude to the death of the father may be instructive on this point. Jung, as a medical student, witnessed his father's last moments and remembered many years later his attitude as one of curiosity and interest in the death rattle of the father. As he remembered the period, after the death he moved into father's room and assumed father's position regarding money. Two consequent dreams were recalled in which father was not dead. In one Jung was

concerned that father would be upset for having been displaced in his room. But this was not the case (Jung, 1961, p. 96). In all it does not seem as though the father's death presented any great emotional upheaval for him. On the other hand, the death of Freud's father when Freud was already forty years of age released in him strong hidden affects and wishes which he detected through an analysis of his dreams.

13  The theme of displacement also had an infantile root in Freud's life. The birth and death of a male sibling within two years of his own birth was reviewed in Freud's self-analysis. However, the theme did not reappear permanently until later life. Its appearance at that time had little of the flavor of a sibling situation, much more that of a parent-child interaction.

14  The postscript to Freud's autobiographical study, added in the 1935 edition, is interesting in this regard: "This autobiographical study shows how psychoanalysis came to be the whole content of my life and rightly assumes that no personal experiences of mine are of any interest in comparison to my relations with that science" (Freud, 1935).

15  Freud's overconcern with authority is documented in Jung's memoirs in recounting their trip to America in 1909. In analyzing each other's dreams Jung asked Freud for some additional personal material, to which Freud is reported to have refused with the statement, "But I cannot risk my authority" (Jung, 1961, p. 158; Billinsky, 1969, p. 43).

#### 4  If Freud Were Moses

1  *Moses and Monotheism, Standard Edition,* vol. 23, pp. 7–137.

2  In the years since its publication in 1939, *Moses and Monotheism* has attracted the attention of many scholars from many fields. Initial reviews of the work came from theological, psychological, sociological, anthropological, psychoanalytic, and Judaic sources. The thrust of the evaluations was generally negative, or at best tolerant even when offered by psychoanalytic colleagues. The basic intrapsychic themes dealt with are those related to Freud's Jewishness and to his struggle with the father in the resolution of the Oedipal conflict. Many have postulated that an apostatic wish on Freud's part is reflected in this book. Others have tied the work to his fear of death. That the book was in part occasioned by Hitler's rise to power in Germany was recognized early and accepted by most scholars. This essay will speak to all of these issues.

3  For more extensive reading on the psychology of "scripts," see S. S. Tomkins, "Script Theory," a paper presented at the annual meeting of the Society for Personology, Asilomar, June 1984. See also "Script Theory: Differential Magnification of Affect," in H. E. Howe, Jr., and R. A. Dienstbier (eds.), *Nebraska Symposium on Motivation,* vol. 26 (Lincoln: University of Nebraska Press, 1979). Chapters 1 and 2 of this volume also deal with this concept.

4  This is true until the third part of *Moses and Monotheism,* which was the most problematic for Freud. It is a point which will be addressed later in this essay.

5 This attitude may be gleaned from Freud's discussion of the development of psychoanalysis, especially Breuer's role as discoverer, in chapter 2 of *An Autobiographical Study* (1925/1935).

6 The outer calm was in no way indicative of dismissal. Over and above the works clearly identified as related to the defections ("The Moses of Michelangelo" and *Totem and Taboo*), Silverstein (1986), attributes some of the motivation for Freud's twelve consequent metapsychological papers (of which seven were never published) to answering the defector's criticisms of psychoanalytic theory.

7 This statement is offered with full knowledge of Freud's well-documented concern with predicting the date of his own death, especially the prediction for age fifty-one (1971). Schur (1972) deals with this issue extensively and Silverstein (1986) reveals it as a possible motivator for the metapsychological series written in 1915. Schur (1972), p. 5) refers to this propensity in Freud as having "a mildly superstitious-obsessive character." My statement refers to Freud's physical state in 1913 compared with his physical state in 1934.

8 Letter to Marie Bonaparte, March 16, 1933, quoted in Jones, vol. 3, p. 175. Also letter to Ferenczi, April 2, 1933, quoted in the same volume of Jones, pp. 177–78. Also H. Nunberg's *Memoirs*, quoted in Roazen, p. 532.

9 Certainly the major biographers, Jones (1953, 1955, 1957), Schur (1972), Roazen (1975), and Gay (1988), have made this point, as well as Bakan (1958), Wallace (1977), Fromm (1958), Sachs (1941), Puner (1947), Oehlschlegel (1947), Robert (1976), and others.

10 See Editor's Note, *Moses and Monotheism*, S. E., vol. 23, pp. 3–5.

11 Trude Weiss-Rosmarin (1939) in her book *The Hebrew Moses: An Answer to Sigmund Freud* devotes the first chapter to this point.

12 An addition to the third essay was written in the summer of 1938 after his arrival in London.

13 The evidence for the first two points are found in Jones, vol. 3, p. 124, the third in S. Freud, *An Autobiographical Study*, p. 14; the fourth point is a derivative of the third.

14 *Moses and Monotheism*, p. 55.

15 The issue of Freud and his Jewishness has attracted a multitude of scholarly comments. A large group of writers following the publication of *Moses and Monotheism* and Freud's death interpreted the work as indicative of Freud's wish for apostasy. Among the early proponents of this hypothesis were Rosmarin (1939), McLean (1940), Velikovsky (1941), and Puner (1948). An early counter to this view was provided by Sachs (1941, 1944), who maintained that Freud believed in assimilation without apostasy. The matter lay fallow for some years, touched off again largely by the publication of two books. One was Bakan's volume (1958) which revived the apostatic wish thesis but this time from the standpoint of Freud's relationship to Jewish mysticism. The other was the long-awaited third volume of the Jones trilogy which dealt extensively with *Moses and Monotheism* and its meaning for Freud. Jones had responded in part to Velikovsky, Oehlschlegel, and Puner in volume two. The arguments were extended and buttressed in the final

book. Jones was thoroughly negative to the idea that Freud at any level harbored an apostastic wish. A position similar to that of Jones may be found in Schoenwald (1956) and Roback (1957). The unconscious wish to reject Judaism is implied in F. Alexander (1938). More recently the discussions of Freud's Jewishness emphasize the ambivalence that he suffered, somewhat more representative of Sachs's view, although the hidden wish to renounce is not overlooked: Roazen (1971), Bergmann (1976), Falk (1977). Oring (1984) returns strongly to Freud's hidden wish to reject his Jewishness. Wallace (1978) points this out more subtly. Gay (1988) in an extended biographical study has presented the most complete set of data bits relating to Freud's Jewishness since the Jones volumes. He, like Jones, tends to minimize the conflictual aspects of the picture, although a review of the data he cites at various places in the book would lead me to believe otherwise.

The position that I have taken on this issue is that *Moses and Monotheism* did not reflect a wish for apostasy on Freud's part since that wish had been fulfilled more than thirty years before when psychoanalysis began to take form as an organizational structure. The doctrine as it developed took on the trappings of a religious movement, an attribution made by many observers. This position will be referred to at other points in this essay.

16  This translation is similar to the ones made by Fromm (1958, p. 58), Bakan (1958, p. 148 ff), and Puner (1947, p. 180).

17  For an extensive review of the Jewish position in Freud's Vienna and Freud's own ethnic background, see the first three chapters in D. B. Klein, *Jewish Origins of the Psychoanalytic Movement* (New York: Praeger, 1981).

18  In real life and at different times, these were his wife Martha and psychoanalysis. The relationship between the two will be explored at a later point in this essay.

19  In 1908, in a letter to K. Abraham quoted in part in E. Jones, vol. 2, pp. 49–50, he says, "You may be sure that if my name were Oberhuber my new ideas would despite all other factors have met with far less resistance." Seventeen years later in a paper entitled "The Resistances to Psychoanalysis" he publicly acknowledged that "anti-Semitic prejudices concerning his person might be a contributory reason for there being so much opposition and for the unpleasant form it so often took" (E. Jones, vol. 3, p. 117).

20  The translation of "his people" to "his interpersonal struggles" is pointed to by his struggle with his Jewishness (his people), a symbol for all things over which he suffered conflict or ambivalence.

21  See "On the History of the Psychoanalytic Movement," *Sigmund Freud: Collected Papers*, vol. 1 (New York: Basic Books, 1959), pp. 287–99. For the comparison, see S. Freud, *An Autobiographical Study* (London: Hogarth Press, 1935), chap. 2, pp. 31–49 (also in *S. E.*, vol. 20).

22  This position is elaborated in the second essay, "If Moses Was an Egyptian," and repeated in part at various points in the third essay.

23  With this analogy we have now introduced the hidden aspects of this work which ostensibly deals with the role of the father as socializer, whether in the history of mankind or the history of individual man. How this work relates to the role of the

mother will become more apparent as the analysis continues. The major features of salience to be noted are omission and distortion, leaving out the female role when its inclusion is demanded and attributing to father that which in every way has been connected previously to the mother.

24 Most of the incidents recorded by the biographers about Freud's father and their early relationship would support the general overevaluation of the mother and the devaluation of the father.

25 Although the material on death wishes toward parents in *The Interpretation of Dreams*, pp. 255–67, and in "The Origins of Psychoanalysis," pp. 307–8, speak of the widespread dreams of death of parents, Freud acts as though a death wish toward the father is a logical derivative rather than an insight about his own relationship to father which was garnered through the analysis of one of his own dreams.

26 Two of the more prominently mentioned goals were a professorship and the Nobel Prize, one of which, the professorship, he did achieve with some outside help. See Jones, vol. 2, p. 19 and vol. 3, pp. 137, 139, 152, 202, 207, 233–34.

27 See M. Schur, *Freud: Living and Dying*, chap. 14, for an extended discussion of this issue.

28 Excellent summaries of her complex qualities are found in Roazen (1975, pp. 45–46) and in Gay (1988, p. 504).

29 Most writers dealing with Freud's life follow his lead and stress the father-son relationship. Jones, in volume 2, p. 409, however, calls attention to a missing factor in the analysis of Freud's personality, namely his deep love for his mother, which he concealed from self and others. Erich Fromm, in *Sigmund Freud's Mission* (1959), picks up Jones's hint and devotes a brief chapter to the discussion of Freud's relationship to his mother. In it he emphasizes the depth of the attachment to the mother and the impact it had on Freud's life. He cites the need for unconditional love, affirmation, admiration, and protection that began in the mother relationship and Freud's attempts in later life to reproduce this with his wife and with older men, contemporaries, and disciples.

Perhaps the most penetrating analysis of Freud's early relationship with his mother and its impact on his personality appears in a well-hidden section of S. S. Tomkins, *Affect-Imagery Consciousness: The Negative Affects*, vol. 2, 1963, pp. 511–29. Tomkins uses Freud's chapter 33, on "Femininity," in the *New Introductory Lectures* (1933) as a projective instrument and points out the centrality of the loss of the mother for Freud and its reverberations on his affect and imagery as these manifest themselves in his theory and in his later relationships. This analysis makes clear the origin of Freud's complex attitudes toward women as reflected both in his theory and in his life.

Among the major biographers Roazen in *Freud and His Followers* (1973) does more with the mother's role in Freud's personality than either Jones or Schur. Roazen cites Fromm's analysis and adds to it the fear of loss of that which was rightfully his (psychoanalysis) as an analog resulting from the loss of the mother by the birth of siblings. A few years later Stolorow and Atwood, extending the lead provided by Tomkins, analyze historical material of Freud's early life with special emphasis on the relationship to his mother. They argue that his inability to recognize the negative aspects of that relationship are reflected, in part, in his theory of psychosexual development, a "defensive-restitutive effort by Freud to protect an idealized image of his mother against profound unconscious ambivalence." This material is found in chapter 2, "Sigmund Freud" in R. D. Stolorow and G. E. Atwood, *Faces in a Cloud: Subjectivity in Personality Theory* (New York: Jason Aronson, 1979). Still another proponent of the underplayed role of the mother is Peter Gay in the most recent biography of Freud (1988). In a section entitled "Woman, the Dark Continent," he reviews various aspects of Freud's relationship to his mother, also calling to attention various places in Freud's writings where the role of the mother is obviously neglected. Gay indicates that Max Schur, in a letter to Ernest Jones in 1955, also pointed to neglected aspects of the women's role (see pp. 503–7).

30    This attitude was present even in the last year of his life. It is clearly indicated in two communications on anti-Semitism written in 1938 that appear in *S. E.*, vol. 23, pp. 289–92 and 301. In the one (which Jones conjectures is written by Freud) Freud quotes an unrecoverable source, a non-Jew, writing in defense of the Jews. In the other his imagery moves suddenly to an old French saying which is translated as,

> A fuss becomes the fop
> A fool's complaints are heard
> A gentleman betrayed
> Departs without a word

31    This point will be elaborated in a later section of this essay. The decline of his own sexuality, roughly at age forty, coincides with the beginning of what emerged as the core of psychoanalytic theory.

32    An example of this is given in my analysis of the Freud-Jung relationship; see chapter 3.

33    The analysis provided by Tomkins and by Stolorow and Atwood (see note 29) speak affirmatively to this question.

34    The evidence for the awareness of his distortion of the relationship with father is contained in a letter to Fliess on October 3, 1897. The relevant content of this letter will be quoted in another context at a later point in this essay (Bonaparte, A. Freud, and Kris, 1957, p. 222).

35    Jones, vol. 2, p. 375, pointed out that Freud came to a different position about the impact of his brother's death. In *"Dichtung und Wahrheit,"* discussing sibling rivalry, Freud comments on the fifteen-month difference in age between Goethe and his next sister, Cornelia, "This slight difference in age almost excludes the possibility of her having been an object of jealousy. It is known that, when their passions awake, children never develop such violent reactions against the brothers and sisters they find in existence, but direct their hostility against newcomers." Are the hard-won insights (1897) always subject to disappearance with time (1917)? Or was his memory of brother Julius nothing more than a screen for his anger toward

sister Anna, born when he was two and one-half? The latter possibility has been pointed out by Schur, p. 341. Yet fifteen years later, in 1932 in *The New Introductory Lectures*, in the chapter on femininity, he was certain that an eleven-month-old child could detect the loss of maternal care by the birth of a sibling, a return to his original position.

36 In a further interpretation of Freud's "Irma" dream Elms had also brought to attention the displacement aspect in the relationship between Freud and Martha during those years. A. Elms (1980), "Freud, Irma, Martha: Sex and Marriage in the 'Dream of Irma's Injection,'" *Psychoanalytic review* 67:83–109.

37 In its major outlines one can trace Freud's struggles during the sixteen-year period of the letter exchange. In the early years, 1887 to 1893, he seems to be somewhat subdued, needing a friend, and in his own mind not very active in his scientific work. That period of time is also characterized by the paucity of the exchange compared with the accelerated activity in the comparable period that followed. Those first seven years produced 33 letters from Freud out of a total of 284 in existence. In the next six years, 1894 to 1899, the number written by Freud was 229. They were filled with theoretical speculations and personal disclosures which had a much more alive, exciting quality about them. One could see internal, intellectual ferment around the problems presented by his patients, his own personal problems, and the derivation of a set of principles by which he could understand both. He progressed from trying to understand the neuroses to trying to understand himself, then to explicating the chief method for how one could understand the neuroses or a neurosis, the dream life.

38 See Draft B, 8/2/93, "The Aetiology of the Neuroses," in Bonaparte et al. (eds.), *The Origins of Psychoanalysis* (1957), especially the remarks about the tolerance of normal men. In addition, the point about Freud's sexual relationship with Martha has been explored at great length in a paper by Elms (1980) (see note 36).

39 The undiscovered anger toward mother as a central factor in Freud's development and in his theory is made by both Tomkins (1963) and Stolorow and Atwood (1979) (see note 29).

40 Paul Roazen's *Freud and His Followers* (1975, pp. 419–88), more than any other biography, speaks clearly to Freud's relationship to all the significant women in his life. Peter Gay (1988) devotes an extended section of a chapter on the relationship of Freud's inner life to his work to the issues relating to "woman, the dark continent."

41 Even the Oedipus myth which Freud used so extensively contained in his rendition a fair amount of poetic license distorting the role of the father. The story begins with a father's fear of displacement, which implies the loss of the object. Oedipus is never threatened by the father with castration; he inflicts retribution upon himself. Furthermore, Oedipus does not seek out his mother as a lover; she is given to him as a prize for his intellectual achievement, solving the riddle of the Sphinx. What is perhaps similar in the Freud and Oedipus stories is the ignoring of any essential role of the mother in the unfolding tale. Perhaps that is what added to its attraction.

42 Also in *The Future of an Illusion* (1927) and *Civilization and Its Discontents* (1928).

### 5 C. G. Jung: The Man and His Work, Then and Now

1 The memory is likely of an interview with Jung filmed for the BBC by Laurens van der Post.

2 The story was told in a seminar given by Hannah which I attended while on a sabbatical leave. The year was 1954–55; the place was the Jung Institute, Zurich.

3 One can infer this from the letter from Jung to Freud (McGuire, 1974, pp. 534–35) written one year to the day before Jung's Siegfried dream. In it he berates Freud openly (a marked change in Jung's usual correspondence demeanor) for taking unfair advantage of his "pupils"—treating them as patients. Jung clearly lays the blame on Freud for what has happened to change their relationship.

4 In chapter 3 this difference between Freud and Jung is traced in their attitudes toward their work and is attributed to the differences in their relationship to their mothers.

### 6 On the Life and Work of Harry Stack Sullivan

1 Chatelaine reproduces a letter written by the eminent psychiatrist Roy R. Grinker, Jr., in 1977, in response to an inquiry by Chatelaine regarding Sullivan's Chicago medical days. Grinker says in part, "I did not know Sullivan while he was in Chicago. . . . When I met him in later life, I felt he was schizoid or a schizophrenic" (Chatelaine, 1981, p. 486). See also Kvarnes and Parloff, 1976, pp. 224–26.

2 In describing Gregory she states, "Gregory, who was only five feet tall *and remained a lifelong bachelor* [emphasis mine], had a sensitive feeling for patients, and as an immigrant, a special understanding of the difficulties of transition to another society" (Perry, 1982, p. 153). The underlined portion of the description is also one she uses for Sullivan and Bellinger, whose histories were plagued with rumored allegations of homosexuality.

3 A clear example of this may be found in discussions about Sullivan's personality in *A Harry Stack Sullivan Case Seminar*, edited by R. Kvarnes and G. Parloff. See pp. 201–35 and especially pp. 225–26. (Kvarnes and Parloff, 1976).

4 Chatelaine places the broken jaw incident some two years later, in 1918, on information from James Inscoe Sullivan (Chatelaine, 1981, p. 273). H. S. Sullivan may have told him that he sustained the broken jaw while riding in the military, which James took to mean in 1918 since Sullivan's sojourn in the National Guard was kept quiet.

5 Earlier we mentioned J. I. Sullivan's disclosure to Perry of H. S. Sullivan's alleged despair at the death of a friend from medical school, a matter which Perry's investigations failed to confirm.

6 Incidentally, it is interesting in this regard that Perry, who seems to have been especially careful to note every return of Sullivan to Smyrna after leaving there in 1908, reports no visits between 1911, when he left for Chicago, until January 1918. The implications of his absence could be very important. Aside from the fact that he had little money, which could have accounted for some enforced absence, it is

quite likely that continuing shame about the Cornell incident, and lack of obvious signs of accomplishment which could have mitigated the shame, could have kept him away until he had a medical degree.

7 Probably the sum was in the neighborhood of $100 to $200, since tuition was $100 per year and initial admission and yearly readmission probably depended on some payment of fees.

8 In this regard his setting it at seventy-five hours of analysis is interesting. It would either mark fifteen weeks at five meetings a week, or roughly thirteen weeks at six meetings a week, the work week at that time of a hospital psychiatrist—in either case reasonably close to the confines of the winter season. The limited time sequence hardly seems consonant with psychoanalytic practice and rather supports the view that he was hospitalized.

9 Perry, in discussing the various name emphases that Sullivan used at different times in his life, e.g. H. F. Sullivan, H. Stack Sullivan, Harry Frances Sullivan, etc., says, "Finally he would settle on the name Harry Stack Sullivan, with no M.D. after his name on most letters after the 1930's" (Perry, 1982, p. 170).

10 Chatelaine for some unexplained reason has chosen to reproduce a copy of Sullivan's medical degree in an appendix of his book.

11 In the original the participants are identified by name.

12 See, for example, his references to early and later sexual experiences of preadolescent groups he claimed to have studied (Sullivan, 1953, p. 158; Sullivan, 1972, p. 171). In these instances the identifying locale of the groups changed but the material remained the same.

13 Clear examples may be found in his exposure of attitudes toward immorality by a social worker and also by a policeman in *Personal Psychopathology* (Sullivan, 1972, p. 360).

14 The only evidence to the contrary is that suggested by Sullivan in his description of the outcome of the "outsiders" in the Kansas and/or mid-east (N.Y.) preadolescent group to which we have referred earlier (Sullivan, 1953, p. 158; Sullivan, 1972, p. 171). If the stories are autobiographical, as some have surmised, then the two social isolates, who are described as homosexuals in adult life, would likely be Sullivan and Bellinger.

15 It is reported by Chatelaine that Adolph Meyer, the psychiatric leader at adjacent Johns Hopkins, was reluctant to send patients to Sullivan at Pratt because of the taint of homosexuality that attended Sullivan's special unit. It is likely that such news was known in psychiatric circles (Chatelaine, 1981, p. 406).

16 Perry quotes J. I. Sullivan as saying that if he reported on their life together "he would have no reminiscences left to write about" (Perry, 1982, p. 209).

17 In *The Interpersonal Theory of Psychiatry* (1953), when introducing the concept of love, he writes, "What should I do to contribute to the happiness or to support the prestige and feeling of worthwhileness of my chum?" (p. 243). He indicated that love existed when the needs of the other became as important as one's own.

# REFERENCES

Abraham, H., and Freud, E. (eds.) (1965). *The Letters of Sigmund Freud and Karl Abraham.* New York: Basic Books.

Alexander, F. (1957). The neurosis of Freud. (Review of vol. 3 of the Jones biography of Freud.) *Saturday review of literature* 40 (November 2): 18–19.

Alexander, I. E. (1988). Personality, psychological assessment, and psychobiography. *Journal of personality* 56: 265–94.

———. (1985). On the life and work of Harry Stack Sullivan: An inquiry into unanswered questions. Working paper. Presented at the annual meeting of the Society for Personology, Chicago.

———. (1984). C. G. Jung: The man and his work, then and now. Address presented at the American Psychological Association annual meeting, Toronto, August. Also in *Resources in education,* June, Microfiche ED252791.

———. (1982). The Freud-Jung relationship: The other side of Oedipus and countertransference: Some implications for psychoanalytic theory and psychotherapy. *American psychologist* 37: 1009–18.

Allport, G. W. (1965). *Letters from Jenny.* New York: Harcourt, Brace and World.

———. (1942). *The use of personal documents in psychological science.* New York: Social Science Research Council.

———. (1937). *Personality: A psychological interpretation.* New York: Holt.

Allport, G. W., Vernon, P. E., and Lindzey, G. (1960). *Study of values.* 3d ed. Boston: Houghton-Mifflin.

Anderson, J. W. (1981). Psychobiographical methodology: The case of William James. In L. Wheeler (ed.), *Review of personality and social psychology.* vol. 2. Beverly Hills: Sage.

Bakan, D. (1958). *Sigmund Freud and the Jewish mystical tradition.* Princeton: Van Nostrand.

Baldwin, A. L. (1942). Personal structure analysis: A statistical method for investigation of the single personality. *Journal of abnormal and social psychology* 37: 163–83.

Beck, S. J. (1944). *Rorschach's test I: Basic processes.* New York: Grune and Stratton.

Bellak, L. (1975). *The T.A.T., C.A.T., and S.A.T. in clinical use.* 3d ed. New York: Grune and Stratton.

Bergmann, M. S. (1970). Moses and the evolution of Freud's identity. *Israel annals of psychiatry and related disciplines* 14: 3–26.

Billinsky, J. (1969). Jung and Freud. *Andover Newton quarterly* 10: 39–43.

Block, J. (1961). *The Q-sort method in personality assessment and psychiatric research.* Springfield, Ill.: Charles C Thomas.

Bonaparte, M., Freud, A., and Kris, E. (eds.) (1957). Sigmund Freud, *The Origins of Psychoanalysis: Letters, Drafts, and Notes to Wilhelm Fliess, 1887–1902.* Trans. E. Mosbacher and J. Strachey. Garden City, N.Y.: Doubleday Anchor Books.

Bromley, D. B. (1977). *Personality description in ordinary language.* New York: Wiley.

Buck, J. N. (1966). *The House-Tree-Person technique revised manual.* Beverly Hills: Western Psychological Services.

Buxbaum, E. (1951). Freud's dream interpretation in the light of his letters to Fliess. *Bulletin of the Menninger Clinic* 15: 197–212.

Carlson, R. (1986). After analysis: A study of transference dreams following treatment. *Journal of consulting and clinical psychology* 54: 246–52.

———. (1981). Studies in script theory: Adult analogs of a childhood nuclear scene. *Journal of personality and social psychology* 40: 501–10.

Carotenuto, A. (1982). *A secret symmetry.* New York: Pantheon Books.

Carson, R. (1969). An introduction to *MMPI* interpretation. In J. N. Butcher (ed.), *MMPI: Research development and clinical application.* New York: McGraw-Hill.

Cattell, R. B., and Stice, G. F. (1957). *Handbook for the sixteen personality factor questionnaire.* Champaign, Ill.: Institute for Personality and Ability Testing.

Chapman, A. H. (1976). *Harry Stack Sullivan: His life and his work.* New York: G. P. Putnam.

Chatelaine, K. (1981). *Harry Stack Sullivan: The formative years.* Washington, D.C.: University Press of America.

Cuadra, C. A., and Reed, C. F. (1954). An introduction to the Minnesota Multiphasic Personality Inventory. (mimeo).

Demorest, A. (1987). *A study of recurring messages in individual imagery.* Ph.D. dissertation, Duke University.

———. (1985). A theory of leitmotifs. Unpublished major area paper, Duke University.

Elms, A. (1980). Freud, Irma, Martha: Sex and Marriage in the "Dream of Irma's Injection." *Psychoanalytic review* 67: 83–109.

———. (1972). Allport, Freud, and the clean little boy. *Psychoanalytic review* 59: 627–32.

Exner, J. E. (1974). *The Rorschach: A comprehensive system.* New York: Wiley.

Falk, A. (1977). Freud and Herzl. *Midstream* 23(1): 3–24.

Fransella, F., and Bannister, D. (1977). *A manual for repertory grid technique.* London: Academic Press.

Freud, E. L. (ed.) (1970). *The letters of Sigmund Freud and Arnold Zweig.* New York: Harcourt Brace Jovanovich.

———. (1964). *The letters of Sigmund Freud.* New York: McGraw-Hill.

Freud, S. (1964). *Moses and monotheism.* In J. Strachey (ed.), *The Standard Edition of the Complete Psychological Works of Sigmund Freud.* Vol. 23. London: Hogarth Press and the Institute for Psychoanalysis.

——. (1959). On the history of the psychoanalytic movement. In *Collected papers*. Vol. 1. New York: Basic Books.

——. (1959). The Moses of Michelangelo. In *Collected papers*. Vol. 4. New York: Basic Books.

——. (1959). Negation. In *Collected papers*. Vol. 5. New York: Basic Books.

——. (1958). *The interpretation of dreams*. New York: Basic Books.

——. (1953). *Civilization and its discontents*. Trans. J. Riviere. London: Hogarth Press.

——. (1952). *A general introduction to psychoanalysis*. Trans. J. Riviere. Garden City, N.Y.: Garden City Books.

——. (1938). *Psychopathology of everyday life*. In A. A. Brill (ed. and trans.), *The basic writings of Sigmund Freud*. New York: Modern Library.

——. (1938). *Totem and taboo*. In A. A. Brill (ed. and trans.), *The basic writings of Sigmund Freud*. New York: Modern Library.

——. (1935). *An autobiographical study*. London: Hogarth Press.

——. (1927). *The future of an illusion*. In *Standard Edition*. Vol. 21.

——. (1917). A childhood recollection from *Dichtung und Wahrheit*. In *Collected papers*. Vol. 4.

Fromm, E. (1958). *Sigmund Freud's mission*. New York: Harper.

Gay, P. (1988). *Freud: A life for our time*. New York: Norton.

Glover, E. (1950). *Freud or Jung*. New York: Norton.

Gough, H. G. (1957, 1964, 1988). *California psychological inventory: Manual*. Palo Alto: Consulting Psychologists Press.

Gough, H. G. and Heilbrun, A. B. (1965). *Adjective check list manual*. Palo Alto: Consulting Psychologists Press.

Grinstein, A. (1968). *On Sigmund Freud's dreams*. Detroit: Wayne State University Press.

Hannah, B. (1976). *Jung, his life and work*. New York: Putnam's.

Hathaway, S. R., and McKinley, J. C. (1943). *The Minnesota Multiphasic Personality Inventory*. Minneapolis: University of Minnesota Press.

Henry, W. E. (1956). *The analysis of fantasy*. New York: Wiley.

Horowitz, M. J. (1979). *States of mind: Analysis of change in psychotherapy*. New York: Plenum Medical.

Jaffé, A. (1971). *From the life and work of C. G. Jung*. Trans. R. F. C. Hull. New York: Harper and Row.

Jones, E. (1959). *Free associations: Memories of a psycho-analyst*. New York: Basic Books.

——. (1958). The birth and death of Moses. *International journal of psychoanalysis* 39: 1–4.

——. (1957, 1955, 1953). *The life and work of Sigmund Freud*. Vols. 1, 2, and 3. New York: Basic Books.

Jung, C. G. (1971). *Psychological types*. Vol. 6. In H. Read et al. (eds.), *The collected works of C. G. Jung*. Trans. R. F. C. Hull. Princeton: Princeton University Press.

——. (1961). *Memories, dreams, reflections*. New York: Pantheon Books.

——. (1953). *Two essays on analytical psychology*. In H. Read, M. Fordham, and

G. Adler (eds.), *The collected works of C. G. Jung.* Vol. 7. Trans. R. F. C. Hull. Princeton: Princeton University Press.

——. (1916/1949). *Psychology of the unconscious.* Trans. B. M. Hinkle. New York: Dodd, Mead.

——. (1925). A view of the field of analytical psychology. 1925 seminar notes. Unpublished manuscript, on file in the library of the Jung Institute, Zurich.

——. (1918). *Studies in word-association.* Trans. N. D. Eder. London: Routledge and Kegan Paul.

Kelly, G. A. (1958). Man's construction of his alternatives. In G. Lindzey (ed.), *Assessment of human motives.* New York: Rinehart.

——. (1955). *The psychology of personal constructs.* New York: Norton.

Klein, D. B. (1981). *Jewish origins of the psychoanalytic movement.* New York: Praeger.

Kvarnes, R. G., and Parloff, G. H. (1976). *A Harry Stack Sullivan case seminar.* New York: Norton.

Lamiell, J. T. (1981). Toward an idiothetic psychology of personality. *American psychologist* 36: 276–89.

Landy, F. J., and Trumbo, D. A. (1976). *Psychology of work behavior.* Homewood, Ill.: Dorsey.

Leary, T. (1957). *Interpersonal diagnoses of personality.* New York: Ronald.

Lewin, K. (1935). The conflict between Aristotelian and Gallilean modes of thought in contemporary psychology. Chapter 1. In *Dynamic theory of personality.* New York: McGraw-Hill.

McCullers, C. (1940). *The heart is a lonely hunter.* Boston: Houghton Mifflin.

McCurdy, H. G. (1961). *The personal world.* Chapter 12. New York: Harcourt, Brace and World.

McGuire, W. (ed.) (1974). *The Freud-Jung letters.* Trans. R. Manheim and R. F. C. Hull. Princeton Bollingen Series. Princeton: Princeton University Press.

McLean, H. V. (1941). A few comments on "Moses and monotheism." *Psychoanalytic quarterly* 9: 207–13.

Morgan, C. D., and Murray, H. A. (1935). A method for investigating fantasies: The Thematic Apperception Test. *Archives of neurology and psychiatry* 34: 209–306.

Murray, H. A. (1955). American Icarus. In A. Burton and R. E. Harris (eds.), *Clinical studies in personality.* Chapter 18. New York: Harper and Brothers.

Murray, H. A., et al. (1938). *Explorations in personality.* New York: Oxford University Press.

Myers, I. B. (1970). *Introduction to type* 2d ed. Gainesville, Fla.: Center for Applications of Psychological Type.

——. (1962). *The Myers-Briggs type indicator: Manual.* Princeton: Educational Testing Service.

Oehlschlegel, L. (1947). Regarding Freud's book on "Moses." *Psychoanalytic review* 30: 67–76.

Oring, E. (1984). *The jokes of Sigmund Freud.* Philadelphia: University of Pennsylvania Press.

Perry, H. S. (1982). *Psychiatrist of America: The life of Harry Stack Sullivan.* Cambridge: Harvard University Press.

———. (1974). Harry Stack Sullivan. In *Dictionary of American Biography*. New York: Scribner. Supplement 4.

———. (1972). Introduction. In H. S. Sullivan, *Personal Psychopathology*. New York: Norton.

———. (1962). Introduction. In H. S. Sullivan, *Schizophrenia as a human process*. (New York: Norton.

Puner, H. W. (1947). *Freud, his life and his mind*. New York: Grosset and Dunlap.

Rangell, L. (1955). The role of the parent in the Oedipus complex. *Bulletin of the Menninger Clinic* 19: 9–15.

Roazen, P. (1975). *Freud and his followers*. New York: Knopf.

Roback, A. (1957). *Freudiana*. Cambridge, Mass.: Sci Art.

Robert, M. (1976). *From Oedipus to Moses*. Garden City: Anchor Books.

Rorschach, H. (1942). *Psychodiagnostics* Trans. P. Lemkau and B. Kronenberg. New York: Grune and Stratton.

Rosenberg, Sam. (1978). *Why Freud fainted*. Indianapolis: Bobbs-Merrill.

Rosenberg, Seymour, and Jones, R. A. (1972). A method for investigating and representing a person's implicit personality theory: Theodore Dreiser's view of people. *Journal of personality and social psychology* 22: 372–86.

Rosenzweig, S. (1978). *Aggressive behavior and the Rosenzweig Picture-Frustration study*. New York: Praeger.

———. (1945). The picture-association method and its application in a study of reactions to frustration. *Journal of personality* 14: 3–23.

Rotter, J. B., and Rafferty, J. E. (1950). *Manual: The Rotter incomplete sentences blank*. New York: Psychological Corporation.

Runyan, W. McK. (1984). *Life histories and psychobiography*. New York: Oxford University Press.

———. (1981). Why did Van Gogh cut off his ear? The problems of alternative explanations in psychobiography. *Journal of personality and social psychology* 40: 1070–77.

Sachs, H. (1944). *Freud: Master and friend*. Cambridge: Harvard University Press.

———. (1941). "The Man Moses" and the man Freud. *Psychoanalytic review* 28: 156–62.

Schafer, R., Zimet, C., Levin, M., and Prelinger, E. (1958). Rating scales for characterological assessment. (mimeo).

Schoenwald, R. (1956). *Freud, the man and his mind, 1856–1956*. New York: Knopf.

Schur, M. (1972). *Freud: Living and dying*. New York: International Universities Press.

Shapiro, K. J., and Alexander, I. E. (1975). *The experience of introversion: An integration of phenomenological, empirical, and Jungian approaches*. Durham, N.C.: Duke University Press.

Silverstein, B. (1986). "Now comes a sad story": Freud's lost metapsychological papers. In P. Stepansky (ed.), *Freud: Appraisals and reappraisals*. Vol. 1, Contributions to Freud Studies. Hillsdale, N.J.: Analytic Press.

Stephenson, W. (1953). *The study of behavior*. Chicago: University of Chicago Press.

Stern, P. (1976). *C. G. Jung: The haunted prophet*. New York: Delta.

Stolorow, R. D., and Atwood, G. E. (1979). *Faces in a cloud: Subjectivity in personality theory.* New York: Aronson.

Storr, A. (1973). *C. G. Jung.* New York: Viking.

Sullivan, H. S. (1972). *Personal psychopathology.* New York: Norton.

———. (1956). *Clinical studies in psychiatry.* New York: Norton.

———. (1953). *The interpersonal theory of psychiatry.* New York: Norton.

———. (1942). H. S. Sullivan. In *Current biography,* p. 814.

Tomkins, S. S. (1984). Script theory. Working paper. Presented at the annual meeting of the Society for Personology, Asilomar, Calif.

———. (1979). Script theory: Differential magnification of affects. In H. E. Howe and R. A. Dienstbier (eds.), *Nebraska Symposium on Motivation.* Vol. 26. Lincoln: University of Nebraska Press.

———. (1963). *Affect, imagery, and consciousness.* Vol. 2. *The negative affects.* New York: Springer.

———. (1952). The Tomkins-Horn Picture Arrangement Test. *Transactions of the New York Academy of Science* 15: 46–50.

———. (1947). *The Thematic Apperception Test.* New York: Grune and Stratton.

Tomkins, S. S., and Miner, J. B. (1957). *The Tomkins-Horn Picture Arrangement Test.* New York: Springer.

Van Der Heide, C. (1952). Discussion of Buxbaum's paper. *Bulletin of the Menninger Clinic* 16: 66–69.

Velikovsky, I. (1941). The dreams that Freud dreamed. *Psychoanalytic review* 28: 487–511.

Von Franz, M. (1977). *C. G. Jung, his myth in our time.* Trans. William H. Kennedy. Boston: Little, Brown and Company.

Wallace, E. R., IV. (1978). Freud's father conflict: The history of a dynamic. *Psychiatry* 41: 33–56.

———. (1977). The psychodynamic determinants of *Moses and Monotheism. Psychiatry* 40: 79–87.

Wechsler, D. (1972). *Wechsler's measurement and appraisal of adult intelligence.* J. Matarazzo (ed.). 5th ed. Baltimore: Williams and Wilkins.

Wehr, G. (1987). *Jung: A biography.* Trans. D. Weeks. Boston: Shambala.

Weiss-Rosmarin, T. (1939). *The Hebrew Moses: An answer to Sigmund Freud.* New York: Jewish Book Club.

White, R. W. (1975). *Lives in progress.* 3d ed. New York: Holt, Rinehart and Winston.

———. (1974). Teaching personality through life histories. *Teaching of psychology* 1: 69–71.

———. (1938). The case of Earnst. In H. A. Murray et al. (eds.), *Explorations in personality.* New York: Oxford University Press.

Wiggins, J. S. (1973). *Personality and prediction: Principles of personality assessment.* Reading, Mass.: Addison Wesley.

Young-Breuhl, E. (1988). *Anna Freud.* New York: Summit Books.

# INDEX

**About the Author**

Irving E. Alexander is professor of psychology at Duke
University. He is the author with Kenneth Joel Shapiro
of *The Experience of Introversion: An Integration of
Phenomenological, Empirical, and Jungian
Approaches*, published by Duke University Press.

Library of Congress Cataloging-in-Publication Data
Alexander, Irving E.
Personology : method and content in personality
assessment and psychobiography / Irving E. Alexander.
Includes bibliographical references.
ISBN 0-8223-0996-3. — ISBN 0-8223-1020-1 (pbk.)
1. Personality. 2. Personality assessment.
3. Psychology—Biographical methods. 4. Freud,
Sigmund, 1856–1939. 5. Jung, C. G. (Carl Gustav),
1875–1961. 6. Sullivan, Harry Stack, 1892–1949.
I. Title.
BF698.A346 1990
155.2—dc20      89-36230 CIP